Contents

"The significant problems we face cannot be solved at the same level of thinking we were at when we created them." — Albert Einstein

— Albert Einstein

1. Embarking on a Celestial Journey

Picture a future where humanity has the wisdom and foresight to safeguard the very essence of life itself—not just on Earth, but among the vast, uncharted reaches of the universe. "Arks Among The Stars: DNA Vaults and the Preservation of Life" is a voyage into that visionary realm. In this book, we will explore the ambitious yet necessary projects that aim to preserve the genetic blueprints of all known life forms through stellar DNA vaults. These cosmic repositories serve as a beacon of hope and survival in the face of existential threats. Imagine a place where time stands still, where safekeeping the biodiversity of our planet is not merely an ideal but a resolute commitment.

Through careful stewardship and relentless innovation, humankind embarks on its most momentous initiative—constructing secure arks among the stars to ensure life's continuity. As you turn the pages of this book, you will discover how this audacious mission balances on the cutting edge of technology and conservation. Whether scientist or student, dreamer or doer, this journey invites you to envision a future where life as we know it is unyieldingly protected, regardless of the cosmic challenges that lie ahead. So, get ready to buy your ticket to the stars; this book is your passage.

2. The Genesis of Cosmic Preservation

2.1. Understanding DNA and Its Importance

To understand the profound significance of DNA in the larger context of cosmic preservation and biological continuity, we must first appreciate what DNA truly represents. Deoxyribonucleic acid, or DNA, is the molecule that encodes the genetic instructions necessary for the growth, development, functioning, and reproduction of all known living organisms. Its double helix structure, characterized by a backbone of sugar and phosphate groups and pairs of nitrogenous bases (adenine paired with thymine and cytosine paired with guanine), serves as the foundational blueprint for life as we know it.

DNA is not merely a chemical compound; it is an intricate system of information, containing within it the legacy of billions of years of evolution. Each organism's genetic material is a tapestry woven from the threads of ancestry and adaptation, showcasing how life has evolved in response to relentless environmental pressures, from the depths of the oceans to the loftiest mountains. In the existential quest to safeguard life against potential extinction threats, whether they come from climate change, habitat destruction, or cosmic calamities, the preservation of DNA emerges as an urgent priority.

The importance of DNA preservation cannot be overstated. By archiving the genetic blueprints of Earth's myriad organisms in DNA vaults, humanity ensures that future generations will have access to the foundation of biological diversity. This endeavor transcends the mere act of saving species; it is about maintaining the mosaic of life itself. Every organism, no matter how seemingly insignificant, plays an integral role within ecosystems, contributing to the resilience and adaptability of the biosphere. Preserving genetic material enables us not just to save species, but to preserve the intricate web of life that supports and sustains the planet.

Historically, humans have practiced various forms of biodiversity conservation, but the advent of modern genetic technologies opens new vistas. While traditional methods such as wildlife preserves and seed banks are valuable, they often rely heavily on the assumption that environments will remain stable enough for the reintroduction of species. The potential for future instability—as predicted under scenarios of climate change and ecological collapse—challenges the efficacy of these strategies. In contrast, DNA vaults represent a revolutionary approach to conservation that acknowledges the uncertainties of the future. By storing genetic material in stable, secure environments, we safeguard the potential for future ecological restoration, enabling the re-establishment of species, or even entirely new synthetic organisms that may be better suited to anticipated environmental conditions.

Central to the significance of these DNA vaults is the sophisticated understanding of genomic information that modern science affords us. The complete sequencing of genomes from a multitude of organisms has illuminated the complexity and interconnectedness of life. With advancements in technology, we can now analyze and manipulate genes with unprecedented precision, allowing for the possibility of engaging in de-extinction efforts or enhancing organisms' resilience to environmental stresses. These ambitious projects underscore the ethical responsibility we hold as stewards of the planet —a responsibility not just to our own species, but to all life forms that inhabit it.

The implications extend beyond Earth. As we dare to dream about humanity's footprint in the cosmos, DNA vaults take on a cosmic dimension. When contemplating interstellar travel and the establishment of colonies on other celestial bodies, the preservation of Earth's biological heritage becomes not only an act of caution; it morphs into a deliberate strategy to seed life throughout the universe. DNA vaults transform into vessels of hope—repositories that carry the genetic legacies of countless species, ready to sow the seeds of life in barren landscapes far beyond our home planet.

Understanding DNA in this context also propels us into the realm of biotechnology and synthetic biology. The potential to learn from and apply findings from different organisms opens the door to creating novel life forms that can interact beneficially with extraterrestrial environments. By utilizing the genetic blueprints preserved in these vaults, humanity could engineer organisms capable of thriving in alien habitats, thereby expanding the parameters of what life can be and where it can flourish.

Moreover, this bold endeavor invites dialogue around ethical considerations. Questions about the manipulation of genetic material, the roles we assign to synthetic organisms, and the ecological impact these decisions may have compel us to tread thoughtfully as we advance into the unknown. One must grapple with the consequences of reintroducing species that have adapted to new ecological niches or manipulating genetic codes for unforeseen outcomes.

In summary, understanding DNA—its structure, role, and implications for life—is crucial for realizing the vision of preserving biological diversity within DNA vaults for both terrestrial and extraterrestrial contexts. As custodians of life, this responsibility calls for a synthesis of scientific innovation, ethical reflection, and deep respect for the intrinsic value of all living organisms. By safeguarding the essence of life encoded within the sequences of DNA, we embolden humanity's quest to illuminate the dark corners of existence, enriching our understanding of life itself and the potential for its flourishing among the stars.

2.2. Historical Attempts at Biodiversity Preservation

Throughout history, humanity has faced the relentless march of extinction, driven by factors ranging from habitat loss to climate change, and from invasive species to natural disasters. The quest for biodiversity preservation has unfolded over millennia, manifesting in various forms and through differing philosophies. While the concept of conserving biological diversity has evolved, early attempts to safeguard our planet's ecological richness laid the groundwork for contemporary initiatives and the ambitious proposals of today aiming for cosmic biodiversity preservation.

Ancient civilizations, particularly in agriculture, demonstrated an early understanding of the need to preserve genetic material. The cultivation of crops like rice, wheat, and corn often involved selecting seeds from the best specimens for replanting. Societies such as the Mesopotamians, Egyptians, and later the Incas recognized the significance of seed selection in maintaining productive harvests. However, these practices were largely incidental rather than systematic efforts aimed at preserving biodiversity as we understand it today.

As scientific inquiry advanced, particularly in the 18th and 19th centuries, the field of natural history blossomed. Pioneers like Charles Darwin began to explore the complex relationships between species and their environments, setting the stage for modern ecology and evolutionary biology. The insights garnered from such studies prompted early conservationists, such as John Muir and Aldo Leopold, to advocate for the protection of particular landscapes and the species that inhabited them, emphasizing that biodiversity was integral to human survival and ecological health.

The 20th century saw the establishment of the first protected areas, including national parks and wildlife refuges, aimed at safeguarding ecosystems and their inhabitants from human encroachment. The establishment of Yellowstone National Park in 1872, recognized as the first national park in the world, marked a defining moment in conservation history. This movement gained momentum, with various nations creating reserves to preserve their natural heritage. However, these efforts often fell short of ensuring the genetic diversity needed for long-term ecological stability, primarily because they were rooted in the notion that allowing nature to run its course without human interference would inherently protect ecosystems.

The comprehensive insight into genetic science that emerged in the latter half of the 20th century shifted the paradigm of conservation towards a more nuanced understanding of biodiversity. The birth of population genetics, pioneered by researchers like Sewall Wright and J.B.S. Haldane, introduced the concept that rather than merely preserving a number of species, conserving genetic variation within those species was imperative for resilience and adaptability in changing environmental conditions.

This era gave rise to initiatives such as seed banks and genetic repositories. The Svalbard Global Seed Vault, inaugurated in 2008, epitomized this new approach. Operating as a global insurance policy for the epitome of agricultural biodiversity, the Seed Vault aims to safeguard seeds from around the world against catastrophic events, from climate upheavals to wars. It represents a significant step towards recognizing the importance of genetic preservation, albeit with ground-level ramifications tied predominantly to agriculture.

As we moved into the 21st century, the recognition of biodiversity and its ecological, economic, and societal significance reached new heights. Advancements in genomics and biotechnology have paved the way for more sophisticated preservation strategies. Initiatives such as the Earth Biogenome Project aim to decode and catalog the genomes of all known species, offering insights into their evolutionary history and adaptations.

Moreover, as concerns have grown regarding the impacts of climate change and habitat destruction, organizations such as the International Union for Conservation of Nature (IUCN) have increasingly folded genetic diversity into their conservation strategies. They underscore the need to not only protect species and habitats but also to maintain the gene pools that facilitate future adaptability and resilience.

In parallel, contemporary discussions about the preservation of life in a cosmic context have emerged, urging the question: how do we take these historical lessons into the cosmos? The idea of storing genetic material beyond Earth marks a radical leap from traditional conservation methods. Envisioning DNA vaults in space entails utilizing the advances in genetic understanding and conservation strategies established on Earth, while responding to stellar threats and opportunities.

Debates surrounding the limitations, ethical implications, and technological feasibilities of this cosmic preservation draw upon historical attempts and the lessons learned from Earth-based conservation challenges. Historical attempts emphasize the critical need for careful stewardship and the integration of genetic and species conservation in the unfolding drama of planetary biodiversity.

Ultimately, these foundations serve as a reminder of humanity's role as custodians of life. By thoughtfully extending our preservation efforts beyond the confines of Earth and incorporating historic insights into contemporary practices, we can forge a comprehensive legacy of biodiversity. In securing life's genetic heritage against cosmic uncertainties, we invite an audacious commitment—one that resonates through time and space, recognizing our shared responsibility to preserve the intricate web of life that spans the universe. As we endeavor to create arks among the stars, we must remember that successful preservation is built upon the lessons taught to us by the struggles of our past. This, in turn, can guide our journey toward a thriving biosphere that can flourish even in the uncharted landscapes of the cosmos.

2.3. The Evolution of Arks in Human Lore

The concept of arks has permeated human lore across civilizations, civilizations which have constantly grappled with themes of survival, preservation, and resurrection. In the grand tapestry of human history, these mythical constructs often emerge as symbols of hope and resilience, embodying humanity's deep-seated desire to protect life against insurmountable odds. From ancient texts to modern science fiction, the idea of the ark serves as a bridge linking our past experiences with future aspirations, particularly in our quest to preserve biodiversity amidst existential threats.

In the ancient world, narratives surrounding arks often converged around the tales of divine intervention and salvation. Prominent among these is the legendary story of Noah's Ark, which recounts a great flood that was to cleanse the Earth of its sins. In this singular narrative, Noah, commanded by a higher power, constructed a massive vessel to safeguard a pair of every living creature, ensuring the continuance of life. This archetype reflects a fundamental human instinct: to seek sanctuary in times of peril. While rooted in faith, such stories resonate with the universal quest for preservation, underscoring the belief that life, in its manifold forms, is sacred and worth saving.

The motifs of refuge and preservation echoed through time and found expression in various cultures. In the ancient civilizations of Egypt, temple complexes served as sanctuaries for gods and the accordingly designated flocks of people. Similarly, the concept of genetic preservation—the safeguarding of life itself—began to take more structured forms, reflecting society's growing understanding of the intricate web that binds all living beings together. While perhaps less dramatic than miraculous floods, these practices encapsulate the wisdom present in tending to the biological heritage of humanity.

As humanity progressed into the Renaissance, a rebirth of interest in the natural world saw explorers venture into the unknown. This era not only expanded geographical horizons but also initiated a burgeoning curiosity about the living organisms inhabiting the newly discovered lands. Curiosity about biodiversity began to flourish, gradually giving rise to an understanding that safety and preservation were not only for the elite or the divine but also essential for the masses. Concepts of natural history emerged, invoking a relationship between humans and the myriad forms of life they observed around them. However, the preservation of that life began to take on new meanings, with early botanical gardens and animal reserves sprouting in an effort to collect and conserve diverse species.

The Industrial Revolution brought about significant changes in human interaction with the environment. The rapid advancement of technology created both a boon and a bane, as biodiversity began to dwindle amidst the expansion of cities and agriculture. It was in this context that the ark of preservation found new interpretations, giving rise to the idea of sanctuaries for wildlife. This transition reflects a pivotal moment in our cultural narrative—where the ark, originally conjured as a means of divine salvation, transforms into a refuge built by human hands. The establishment of national parks and wildlife sanctuaries can be seen as a modern extension of ancient protective arks—albeit now rooted in scientific principles and ecological understanding.

As the 20th century dawned, conservation efforts gained momentum, ignited by awareness of alarming rates of species extinction. Organizations dedicated to preserving wildlife emerged, alongside groundbreaking treaties aimed at protecting endangered species. Amid this backdrop, the notion of arks also evolved to include the wider initiative of biodiversity conservation on a more extensive scale. The first glimpses of modern DNA technology foreshadowed more ambitious preservation methods, echoing the age-old instinct to safeguard life.

By the 21st century, the conversation around cosmic preservation began to intertwine with the established narrative of arks in human lore. As humans pondered the political, ethical, and practical implications of space colonization, the ideas of arks took on fresh significance. The vastness of the cosmos presents unthinkable perils, but it also offers extraordinary potential for the continuation of life beyond Earth. The conception of DNA vaults, or arks of a new kind, emerges as a meticulously planned refuge that transcends the terrestrial plane. These stellar repositories manifest the human response to cosmic challenges —akin to the ancient arks that preserved earthly life against calamity.

In seeking to create sustainable arks among the stars, humanity draws upon the wisdom of our ancients while delving deep into contemporary science. The juxtaposition of historical and modern understandings creates a rich narrative; it evokes profound questions about the relationships we cultivate with nature, technology, and each other. What ancient instincts can guide us as we venture into the challenges of space exploration and preservation? How can we ensure that our efforts honor the delicate balance of life while expanding into the cosmos?

Thus, the evolution of arks in human lore encapsulates both our legacy and our aspirations. As beacons of hope and custodians of genetic memory, arks compel us to redefine our relationship with life, harnessing the lessons of the past to pave a resilient path for the future. Through this lens, we come to glimpse a future in which the concepts of conservation, preservation, and resurrection are not merely rhetoric, but are entrenched in our collective consciousness, motivating us to safeguard the intricate web of life that has endured through time—and continues to inspire our foray among the stars.

2.4. Celestial Stewardship Through the Ages

Throughout the annals of human civilization, the narrative of stewardship—both earthly and celestial—has evolved alongside humanity's understanding of its place in the universe. From ancient mythologies reflecting humanity's impulse to preserve and protect life, to modern science initiatives committed to safeguarding biodiversity, this concept manifests in increasingly ambitious ways. The age of celestial stewardship invites us to reimagine these efforts, transforming the aspiration of preserving life into an interstellar endeavor fully realized through innovation, collaboration, and ethical consideration.

Early human civilizations perceived themselves as guardians of the natural world, establishing harmonious relationships with the ecosystems around them. Such perspectives are encapsulated in the spiritual and cultural traditions of many indigenous peoples, who recognized the intricate connections binding all living beings. It is within these ancient paradigms that we find the seeds of celestial stewardship, where the principles of balance and respect for nature can be extrapolated to include the wider cosmos. Over time, these relationships paved the way for the burgeoning field of environmental conservation, fundamentally shifting our understanding of responsibility from a local to a planetary—now cosmic—scale.

As scientific knowledge advanced, particularly in the realm of genetics, humanity's capacity for stewardship expanded exponentially. The understanding that life is cradled within the coils of DNA demonstrated that preservation is not merely the survival of individual species but the safeguarding of genetic diversity itself, an ecosystem's lifeblood. The evolution of selective breeding practices into modern genetic preservation initiatives illustrates this shift. Our foray into the realm of DNA vaults epitomizes humanity's profound responsibility: not only to maintain existing life forms but to prepare for unprecedented challenges that lie beyond our blue planet.

The advent of space exploration has further intensified these responsibilities. As humanity casts its gaze toward the stars, we face new dilemmas: How do we carry forward the stewardship philosophy in a universe filled with risks and potential crises? The establishment of DNA vaults in space symbolizes the culmination of centuries of thought and practice into one audacious but necessary project. Each vault represents more than a storehouse of genetic material; it embodies humanity's resolve to learn from history and act in anticipation of unknown futures.

Throughout this evolving paradigm, the role of technology has been crucial. The past few decades have witnessed an unparalleled advancement in genomic technologies, creating opportunities that were unimaginable even a generation ago. From sequencing entire genomes to successfully cloning endangered species, these technologies have forged new paths for biodiversity preservation. As we transition these tools into the cosmic arena, new frameworks for managing and preserving life emerge, embedding the principles of stewardship into the very fabric of cosmic exploration.

The ethical considerations entwined with this endeavor cannot be understated. As we consider the implications of manipulating genetic material, the moral question arises: To what extent do we intervene in the natural processes of life? True celestial stewardship demands that we approach these technologies with caution, ensuring that scientific advancement aligns with our ethical responsibilities. We must grapple with concepts of justice, equity, and respect—not only for life on Earth but also for future life forms among the stars.

Economic and political dimensions must also be navigated in this new arena of stewardship. The collaboration—both among nations and with various organizations—will be pivotal in realizing the vision of cosmic preservation. Global partnerships foster collective responsibility, transcending borders to address shared risks and opportunities. Such alliances echo the interconnectedness of ecosystems, reflecting the same principles that underpin biodiversity conservation on Earth.

As stewards, the legacy we cultivate today reverberates into the future. The lessons learned from our past guides our present, urging us to empower the next generation of custodians through education, awareness, and advocacy. Instilling a culture of stewardship, one that embraces innovation while respecting tradition, is essential to the sustainability of our endeavors. Every individual bears the potential to contribute to this narrative, whether as a scientist, artist, writer, or a concerned citizen.

In this era of interconnected challenges—from climate change to the exploration of other planets—the call for stewardship has never been more urgent. Acknowledging our role in this grand cosmic tapestry compels us to rise to the occasion. As we work to design and deploy arks among the stars, we undertake a shared commitment to protect the essence of life itself—not just for our generation, but for all those who will follow in our footsteps. The vision of celestial stewardship transcends mere survival; it embodies the very spirit of our humanity —the intrinsic desire to foster life, to embrace the unknown, and to leave a legacy that honors the intricate web of life that sustains us. In pursuing this mission, we celebrate the resilience of existence and illuminate the potential for life to flourish amidst the stars.

2.5. Earth's Role in the Great Cosmic Web

Earth occupies a unique position within the vast tapestry of the universe, intricately woven into the Great Cosmic Web—a vast and complex interrelationship among all celestial bodies, energy fields, and life forms. This web connects planets, stars, galaxies, and the fabric of spacetime itself, encompassing the totality of existence. As humankind ventures into the cosmos, understanding Earth's role within this universal network becomes crucial, especially in the context of preserving biological diversity and securing the legacy of life that has flourished under the sun for billions of years.

At the heart of this cosmic connection lies the understanding that Earth is not just an isolated entity; it is profoundly integrated into the greater universe's dynamics. The elements that compose the planets —including Earth—have originated in the crucibles of stars, ignited by gravitational forces and nuclear reactions. As these stars exhaust their lifetimes, they explode in supernovae, dispersing the building blocks of life, such as carbon, oxygen, and nitrogen, across interstellar space. These elements coalesce into new bodies under the influence of gravity, thus ensuring that life as we know it can propagate throughout the cosmos. This ebbs and flows of matter and energy illustrate the interconnectedness of all celestial phenomena, mirroring the intricate connections among living organisms on Earth.

As custodians of this vibrant blue planet, humanity's role is to serve as proactive stewards not only for Earth but for the cosmic legacy we share with the universe. This imperative is reflected in our commitments to ensure continuity of life, expressing our ethical obligation to maintain the integrity of biological diversity. The advent of genetic technology and the establishment of DNA vaults represent a response to that call—an acknowledgment that safeguarding life must extend beyond terrestrial boundaries.

The idea of sealing Earth's biological heritage in DNA vaults is a bold endeavor to prepare for future uncertainties. These vaults are envisioned as cosmic capsules—repositories housing the genetic blueprints of organisms from various ecosystems. By securing this genetic information, Earth becomes a vital hub in the broader cosmic web, facilitating the potential to reconstruct and reintroduce life forms to other celestial environments. Such actions take on an almost mythological significance, echoing the ancient narratives of preservation that emphasize humanity's guardianship role. By investing in these comprehensive preservation strategies, humankind acknowledges its historical responsibilities while acknowledging its future aspirations.

The creation of vaults among the stars could lead to new life forms thriving on previously barren planets, thus reinforcing the notion that life is a cosmic venture. This potential translocation signifies a profound act of cosmological re-creation, wherein humanity transforms the landscapes of alien worlds—outposts not only for exploration but for the nurturing of life, helping to extend the range of Earth's biosphere into the infinite expanse of the universe.

In this context, genetic diversity emerges as both a terrestrial treasure and a cosmic commodity. The DNA vaults become symbols of hope, safeguarding not only the genetic material but also the stories of countless organisms that have withstood the trials of time. Each strand of DNA encodes not simply the genome of an organism but also a part of Earth's evolutionary journey—documenting how life has adapted to myriad challenges. These vaults serve as time capsules, preserving the narratives of evolution in the face of extinction and equipping humanity with the potential to resurrect life in distant worlds, fostering new ecosystems that echo the variety found on Earth.

However, the ethical considerations surrounding the transition of life forms from Earth to space must not be overlooked. The complex question of where our responsibilities end when we allow life to thrive in foreign ecosystems opens myriad discussions. The implications of introducing genetically preserved organisms into environments that have evolved independently for eons require careful deliberation. We must tread softly, respecting both the adaptive resilience exhibited by native species and the potential impacts of newly interjected life forms.

Moreover, engaging with the Great Cosmic Web invites a holistic perspective that encompasses not just biological but also geological, environmental, and perhaps even spiritual dimensions of life. As stewards of Earth, our role intertwines with the ethical practice of aligning our actions with sustainable development—acknowledging that each decision, whether terrestrial or interstellar, reverberates across the fabric of existence.

This deeper understanding of Earth's role in the cosmic expanse encourages a shift in mindset. Rather than viewing ourselves merely as inhabitants of a planet, we must position ourselves as intergalactic ambassadors of life, guardians of genetic knowledge, and advocates for biodiversity. A commitment to Earth's rich biological heritage empowers our endeavors—the preservation of life will ultimately be informed by the understanding of how that life interacts with the broader universe.

As we strive to create arks among the stars, it is imperative to remember that we inherit not only a world teeming with life but also the responsibility to protect and maintain that life across the cosmos. The challenge ahead calls for innovation, collaboration, and profound reverence for the tapestries we are co-creating—one that resonates with the intricate connections of the Great Cosmic Web. By honoring our role as custodians of Earth's diversity, we pave the way for an expansive future where life, in all its forms, continues to flourish against the backdrop of infinity. As we prepare for interstellar arks, let us look inward at the mission before us—the sacred act of preserving life. It is in this noble pursuit that humanity's legacy will align harmoniously with the greater cosmos, etching our role into the very fabric of existence itself.

3. Scientific Foundations of DNA Vaults

3.1. The Biochemistry of DNA

The intricate biochemistry of DNA serves as the foundation upon which the preservation of life, both on Earth and among the stars, is built. Deoxyribonucleic acid (DNA) is a complex molecule composed of two intertwined strands forming a double helix structure, a configuration that not only gives it physical stability but also encodes the vast amount of information necessary for the functioning of living organisms. Each strand is made up of a sugar-phosphate backbone, connected by pairs of nitrogenous bases—adenine (A) with thymine (T), and cytosine (C) with guanine (G). These sequences of bases function as a genetic language, dictating everything from physical characteristics to behavioral traits, evolving through natural selection and adaptation over billions of years.

Understanding the biochemistry of DNA goes beyond its mere structure; it encompasses the various processes that it undergoes, such as replication, transcription, and translation. Replication is the process through which DNA makes a copy of itself, a critical step in cellular division that ensures genetic information is accurately passed to offspring. Transcription involves the synthesis of messenger RNA (mRNA) from a DNA template, which subsequently translates into proteins that perform most life functions. This fundamental triad of processes—replication, transcription, and translation—positions DNA as not only the blueprint of life but also as the connective tissue holding the narrative of evolution, adaptation, and survival.

In the era of genetic science, the implications of DNA preservation and analysis have unlocked advanced methodologies that promise significant advancements in conservation. The complete sequencing of genomes from various organisms provides critical insights into the genetic diversity essential for resilience and adaptability in ecosystems. This colossal project serves as a touchstone for biodiversity efforts, enabling scientists to identify genetic variations within species that may influence their survival in rapidly changing environments.

DNA preservation endeavors tie intimately into the conception of DNA vaults, designed to maintain the integrity of genetic material across vast stretches of time and distance. The preservation of DNA is fraught with challenges, primarily because the molecular structure is susceptible to damage from environmental factors such as radiation, heat, and moisture. Additionally, as time elapses, the potential for mutations increases, making it essential to employ methods that ensure both the stability and accessibility of genetic information.

Cryopreservation, a commonly utilized technique in laboratories, presents a viable method for storing DNA at extremely low temperatures, significantly slowing down the processes that lead to degradation. In cryopreservation, DNA samples are often mixed with cryoprotective agents before being cooled to temperatures as low as negative 196 degrees Celsius, achieving a glass-like state that prevents ice crystal formation and cellular damage. This technique has proven essential for preserving genetic materials from endangered species or organisms facing extinction, providing scientists with a reservoir of genetic resources for future restoration efforts.

While the primary focus is on preservation on Earth, establishing DNA vaults in space introduces an additional layer of complexity and excitement. The advancements in cryopreservation, coupled with vacuum storage technologies, contribute to the development of a robust framework for maintaining the integrity of DNA in extraterrestrial environments. As cosmic journeys take us beyond our terrestrial confinements, considerations around cosmic radiation, cosmic temperature fluctuations, and microgravity conditions become paramount. The idea of DNA vaults orbiting Earth or located on other celestial bodies represents a frontier where biochemistry, engineering, and astronomy converge, shaping humanity's endeavor to ensure that the legacy of life continues within the universe.

Furthermore, an understanding of gene editing technologies, such as CRISPR-Cas9, expands the possibilities of genetic manipulation post-preservation. While the primary objective of preservation is to safeguard existing genetic diversity, these tools empower scientists to explore alternatives for reviving extinct species or enhancing the resiliency of certain organisms through genetic modification. The future of DNA vaults may well include the potential not just for preservation but also for revivification, drafting new narratives of life in environments entirely different from their origins.

However, this fusion of power and responsibility carries profound ethical implications. The manipulation and preservation of DNA bring forth questions of ownership, the ecological impacts of reintroducing genetically modified organisms, and the potential consequences of human intervention on natural ecosystems. The role of ethics in this discussion cannot be overstated; understanding the biochemistry of DNA requires grounding our scientific pursuits in moral contemplation. It invites a dialogue on the extent to which humanity ought to intervene—not only in its own evolutionary trajectory but also in the ways in which life can be directed on distant worlds.

At the intersection of science, ethics, and conservation lies a tapestry woven from the strands of DNA—an intricate manifestation of life's potential across time and space. As we stand at the frontier of cosmic exploration, the preservation of DNA offers a profound opportunity to become stewards not only of Earth's biodiversity but also of life's potential among the stars. The commitment to preserving our genetic heritage through vaults across the universe embodies a collective responsibility—a vow to honor the narrative of life, ensuring that humanity's footprint becomes a thread woven into the expansive fabric of the Great Cosmic Web. Thus, the biochemistry of DNA transforms from a mere scientific study into the heartbeat of our continuity, echoing amidst the galaxies as we endeavor to safeguard life against the backdrop of infinity. The journey that starts from understanding DNA culminates in a vision that stretches across time and space, where the essence of existence is preserved and cherished, ready to be awakened in worlds yet undiscovered.

3.2. From Test Tubes to Stars: Technological Advancements

Technological advancements have driven remarkable progress in the field of biological preservation, laying the groundwork for humanity's ambitious endeavors to safeguard the essence of life not only on Earth but also among the stars. The journey from traditional biological practices to cutting-edge technologies reflects human ingenuity's convergence with scientific inquiry, enabling the ambitious dream of creating DNA vaults—repositories that may one day house the genetic legacy of Earth's biodiversity in the cosmic expanse.

Historically, the preservation of life has relied on more rudimentary techniques, such as seed banks or animal reserves, which aimed to protect biodiversity within terrestrial confines. However, the advent of molecular biology has transformed the landscape of conservation by providing tools that delve deeper into the fundamental units of life. Discoveries in genetic sciences have introduced mechanisms for preserving genetic material at a molecular level, facilitating the design of vaults that take advantage of modern technology to safeguard DNA for generations—or even eons—to come.

Among the most significant advancements is the development of effective DNA preservation techniques. Traditional methods of biological preservation often faced challenges like degradation over time, contamination, and inefficiencies in maintaining the integrity of genetic material. Advances in cryopreservation have revolutionized these practices, enabling scientists to preserve DNA and cell samples at ultra-low temperatures, effectively halting biological processes that lead to decay. By utilizing liquid nitrogen or other cryogenic methods, samples can be maintained in a stable and viable state, ensuring their usability for future research or restoration efforts.

Additionally, the rise of high-throughput sequencing technologies has drastically accelerated genome sequencing processes, allowing researchers to map and store vast amounts of genetic data efficiently. The integration of bioinformatics has further streamlined the management and analysis of this data, enabling the construction of comprehensive databases that document genetic variations and functional characteristics across species. These databases not only facilitate species identification but also provide insights into genetic resilience and adaptability—a crucial factor in the context of climate change and ecological challenges.

The development of nanotechnology has also made significant impacts in preservation approaches. Nanostructures and materials can be engineered on an atomic scale to create robust frameworks for encapsulating DNA while shielding it from environmental factors that could compromise its integrity. Innovative approaches deploy nanosensors to monitor the health of genetic samples, ensuring optimal storage conditions. The incorporation of these technologies emphasizes the role of miniaturization and precision in addressing complex biological preservation challenges.

Moving beyond DNA preservation on Earth, technological advancements have paved the way for the exploration of extraterrestrial vaults. As humanity prepares to venture beyond its home planet, the challenge of creating secure, self-sustaining environments for preserving genetic material in space arises. The potential for DNA vaults on lunar or Martian soil takes into account the unique conditions of these celestial bodies, such as exposure to radiation, fluctuating temperatures, and microgravity. Innovations in materials science are crucial for designing vaults capable of withstanding these environmental stressors while ensuring the viability of the genetic material stored within.

Moreover, the role of artificial intelligence (AI) in managing and monitoring DNA vaults cannot be overstated. AI-driven solutions can analyze vast datasets, optimizing storage conditions, predicting potential failures, and adapting strategies in real-time to ensure the preservation of genetic material. The interplay of AI and robotics enhances the efficiency and accuracy of DNA preservation endeavors, allowing for intelligent, adaptive systems that operate autonomously.

As we contemplate the design of interstellar DNA vaults, the architectural considerations become paramount. These facilities must not only function efficiently but also be durable enough to withstand the challenges posed by the cosmos. From materials selection to energy sources, each facet of the design must harmonize with principles of sustainability and resilience. Advanced techniques in 3D printing and modular construction allow for the creation of vault components suited for transportation and assembly in space delving into the realms of architectural innovation.

The ethical dimensions accompanying these technological advancements also provoke critical discussions. As we explore the potential to manipulate genetic material and preserve life forms in space, ethical concerns surrounding intervention, ownership, and ecological balance become increasingly prominent. Rigorous standards must be established to navigate the responsible use of technology, ensuring that our quest for preservation does not lead to unintended consequences or inequities.

Ultimately, the progression from test tubes to the stars illustrates humanity's relentless drive to innovate in the name of preservation. By embracing the intricate relationship between technology and biology, we empower ourselves to protect life's diverse tapestry from existential threats. The fusion of advancements in cryobiology, nanotechnology, and artificial intelligence position humanity to undertake the profound challenge of cosmic preservation—securing the legacy of life in vaults that, one day, may orbit distant stars or reside on uncharted worlds.

In summary, as we stand poised at the intersection of technological progress and the philosophical imperative to preserve life, the ongoing exploration of how best to construct and utilize DNA vaults reinforces our commitment to stewarding life across the cosmos.

From crafting the architecture of these vaults to monitoring their intricate contents, the journey toward cosmic preservation is lit by our dedication to ensuring that life, in all its myriad forms, endures far beyond the horizons of our Earth.

3.3. Comparative Analysis of DNA Preservation Approaches

In the realm of biodiversity and genetic preservation, a myriad of approaches have surfaced, each with its strengths and limitations. The urgency of safeguarding Earth's biological wealth against potential existential threats—whether environmental, anthropogenic, or cosmic—drives the need for comparative analysis of these methods. By examining various DNA preservation techniques, we can identify the most effective practices that may be applied, not only on Earth but also in the ambitious endeavor of creating DNA vaults among the stars.

Traditional methods of genetic preservation primarily include cryopreservation and the use of seed banks. Cryopreservation harnesses incredibly low temperatures to halt biochemical reactions that lead to cellular degradation. This technique has gained prominence in the fields of animal and plant conservation, allowing for the preservation of viable genetic material for extended periods. While effectively maintaining the integrity of DNA, cryopreservation presents certain logistical challenges, including the need for constant power supply and the risks associated with temperature fluctuations during transport. Moreover, durability under long-term storage remains a concern as cellular structures might still succumb to crystallization effects and other forms of cryoinjury over extensive periods.

Conversely, seed banks function as repositories for the seeds of various plant species, preserving their genetic diversity for potential future cultivation. While they represent a vital resource for agricultural biodiversity and food security, seed banks face limitations in terms of species representation. As not all plant species produce seeds, and as certain seeds lose viability over time, relying solely on this approach could leave critical gaps in the preservation of the planet's genetic diversity. Furthermore, seed banks are intrinsically linked to Earth's environmental conditions; they cannot ensure the survival of organisms outside their specific habitats or those that require specific soil and climatic conditions for growth.

Modern biobanking, another approach, seeks to combine the advantages of both cryopreservation and seed banks, utilizing advanced techniques to handle tissues, cells, and even whole organisms. It allows for the preservation of a broader array of genetic material, pushing the boundaries of what can be stored over time. Biobanks have emerged as a crucial tool in conservation biology, enabling genetic studies and applications in restoration ecology. However, they often struggle with complications related to rare species and the complexities of genetic manipulation, not to mention the financial costs tied to maintaining such facilities with continuously viable storage environments.

In recent years, the development of DNA vaults presents an ambitious new frontier in genetic preservation, especially in the context of preparing for cosmic exploration. These vaults aim to encapsulate not only the genetic material of various species but also their entire genetic heritage. Strategies for vault design encompass sophisticated cryogenic technologies, vacuum storage, and unique construction materials that protect against cosmic radiation and extreme temperatures. The potential for long-term stability significantly surpasses terrestrial approaches, allowing humanity to envision a future where the origin of life can be administered on distant worlds.

To truly assess the viability and reliability of different DNA preservation methodologies, we must also consider emerging technologies. Synthetic DNA constructs represent a pioneering approach that mimics the sequences of naturally-occurring DNA while enabling the development of entirely new sequences for targeted applications. This method could be used to design organisms tailored for life in specific off-world environments, thus situating such developments as an evolutionary step forward from standard practices.

As we transition into the cosmic realm, several factors must be weighed when comparing preservation approaches—specifically the environmental suitability for longevity. Space vaults must factor in cosmic radiation, microgravity, and temperature fluctuations. Requirements for these preservation techniques extend beyond our knowledge of Earth-based methodologies. Each technique will require an adaptation strategy capable of working harmoniously with the unique features of extraterrestrial environments.

In conclusion, the comparative analysis of DNA preservation approaches reveals complex interrelations that inform not only terrestrial ecological strategies but also cosmic aspirations. By rigorously examining the advantages and limitations of each technique, researchers can lay the groundwork for innovative methods tailored toward the dual purpose of conservation and cosmic exploration, thus advancing our quest to preserve the rich tapestry of life we hold dear. As humanity sets its sights on the stars, blending the wisdom of past methodologies with modern advancements will be pivotal in fostering a future where life endures across the cosmos.

3.4. Cryogenics and Vacuum Storage in Space

Cryogenics and vacuum storage represent two critical aspects of preserving biological materials, especially in the context of cosmic endeavors such as the establishment of DNA vaults among the stars. As humanity aspires to secure the genetic heritage of Earth for future generations and potentially introduce biological diversity to extraterrestrial environments, understanding and implementing these technologies become paramount.

Cryogenics, the science of producing and studying very low temperatures, plays a pivotal role in DNA preservation. By significantly reducing the kinetic energy of molecules, cryogenic conditions inhibit biochemical activities that lead to the degradation of DNA. For biological specimens, ideal storage conditions can be achieved at temperatures below −150 degrees Celsius, often facilitated through the use of liquid nitrogen or other cryogenic agents. At these temperatures, the processes of enzymatic activity and cellular metabolism slow to a halt, effectively suspending the state of the organism and maintaining genetic integrity over time.

When considering the preservation of genetic material on a cosmic scale, the challenges multiply. For example, exposure to radiation in space can induce harmful mutations or damage DNA molecules, making them unviable for future use. This potential risk necessitates innovative approaches to DNA storage that not only protect from extreme temperatures but also shield against radiation. Vacuum storage plays a significant role here, as it involves removing air, moisture, and other contaminants from the storage environment, reducing the risk of oxidation and molecular damage. When coupled with cryogenic techniques, vacuum storage can provide a double shield, ensuring DNA remains intact for extended periods even in the harsh conditions space presents.

The integration of cryogenics and vacuum storage technologies led to the conceptualization of futuristic DNA vaults specifically designed to withstand the rigors of space. Such vaults would ideally be constructed using materials engineered to endure cosmic radiation while effectively managing temperature fluctuations. For instance, advanced insulation materials that minimize heat transfer and resist radiation damage will be fundamental in safeguarding the delicate biological specimens housed within the vaults. Additionally, construction methods may involve multi-layered containment structures similar to those used in terrestrial laboratories, further enhancing the resilience of these cosmic repositories.

In the vacuum of space, where gravitational effects are minimal, the design of DNA vaults would incorporate unique considerations. Materials must meet stringent requirements not only for protection against external factors but also for performance within an environment devoid of atmospheric pressure. Elevating sustainability becomes vital as well; utilizing in-situ resources on other celestial bodies for the construction and maintenance of these vaults can ensure a lower cost and reduced complexity in logistics.

Managing the logistics of cryogenic and vacuum storage systems in space involves sophisticated monitoring and transportation systems. Automated temperature and pressure control systems, potentially enhanced by AI-driven analytics, will be critical to ensuring genetic samples are stored in optimal conditions. Data from these systems can help analyze potential threats to the integrity of the stored DNA, facilitating preemptive actions before issues arise. The predictive capabilities of AI can improve the reliability of storage systems by minimizing human error and adapting to changing conditions in real-time.

Moreover, advancements in nanotechnology can further amplify the efficacy of cryogenic and vacuum preservation techniques. Nanostructured materials might be integrated into the vaults to provide additional protection against radiation and temperature extremes. For example, nanoparticles engineered to disperse heat or absorb radiation can greatly enhance the storage environment for genetic materials.

As humanity forges ahead on its journey to become an interstellar species, the deployment of cryogenics and vacuum storage technologies will prove instrumental in the preservation of life in cosmic contexts. Each DNA vault not only serves as a repository for Earth's genetic legacy but as a testament to human creativity and resilience. Ensuring the survival of these genetic materials against cosmic uncertainties is not merely a technical challenge; it embodies our ethical responsibility as custodians of life, influencing how we navigate both the terrestrial and cosmic realms. Thus, the combination of cryogenics and vacuum storage will play an integral role in humanity's broader mission to safeguard the future of biodiversity, ensuring that life, in its myriad forms, can continue to flourish, even among the stars.

3.5. Managing Mutations Beyond Earth

In an age where humanity increasingly understands the interconnectedness of life forms and the delicate balance of ecosystems, the need to manage mutations beyond Earth becomes crucial, particularly as we endeavor to establish DNA vaults in space. This intricate venture compels us to consider how mutations can be monitored, managed, and even harnessed as we seek to preserve our biological legacy and explore the planets beyond our home.

First and foremost, it is vital to understand the nature of mutations themselves. Mutations are alterations to the genetic material of an organism and are fundamental to the process of evolution. They can arise through various mechanisms, including errors in DNA replication, exposure to radiation, and even environmental factors such as chemical pollutants. While many mutations are neutral or even detrimental, others can provide beneficial adaptations, equipping organisms with improved survival skills in new environments. As we contemplate the preservation of DNA vaults, we must recognize that these mutations may play a significant role in the long-term sustainability of life, particularly in space.

Managing mutations in extraterrestrial environments will require innovative strategies, particularly as we consider the potential impacts of space travel and the unique conditions of celestial bodies. In space, organisms face challenges that can induce stress and result in mutations at higher rates compared to Earth's environments. Cosmic radiation is a significant concern, as high-energy particles can inflict DNA damage, leading to structural alterations and eventual mutations. Therefore, strategies to mitigate these radiation effects will be paramount.

One approach lies in understanding the specific mechanisms of DNA repair that organisms have evolved over millennia. From bacteria to mammals, various repair pathways exist to correct damage before it leads to a permanent mutation. As we contemplate the implications of establishing DNA vaults on other planets, we must prioritize the preservation of these repair pathways. Engineering organisms with enhanced DNA repair capabilities could potentially mitigate the impact of cosmic radiation—making them better suited for survival in these extreme environments.

Furthermore, utilizing advanced technologies, such as synthetic biology, will allow us to manipulate genetic codes to intentionally introduce beneficial mutations or eliminate detrimental ones. This akin to crafting a genetic toolbox tailored for survival in extraterrestrial habitats. By encoding specific traits that augment resilience against radiation or provide metabolic advantages in low-gravity environments, humanity could purposefully steer evolutionary trajectories to suit adaptations necessary for life beyond Earth.

Additionally, the role of bioinformatics will play a critical part in managing mutations in space. Developing sophisticated algorithms and models will enable researchers to analyze vast amounts of genetic data, identifying patterns and predicting outcomes. With the ongoing sequencing of diverse genomes, we can construct comprehensive databases that record mutation rates and types across various organisms. By comparing this data with environmental parameters in extraterrestrial settings, researchers could devise predictive models that inform the engineering of life forms optimized for space.

Moreover, establishing monitoring protocols for mutations over time in extraterrestrial environments will be indispensable. DNA vaults must include mechanisms for long-term assessment of stored genetic materials, enabling scientists to track any emergent mutations and evaluate their potential implications for future ecological restorations or terrestrial reintroductions. This entails both molecular techniques to study changes at the DNA level and ecological assessments to ascertain how these mutations influence overall fitness in extraterrestrial contexts.

Ethical considerations must accompany these scientific endeavors as we delve deeper into managing mutations. The responsibility of preserving life—and potentially altering its course—requires a thoughtful dialogue about the objectives of such actions. How do we balance the potential benefits of using genetic engineering with the ethical implications of playing a god-like role in directing the evolution of life? Questions of biodiversity, ecological balance, and respect for natural organisms weigh heavily on our shoulders.

Furthermore, in designing these vaults and artificial ecosystems conducive to life preservation, we must ensure that they are not merely tested on terrestrial species but also consider the ethical ramifications of inserting modified organisms into extraterrestrial environments. We must seek to resurrect the ideals of preservation rooted in ecological harmony, ensuring that our aspirations to manage mutations do not come at the expense of ecological integrity.

Lastly, international cooperation will be necessary as we embark on this cosmic journey. Collaborative efforts among nations and organizations sharing technologies, data, and ethical guidelines can promote comprehensive approaches to managing mutations in space. As custodians of the cosmic libraries, scientists and researchers must work together to share findings and best practices, aligning their missions to safeguard living forms across galactic domains.

The management of mutations beyond Earth stands at the intersection of biology, ethics, and our exploration of the universe. Together, these facets weave an intricate narrative that highlights not only the wonders of life itself but also the profound responsibilities that accompany our quest for preservation in the cosmos. Through strategic foresight, technological innovation, and ethical reflection, humanity can embark on its most audacious journey—securing life beyond Earth while honorably navigating the complexities of existence. Thus, as we prepare to build interstellar DNA vaults littered across the cosmos, the management of mutations becomes fundamentally woven into our shared narrative of survival and stewardship, guiding the way for future generations.

4. Designing the Vaults: Architectural Marvels

4.1. Materializing the Functional Design

As we embark on the monumental task of designing the ultimate DNA vaults—repositories for preserving the very essence of life across the cosmos—our focus must be on the functional design that encapsulates both the practicalities of storage and the broader ethical considerations tied to our role as custodians of biodiversity. The pivotal challenge lies in ensuring that these vaults do not merely serve as passive containers of genetic material, but rather as dynamic, responsive systems capable of sustaining life across eons.

To materialize a functional design, we must first delve into the specific requirements for safeguarding DNA against a spectrum of environmental hazards that space presents. The cosmic environment is marked by extreme temperatures, unpredictable radiation levels, and microgravity impacts, all of which can compromise the structural integrity of biological materials. The vaults must be constructed from advanced materials that exhibit resilience against these factors. This could involve using polycarbonate composites or aerogels—substances known for their low weight yet formidable insulating properties. Such materials can effectively endure harsh conditions while providing a stable internal environment for the preservation of genetic material.

One of the fundamental design principles for these vaults is the creation of a robust isolation chamber that minimizes the risk of contamination. Implementing sterile containment protocols will be critical, ensuring that the genetic samples remain untarnished over long storage periods. An effective approach could incorporate a series of redundant seals and sterilization measures within the architecture of the vaults, allowing for definitive barriers against cosmic dust and radiation while facilitating safe access for retrieval or analysis when necessary.

In addition to structural integrity, the function of the vaults must incorporate sophisticated systems for monitoring and maintaining optimal internal conditions. Consideration must be given to temperature control, with cryogenic systems that utilize advanced refrigeration technologies to maintain low temperatures conducive to the preservation of DNA. These systems could be paired with heat exchangers and automated feedback loops that respond to any deviations from set parameters, thus ensuring consistent storage conditions regardless of external variations.

While temperature management is essential, the vaults must also function within a vacuum environment to mitigate oxidative damage and moisture penetration. The design could incorporate both cryogenic and vacuum technologies, creating a dual-layered defense that removes air while maintaining a gel-state or liquid nitrogen atmosphere where DNA's structural integrity is preserved. Employing vacuum sealing techniques, akin to those seen in vacuum-packed food products, can effectively protect biological materials against the gradual decay that can result from prolonged exposure to environmental factors.

The challenges posed by microgravity necessitate unique design adaptations for the vaults, particularly in how the samples are stored and organized within their confines. Clamping mechanisms or suspension systems could be utilized to keep specimens in place, preventing physical agitation or movement that might occur due to shifts in orientation. Additionally, embedding magnetic or smart technologies could facilitate the localization and retrieval of samples without needing extensive manual intervention, promoting efficiency in managing the vault's contents.

Robust illumination plays a critical role in the functional design, as light exposure can adversely affect biological materials. This consideration evokes the possibility of designing advanced lighting systems —such as LED strips with customizable wavelengths—wherein only specific wavelengths can penetrate the vault's interior safely. By leveraging smart sensors and AI, these lighting systems can adjust automatically to the presence or absence of genetic samples, negating unnecessary exposure when retrieval or analysis is not occurring.

The integration of sustainability features into the design aligns with our overarching ethos of stewardship. Utilizing renewable energy sources, such as solar power or even nuclear batteries, could provide self-sustaining energy solutions for the vaults without necessitating resupply missions. This autonomy ensures that the vaults can operate independently for years, remaining functional regardless of external logistical challenges faced by Earth-bound operations.

To address the prospect of continuous environmental adversities, the architectural design could also incorporate fail-safe mechanisms. These systems would activate upon detecting critical malfunctions or potential breaches—intentionally triggering self-healing protocols or re-instilling appropriate internal conditions. Such responsive technologies not only enrich the vault's longevity but also catalyze advancements in materials science.

As we consider the design of DNA vaults, it is imperative to engage in collaborative dialogues that bring together experts from various disciplines, including materials science, genetics, engineering, and bioethics. The function of these vaults extends beyond mere architectural features; they embody the principles of our shared responsibilities as humans as we navigate our profound obligation to preserve life among the stars.

In materializing the functional design of DNA vaults, we forge a pathway that intertwines innovation with a deep respect for ethical considerations, ensuring that these repositories not only protect our biological legacy but also embrace our role as guardians of life's continuity. By establishing a foundation that harmonizes practicalities with profound reflections on the meaning of preservation, this design endeavor intends to ensure that future generations may benefit from the genetic riches safeguarded within these architectural marvels—a legacy not just constrained to Earth, but expanded across the cosmos.

4.2. Robust Illumination and Temperature Control

The tasks of robust illumination and temperature control are paramount in any DNA vault designed for long-term preservation of biological materials, especially as humanity seeks to secure the genetic blueprints of life on Earth and beyond. These factors are intertwined and pivotal in creating an environment that maintains the integrity of stored genetic material over potentially vast epochs.

First, robust illumination within a DNA vault goes beyond merely providing light; it is about ensuring that the wavelengths employed do not degrade or compromise the biological samples. Ultraviolet (UV) light, for example, while effective as a tool for certain laboratory applications, poses a significant risk to the structural integrity of DNA. The high-energy photons associated with UV radiation can induce mutations by causing the formation of pyrimidine dimers—compounds that disrupt the normal base pairing of DNA, leading to replication errors. Therefore, selecting lighting technology must consider these factors; LED lights, for instance, could be customized to emit wavelengths safe for biological materials, operating under the notion of minimal effective exposure.

Moreover, the design must incorporate intelligent lighting systems that not only control the illumination based on activity but can also respond to the presence of human operators or automated systems. Integrating motion sensors and adaptive lighting protocols can minimize unnecessary exposure to sensitive materials. When a vault is not in use, the illumination should be dimmed or turned off entirely, ensuring that only necessary lighting aids retrieval or analysis.

Temperature control represents another foundational pillar in the preservation of DNA. The degradation and eventual loss of genetic information can occur rapidly at higher temperatures, making temperature stability essential. Ideally, DNA should be stored at temperatures that inhibit molecular activity, typically below −80 degrees Celsius, although certain delicate samples might require even lower cryogenic temperatures. The infrastructure design must integrate sophisticated cryogenic systems capable of sustaining these conditions over extended periods.

Insulation materials are crucial for maintaining these temperatures, particularly in the face of external thermal fluctuations that could jeopardize internal stability. Multi-layered insulation systems, akin to those used in space applications, can prevent heat transfer from outside, preserving the stability of the internal cryogenic environment. Additionally, the vault's design should enable continuous monitoring of internal temperatures, utilizing advanced sensors connected to automated systems that alert to any deviations from established parameters. These protocols will also draw upon historical data, allowing the systems to predict and adapt to environmental changes proactively.

Furthermore, redundancy becomes a critical aspect of both temperature control and illumination systems. Dual cooling mechanisms ensure that if one system fails, a backup is in place to prevent the catastrophic degradation of biological samples. Similarly, employing multiple parallel lighting systems can safeguard against the failure of any single component, ensuring a consistent environment for the genetic materials.

Another complementary feature includes the integration of machine learning algorithms that analyze environmental data to optimize temperature and lighting conditions over time. By continuously assessing multiple variables—including ambient temperature arrangements, vault air circulation patterns, and humidity levels—these algorithms can make real-time adjustments, preserving the ideal conditions for sample integrity.

For the broader design, a detailed approach to materials and engineering practices ensures that both illumination and temperature systems work synergistically. Materials selected for constructing the vault must not only limit radiation but also resist thermal expansion and contraction that could affect the structural integrity of the storage environment. This could imply the use of advanced composites or alloys with stable thermal properties. In this context, vacuum storage coupled with cryogenics creates an enhanced barrier to molecular degradation through dual-action insulation.

Beyond the mechanics, ethical considerations also factor into the mission of robust illumination and temperature control. The goal here is to act as responsible stewards of life, preserving not just the biological essence encapsulated in the DNA but also honoring the intricate web of life that those genes represent.

In conclusion, the intertwined disciplines of robust illumination and temperature control within DNA vaults form a critical bedrock for preserving life's genetic material. As humanity extends its aspirations beyond the confines of Earth, ensuring that every aspect of these systems works harmoniously will prove fundamental, not only to the longevity of our genetic heritage but also to the ethical fulfillment of our responsibilities as custodians of biodiversity. By marrying innovative technology with pragmatic design, the vision for cosmic vaults dedicated to the protection of life can become a reality—securing the essence of existence as humanity reaches for the stars.

4.3. Gravity and its Artificial Counterparts

The exploration of gravity and its artificial counterparts dives into an essential aspect of our ambition to construct DNA vaults among the stars. While gravity is a fundamental force that governs the behavior of matter, its manipulation is pivotal for facilitating life in extraterrestrial environments. To truly realize our vision of preserving the genetic blueprints of Earth's biodiversity not just for posterity but also for potential revival in extraterrestrial locales, we must understand how to manage gravitational effects—both natural and technological.

Gravity, as a force exerted by celestial bodies, profoundly affects living organisms. On Earth, gravity plays a crucial role in biological rhythms, physiological processes, and various interactions within ecosystems. The manifestation of life as we know it has co-evolved alongside the specific gravitational conditions of our planet. Every aspect, from the growth patterns of plants to the circulatory systems of animals, is intricately designed to function optimally under the influence of Earth's gravitational field. These adaptations bring forward profound questions about the viability of life when subjected to microgravity or even artificial gravitational conditions in space.

The environments beyond Earth present unique challenges. On the Moon, gravity is approximately one-sixth that of Earth's, while on Mars, it is about one-third. Such differences can alter fundamental biological functions: cellular processes may be affected, and the laboriousness of movement can lead to physiological adjustments. The risks of muscle atrophy, bone density loss, and fluid redistribution due to lower gravity are pressing concerns for any long-term human habitation or biological preservation efforts in those settings. Creatures that have adapted to thrive under Earth's gravitational pull might encounter significant challenges in maintaining their functionality without tailored interventions.

To counteract the potential adverse effects of low or microgravity, researchers have begun exploring the feasibility of generating artificial gravity through centrifugal forces. By rotating habitats or specific vault environments, we can create a simulated gravitational effect that better emulates Earth's conditions. This technique not only holds promise for supporting human occupants in space but can also provide a more stable environment for biological samples during extended missions, therefore preserving the integrity of DNA and cellular structures under controlled gravitational conditions.

The establishment of rotating habitats raises interesting engineering challenges. As we design these habitats, the speed and radius of rotation must be carefully calculated to generate the required gravitational force without inducing detrimental effects, such as excessive centripetal forces that could affect biological processes. Various models and simulations can guide these designs, ensuring that we understand the implications of artificial gravity adequately.

Moreover, understanding artificial gravity's role in ecological conservation extends beyond temporary habitats. These gravitational technologies could be integrated into the architecture of DNA vaults in space. For instance, using centrifugal systems may help ensure that fluids required for cell maintenance remain stabilized, reducing the likelihood of cellular erosion caused by the microgravity environment. This approach would help maintain biological viability over extended periods of preservation in a vault setting.

Yet, the implementation of artificial gravity raises ethical and practical questions. Can we justify manipulating gravitational conditions for the benefit of biological preservation? Are we potentially altering the evolutionary pathways of Earth's species through these interventions? Addressing these questions requires balancing technical feasibility with ethical considerations, ensuring that researchers approach this exploration with respect for the organisms preserved and the environments they may potentially inhabit.

As research into gravity manipulation advances, we must also contemplate the implications for various extraterrestrial arrangements and habitats. Should the eventual establishment of settlements on celestial bodies become a reality, the configurations and structures of these domains must incorporate advanced methods of gravity control. To this end, interdisciplinary collaboration among physicists, biologists, engineers, and ethicists will be essential, working collectively to forge a comprehensive understanding of how artificial gravity can coexist with human intervention in ecological and cosmic contexts.

In summary, the concept of gravity and its artificial counterparts is crucial for preserving life's genetic heritage amid the stars. As we seek to create functioning DNA vaults and facilitate the potential transplantation of Earth-based organisms into new domains of existence, our success will hinge on our ability to manage gravitational conditions. By blending traditional ecological insights with innovative technological solutions, we can pave the way not only for life preservation but also for the thriving of that life beyond Earth's atmosphere. Ultimately, our relationship with gravity will define the parameters within which we secure and celebrate the vast biological richness encapsulated within the vaults of our cosmic ambitions.

4.4. Sustaining Life in Zero Gravity Environments

Sustaining life in zero gravity environments embodies a complex interplay of biological, technological, and ethical considerations pivotal to the success of humanity's mission to preserve life across the cosmos. As we strive to establish vital DNA vaults beyond Earth, it becomes imperative to explore how life can be sustained in conditions remarkably different from those on our home planet. This exploration entails understanding the profound impacts of microgravity on biological systems, leveraging advanced technologies to simulate Earth-like conditions, and establishing practices that ensure the viability of life stored in these cosmic repositories.

Microgravity environments, such as those experienced in space or on celestial bodies like the Moon and Mars, present unique challenges for sustaining life. The absence of gravitational force affects not only how organisms function but also fundamental biological processes, including fluid dynamics, nutrient absorption, and cellular behavior. For instance, the effects of microgravity on plants can manifest in altered root growth patterns and stem elongation, with roots demonstrating an inability to orient themselves properly in search of water and nutrients. Similarly, animal physiology can suffer, leading to muscle atrophy, bone density loss, and changes in cardiovascular function as the body adapts to a weightless environment.

To counter these challenges and create viable ecosystems within DNA vaults, advanced technologies that simulate Earth's gravitational conditions must be implemented. The concept of artificial gravity, generated through centrifugal forces, stands at the forefront of these solutions. Rotational habitats—whereby structures are designed to rotate and create a directed force that mimics gravity—can help maintain physiological norms necessary for biological function. These rotating systems can not only facilitate the survival of organisms housed within the vaults but also nurture the biological diversity essential for future generations.

Incorporating bioreactors that leverage artificial gravity can further support life sustainability within these vaults. These systems could employ specially designed chambers that utilize rotation to promote nutrient flow and waste removal, effectively simulating natural conditions experienced on Earth. Such integrations promise to enhance the resilience of organisms, allowing them to adapt to the conditions they would face in their eventual reintroduction to extraterrestrial environments.

Simultaneously, synchronized monitoring systems to assess and maintain the health of organisms in these vaults become critical. Employing artificial intelligence (AI) and machine learning algorithms can optimize conditions by analyzing growth patterns, metabolic activity, and overall health in real time. These adaptive systems will facilitate the identification and mitigation of potential risks before they compromise the stored genetic materials. By leveraging robust data management frameworks, researchers can capture vast datasets regarding organism responses to microgravity—a foundational knowledge that will inform the design of life-sustaining protocols in DNA vaults.

Moreover, the interplay between life and technology extends to the consideration of nutrient provision and waste management, two vital components for sustaining life in isolated systems. The careful engineering of closed-loop life support systems will be essential as these environments are created. These systems should focus on recycling waste into nutrients, thereby creating a self-sustaining ecosystem within the vaults. By incorporating advanced aquaponics or hydroponics systems into the design, the vaults can produce necessary nutrition while simultaneously maintaining an equilibrium that supports various biological processes.

Another significant consideration involves the microbial community that thrives in tandem with plant and animal life. Harnessing beneficial microorganisms will enhance nutrient cycling and bolster the resilience of the biological systems housed within the vaults. As space environments can expose organisms to extreme conditions, building robust ecosystems that incorporate bacterial, fungal, and plant symbiosis can ensure a balanced approach to sustaining life.

In the pursuit of preserving life across the cosmos, ethical considerations must govern these technological explorations. The question of how much we should intervene and manipulate life becomes increasingly prominent as we endeavor to adapt organisms for extraterrestrial habitation. Treating these organisms with respect requires a commitment to maintaining their evolutionary narratives while ensuring their survival.

Furthermore, international cooperation in addressing these challenges emerges as a critical pathway for success. Collaboration among space agencies, research institutions, and governments sets the stage for developing shared frameworks and protocols regarding life preservation in space. Such cooperative strategies will promote the exchange of knowledge and best practices, ensuring that global stewardship informs humanity's endeavors in cosmic conservation.

Ultimately, sustaining life in zero-gravity environments necessitates a combination of biological understanding, advanced technology, and ethical foresight. By integrating artificial gravity systems, closed-loop life support mechanisms, and robust monitoring frameworks, we monumentalize humanity's dedication to preserving life across the cosmos. As we develop technologies and strategies to sustain life in the harsh realities of space, we not only fulfill our obligations as caretakers of Earth's biodiversity but also redefine our role within the broader context of the universe. Through these endeavors, we endeavor to ensure a future where life continues to flourish, both on our home planet and among the stars.

4.5. Blueprints of an Interstellar Arks

In the quest to envision blueprints for interstellar arks, we step into the realm of creative engineering, where imagination marries science to form structures that can transcend the boundaries of our terrestrial experiences. The construction of these cosmic vaults represents humanity's most audacious undertaking: a dedicated mission to preserve the genetic legacies of Earth's biodiversity, enabling adaptation and resilience in environments yet unknown.

The foundation of these blueprints lies in a comprehensive understanding of what interstellar arks must achieve. First and foremost, these structures need to safeguard the DNA and the living genetic imprint of multiple organisms against an array of cosmic threats, while also providing an amenable environment for potential biological restoration or reintroduction into extraterrestrial settings. It is imperative that the design facilitates stabilization against cosmic radiation, extreme temperatures, and microgravity conditions.

The dimensionality of interstellar arks draws from both form and function. These repositories could take various shapes, from large, cylindrical habitats reminiscent of bio-domes to intricate modular systems that can expand and adapt depending on the stored genetic diversity. The architecture could incorporate materials engineered not only for insulation but also for radiation shielding, utilizing lead composites or polyethylene for radiation attenuation while maintaining lightweight structures suitable for interstellar travel.

In this visionary architecture, we must account for multiple levels of preservation. Each level could represent different organisms or genetic strains, organized strategically for easy access and minimal cross-contamination. The lower levels might house cryogenically preserved samples, complete with a sophisticated cooling system that harnesses either passive solar energy or active thermoelectric elements to prevent temperature fluctuations over eons. These lower vaults would be insulated with advanced phase-change materials that actively absorb or release heat as necessary, maintaining a consistent cryogenic environment.

Above these cryogenic reserves, the next level might host organisms maintained in bio-domes, featuring live ecosystems where flora and fauna could be cultivated under controlled conditions. Utilizing hydroponics and aquaponics systems, these micro-ecosystems would facilitate genetic biodiversity and allow for research on how organisms adapt to limited resources and altered conditions—a critical component of resilience engineering. The architecture of this level could be modular, allowing for easy expansion and optimization as further genetic materials are obtained or synthesized.

As we ascend through the interstellar ark, we must consider the technological integration necessary for monitoring and management. Each level could be outfitted with advanced sensors that continuously collect data about temperature, humidity, radiation levels, and the health of biological specimens. These sensors would be linked to an artificial intelligence (AI) system designed to analyze fluctuations and predict potential failures. This AI could also facilitate autonomous decisions about adjusting variable settings within the ark, ensuring optimal storage conditions at all times.

A compelling feature of the arch design is the incorporation of an observational level, perhaps a panoramic dome, enabling humans or robots to visually inspect and interact with the various ecosystems maintained within. Equipped with augmented reality interfaces, custodians could engage in virtual monitoring, directly interacting with biological specimens and receiving real-time data without the need to physically enter the vaults, preserving the integrity of the environments.

Power sources for these interstellar arks must be renewable and self-sustaining. The potential deployment of advanced solar panels, along with compact nuclear reactors, could provide reliable energy. It would be beneficial to incorporate energy-recycling systems capable of repurposing waste heat and biological excretion back into energy production processes, echoing the closed-loop systems prevalent in nature.

Moreover, as we develop architectural blueprints, the ethical considerations of artificial habitats cannot be overlooked. The design of interstellar arks must not only actively preserve life but also strive to respect the complexity of ecological interactions. Plans should be imbued with the acknowledgment that every organism plays a role in its ecosystem, and thus should facilitate opportunities for co-evolution and symbiosis.

Lastly, the narrative woven into these blueprints extends beyond functionality; they must inspire the spirit of adventure and stewardship that defines humanity's mission in the universe. By designing interstellar arks that embody hope, resilience, and deep respect for life, we can signal our intentions to preserve not just genetic material but the very essence of biodiversity across the cosmos.

In conclusion, the blueprints of interstellar arks will reflect humanity's profound commitment to securing the genetic legacy of life as we explore the stars. Through thoughtful design, advanced technology, and ethical considerations, these arks will ensure that the tapestry of life continues to thrive, both within their walls and in the uncharted territories we face beyond our home planet. The responsibility we undertake in realizing these designs is monumental; the future of biodiversity may well depend on our ingenuity, determination, and respect for the intricate web of life that binds all organisms to the universe. The journey to create these celestial repositories will not only define our relationship with the cosmos but also illuminate our understanding of what it means to be guardians of life itself.

5. Implementing Advanced Technologies

5.1. The Role of Artificial Intelligence in Preservation

The integration of artificial intelligence (AI) into the preservation of genetic material marks a transformative advancement in both the biological sciences and our ambitious cosmic initiatives. As humanity strides towards the goal of interstellar DNA vaults—repositories designed to safeguard the genetic blueprints of life—AI emerges as a potent ally in managing, monitoring, and optimizing the multifaceted tasks involved in these complex endeavors.

Initially, one must appreciate the magnitude of data generated through DNA analysis, genetic sequencing, and biosystems monitoring. In the modern context, each organism's genetic information translates into vast datasets that require adept management for analysis and interpretation. AI algorithms, particularly those based on machine learning techniques, have proven exceptionally capable of recognizing patterns within large data sets and extracting actionable insights. By implementing AI-driven data analytics within DNA vaults, researchers can optimize the preservation conditions and improve our understanding of genetic diversity.

Monitoring the health and integrity of biological samples stored within these vaults is an ongoing necessity. AI systems can be programmed to continuously evaluate key environmental parameters— such as temperature, humidity, and radiation levels—while employing predictive analytics to identify deviations from established thresholds that could jeopardize genetic material. In the event of anomalies, AI can automate corrective actions, adjust storage conditions, or alert custodians, thus preventing detrimental outcomes to the stored DNA.

Moreover, as scientific exploration and experimentation progress, AI technologies can facilitate bioinformatics by providing the infrastructure necessary to navigate the complexities of genomics. AI can accelerate genomic data processing by employing sophisticated algorithms for sequence alignment, variant calling, and evolutionary analysis. This rapid processing empowers researchers to conduct comparative studies regarding genetic resilience and adaptability, yielding insights that inform conservation strategies.

In the context of constructing interstellar DNA vaults, the role of AI extends beyond mere storage management. Advanced algorithms can simulate various storage environments and their consequences on biological materials, enabling optimal design choices before the physical construction of the vaults. Through virtual modeling, researchers can experiment with various architectural configurations and their corresponding effects on DNA viability, thus paving the way for innovations that prioritize preservation.

As interstellar missions are planned, AI's capabilities will be indispensable in optimizing the logistics of long-duration space missions. From orchestrating the transportation of genetic materials to calculating optimal launch trajectories and resource allocations, AI-driven systems can ensure that every operation proceeds with efficiency and precision. The ability to analyze real-time data from spacecraft systems—brought together by AI—could redefine our approach to interstellar logistics and management.

Artificial intelligence also enables innovative interfaces for interacting with the DNA vaults. Through the integration of machine learning models into user interfaces, researchers and custodians can gain insights into the health of the stored genetic samples through intuitive visualizations and analytics. These interfaces can facilitate both remote and immediate interactions, allowing custodians to monitor their vaults without the need to compromise the containment environments.

The ethical implications of implementing AI in genetic preservation must also be paramount in our discussions. Questions regarding data ownership, algorithmic transparency, and biases in genetic analysis prompt a necessary dialogue about the moral responsibilities associated with AI's role in conservation. Practices that ensure equity, accountability, and democratic oversight become vital in this endeavor. The use of AI in ecological stewardship should reflect a commitment to inclusivity, ensuring that diverse stakeholders—from scientists to indigenous communities—contribute to shaping the trajectory of these technologies.

Furthermore, as human presence disperses into the cosmos, the intersection of AI and ethics will become even more critical. The decision-making processes AI systems employ must be rooted in ethical frameworks that reflect our collective commitment to biodiversity preservation. A carefully considered approach to programming AI for ecological stewardship will shape the systems that manage our cosmic heritage.

In summary, the role of artificial intelligence in the preservation of genetic material epitomizes the marriage of technological innovation with ecological consciousness. By harnessing AI's capabilities, humanity can elevate its efforts in safeguarding the intricate tapestry of life while embarking on a journey among the stars. As we engineer DNA vaults to protect our planet's genetic diversity, AI will serve as a critical partner in managing complexities, enhancing operational efficiency, and ensuring that our legacy—our precious biological heritage—is preserved and celebrated across the cosmos. Ultimately, this collaboration will stand at the forefront of humanity's responsibly dictated stewardship, illuminating pathways to a sustainable future in which life thrives in dynamic harmony with technology, both on Earth and beyond.

5.2. Utilizing Nanotechnology for DNA Repair

The application of nanotechnology in the context of DNA repair presents a revolutionary advance in our understanding of genetic preservation and restoration, particularly as humanity embarks on the ambitious project of creating interstellar DNA vaults. As we prepare to safeguard the genetic legacy of Earth's biodiversity, harnessing this cutting-edge technology enables us to manage and rectify the inevitable degradation that accompanies the passage of time and exposure to various environmental stressors, including those found in space.

Nanotechnology, concerned with dimensions typically between 1 and 100 nanometers, leverages the unique properties of materials at this scale to manipulate and repair biological systems with astounding precision. When applied to DNA repair mechanisms, nanotechnology offers innovative strategies that could enhance the resilience of genetic material, both during storage in DNA vaults and in the potential reintroduction of organisms to extraterrestrial environments.

At the molecular level, the DNA double helix, while robust, is susceptible to damage from various intrusions, including spontaneous mutations, environmental factors, and radiation diseases. The introduction of nanoparticles engineered to interact specifically with DNA allows for precise targeting of damaged sites, enabling repair mechanisms akin to natural cellular repair pathways but at a vastly accelerated rate. These nanoparticles can be designed to act as carriers for DNA repair enzymes, delivering them directly to the sites of damage where they are needed most. By infiltrating the cellular environment and recognizing specific markers of DNA damage, these nanomaterials can facilitate localized repair efforts with high efficiency.

The ability to develop targeted nanoparticles extends to the incorporation of molecular recognition elements, such as aptamers or antibodies, which can guide repair enzymes to precisely the locations needing intervention. Specifically tailored nanoparticles could be engineered to bind to distinct types of DNA lesions, ensuring that they deliver the necessary repair machinery only when required—a critical factor that minimizes potential off-target effects and bolsters the overall fidelity of the repair processes. This capability is paramount in the context of cosmic exposure, where DNA might endure damage from cosmic radiation or environmental factors faced during space travel.

In exploring the specific types of nanoparticles employed in DNA repair, we find a myriad of options, from liposomes, dendrimers, and gold nanoparticles to quantum dots. Each of these materials presents unique advantages, including biocompatibility, ease of functionalization, and the capacity to carry multiple therapeutic agents. Gold nanoparticles, for instance, are particularly promising due to their tunable surface properties and compatibility with biological systems, creating a platform for effective targeted delivery of repair enzymes or even fragments of DNA designed to replace or supplement damaged sequences.

Moreover, the application of nanotechnology extends beyond simply repairing damaged DNA; it also encompasses the realm of strengthening and enhancing DNA stability. Nanomaterials can be engineered to scaffold around DNA strands, providing a protective barrier that fortifies genetic material against oxidative stress from exposure to high-energy radiation or extreme temperatures—conditions prevalent in both space and within contemporary terrestrial environments punctuated by human activity.

In addition, the incorporation of smart nano-devices that respond to environmental cues is another exciting frontier in the intersection of nanotechnology and DNA preservation. Such devices could autonomously monitor the stability and integrity of stored genetic material, prompting corrective interventions when specific thresholds of damage or degradation are detected. This continuous monitoring capacity not only bolsters preservation strategies but also aligns with the broader goals of sustainability and resilience in the context of cosmic custodianship.

The application of nanotechnology for DNA repair also generates foundational ethical discussions. As we contemplate the manipulation of genetic material, we confront questions related to the limits of technological progress and the moral implications of intervening at such a fundamental level. How do we define intervention in the natural order of life? What responsibilities do we assume when we design organisms to exhibit enhanced resilience in cosmic environments? The potential benefits derived from these advancements compel us to navigate these questions carefully, ensuring that our technological pursuits do not deepen inequalities or create unintended ecological consequences.

Furthermore, international collaboration will play a vital role as we expand our understanding of nanotechnology's applications in DNA preservation and restoration. Engaging transdisciplinary teams from various sectors—including molecular biology, nanotechnology, bioethics, and ecology—will facilitate the establishment of guidelines and protocols that underpin responsible and equitable practices in implementing these advanced techniques.

As humankind stands on the precipice of this extraordinary journey among the stars, leveraging nanotechnology as a cornerstone for DNA repair represents a beacon of hope for preserving genetic diversity and fostering life in extraterrestrial environments. Acting as facilitators of resilience and adaptivity, these microscopic wonders form a key element in our grand vision of securing Earth's biological legacies across the cosmos. The commitment to employing nanotechnology—rooted in scientific rigor and ethical reflection—embodies our responsibility as custodians of life, ensuring that the tales encoded within our genetic material not only endure but also thrive across the vast expanses of the universe.

5.3. Bioinformatics and Data Management

In the age of big data, bioinformatics and data management stand as pillars that support the ambitious framework of preserving life through interstellar DNA vaults. As humanity ventures into the realm of the cosmos, the capacity to efficiently store, retrieve, analyze, and update vast amounts of genetic data becomes a compelling necessity. This subchapter delves into the systems and technologies that will enable comprehensive bioinformatics infrastructures tailored for the extraterrestrial context.

The sheer volume of data generated through genomic sequencing is staggering. A single genome can encompass billions of base pairs, and with thousands of species across myriad ecosystems, the challenge of managing this biological data cannot be overstated. Bioinformatics —the intersection of biology, computer science, and information technology—provides the tools required to sift through these mountains of genetic data and extract meaningful insights. As we contemplate the deployment of DNA vaults across the stars, we need robust systems that can efficiently store and analyze not just the genomic sequences but also the annotations, genetic relationships, ecological interactions, and context around these diverse organisms.

Central to this enterprise is the development of a unified data architecture that encompasses standardized protocols for data collection, storage, and retrieval. Given the complexities of genetic data and the need for interdisciplinary collaboration, establishing these standards is paramount. Researchers from diverse fields—genetics, ecology, space science, and information technology—must collaborate to create a framework that ensures consistency while allowing flexibility to adapt as new data accumulate. This architecture will be foundational in developing databases that aggregate genetic sequences, phenotypic data, environmental conditions, and experimental results relevant to biological preservation.

Cloud computing serves as a powerful ally in this effort. By leveraging cloud infrastructures, DNA vaults can ensure the accessibility of genetic data across vast distances and varied locations. The ability to access and analyze data dynamically—whether from Earth, a lunar outpost, or a Martian habitation module—becomes essential in real-time decision-making and strategic planning for genetic conservation efforts. By integrating bioinformatics databases into cloud systems, scientists can collaborate seamlessly regardless of their physical location, enabling global insights to inform local actions.

Machine learning and artificial intelligence further revolutionize data management in bioinformatics. These technologies can sift through extensive datasets to recognize patterns, make predictions, and identify relationships among genetic traits and their environmental influences. For instance, AI algorithms could analyze genomic data of various species to predict their resilience in changing extraterrestrial environments, which is crucial in the selection process for organisms intended for preservation in DNA vaults.

Another vital aspect of bioinformatics relates to the annotation of genetic information. Annotations provide critical context to genetic sequences, linking them to functional elements, evolutionary history, and ecological roles. As DNA is sequenced and stored within vaults, thorough annotation processes will ensure that each genetic entry embarks on its journey with an accompanying understanding of its significance. Researchers must develop sophisticated pipelines to facilitate the visualization and exploration of this annotated data, thereby enhancing comprehension among scientists and custodians alike.

Data security is also an essential consideration. The immense responsibility of preserving the biodiversity of Earth extends beyond just collection; it encompasses safeguarding this valuable information against loss or tampering. As we create bioinformatics platforms, robust security measures must be implemented to ensure that unauthorized access is prevented, and integrity is upheld. Employing measures such as encryption and multi-factor authentication will be crucial in protecting genetic information, especially as the stakes rise and the potential consequences of compromise escalate.

Interoperability is another crucial factor in data management across cosmic vaults. Different research institutions may employ varied data collection protocols and software systems. Interoperability ensures that knowledge can be shared flexibly and effectively, fostering collaboration and allowing for the integration of diverse datasets into broader biological analyses. The adoption of standards, such as those outlined by the Global Alliance for Genomics and Health, will facilitate smoother data exchange and ensure that the broadest spectrum of genetic diversity is captured and understood.

Additionally, engaging with citizen science plays a significant role in augmenting bioinformatics efforts. By opening platforms for public collaboration, enthusiasts and amateur scientists can contribute to the data collection process. This crowdsourced information, captured through various means including mobile apps and web tools, can complement the professional data gathered by institutions and provide opportunities for new insights into genetic diversity.

Ultimately, the design of bioinformatics strategies for managing genetic data in the context of DNA vaults must embody the principles of accessibility, collaboration, and sustainability. As humanity seeks to preserve and potentially revive biological systems across the cosmos, the frameworks hired for data management and bioinformatics must reflect our commitment to the responsible stewardship of life's diversity.

In conclusion, the integration of effective bioinformatics and data management practices serves as the backbone of our cosmic preservation initiatives. These systems will empower future generations of custodians to make informed decisions as they safeguard the essence of Earth's biodiversity amid a universe of uncharted possibilities. By leveraging advanced technologies and fostering collaborative frameworks, we can ensure that the narratives embedded within genetic materials endure, allowing life to flourish among the stars.

5.4. Quantum Computing in Gene Sequencing

In the quest to revolutionize gene sequencing, quantum computing offers an unprecedented avenue for advancements that could reshape biotechnology's landscape, especially in the context of cosmic preservation. This cutting-edge technology signifies a paradigm shift in how genetic data is processed and understood, allowing for complex calculations that far exceed the capabilities of classical computing. As we aim to create interstellar DNA vaults, we must explore how quantum computing can enhance our approaches to gene sequencing, ultimately safeguarding the intricacies of life on Earth for the future.

Quantum computing leverages the principles of quantum mechanics, utilizing quantum bits or qubits, to perform computations at scales and speeds that classical computers cannot achieve. A qubit can represent a 0, a 1, or any quantum superposition of these states, enabling a higher degree of parallelism in computation. This virtually limitless processing capability allows for solving intricate problems, such as those found in genomics, much faster than traditional methodologies.

In genetics, one of the most daunting challenges lies in deciphering the vast amounts of data generated by sequencing the genomes of countless organisms. The sheer volume of data produced is monumental, necessitating sophisticated analytical techniques to extract meaningful insights. Quantum computing can significantly expedite tasks such as genome assembly, where different fragments of DNA are pieced together to determine the complete genome sequence. Quantum algorithms can sort through large-scale genomic data exponentially faster, allowing researchers to identify patterns, variations, and anomalies within sequences, thus enhancing our understanding of genetic diversity and resilience.

Moreover, quantum computing is poised to facilitate the modeling of complex biomolecular interactions, a key component in understanding how genetic variations influence phenotypes. Classical methods often struggle with the intricate dynamics of proteins, RNA, and other biomolecules. Quantum simulations of these interactions can provide insights into biochemical pathways, allowing scientists to predict how mutations may affect biological processes. This capability is particularly valuable when considering organisms for preservation in interstellar vaults, where adaptability to extraterrestrial environments will be critical.

The intersection of quantum computing and artificial intelligence (AI) further amplifies its potential in gene sequencing. By integrating AI-driven solutions with quantum computational power, researchers can develop hybrid systems that learn from vast datasets and refine their algorithms in real time. Machine learning models, powered by quantum computing, can enhance gene prediction accuracy and improve our understanding of complex disease mechanisms by simulating genetic interactions at unprecedented scales. This approach would not only yield richer data but also pave the way for precision breeding and genetic modifications aimed at improving resilience in space environments.

Quantum algorithms such as Grover's or Shor's algorithm offer additional potential by optimizing search processes across vast databases of genomic information. Grover's algorithm, for instance, allows for quadratic speed-up in searching unsorted databases, which could significantly reduce the time required to identify specific genetic sequences or mutations among extensive genomic datasets. Shor's algorithm, while primarily focused on factorization problems, inspires thoughts about tackling complicated computational issues inherent in genetic data encryption and security—a factor that might be crucial as we preserve life across the cosmos.

When positioning quantum computing within the context of cosmic preservation, we must also consider the implications of such a powerful tool. The capabilities unlocked by quantum computing could lead to sweeping advancements in synthetic biology, where engineered organisms are designed with specific traits for adaptation to extraterrestrial environments. While these prospects are promising, they also necessitate serious ethical considerations. The manipulation of life through advanced biotechnologies, informed by quantum computing, invites a dialogue around the moral dimensions of playing an active role in life's evolutionary pathways.

Additionally, as we transition to a paradigm where quantum computing becomes integral to biological research, training the next generation of scientists in both quantum mechanics and biological sciences will be essential. Educational programs must evolve to prepare individuals who can adeptly navigate and harness these technologies' potential benefits. By fostering interdisciplinary expertise, we inspire a new cohort of custodians capable of leveraging quantum advancements to protect life amid the uncertainties of the cosmos.

In summary, quantum computing significantly enhances our ability to navigate the complexities of gene sequencing, creating a future where we can better analyze, manipulate, and preserve genetic diversity. By unearthing the complexities of life at unprecedented scales, quantum computing serves as a harbinger of innovation in our cosmic preservation efforts. As we endeavor to safeguard Earth's genetic legacies for generations to come, embracing quantum technologies empowers humanity to rise to the challenges posed by life in the universe—as protectors of its essence amidst the stars.

5.5. Interactive Interfaces for Monitoring DNA Vaults

In a future where humanity boldly ventures into the vastness of the universe, the preservation of life's essence takes center stage, particularly through the establishment of interstellar DNA vaults. These vaults, designed to safeguard Earth's biological legacy, require innovative interactive interfaces to monitor and manage the intricate genomic treasures they house. The relationship between advanced technology and biological preservation is paramount, entrusting humanity's responsibility to shield the blueprint of life against cosmic uncertainties.

The intricacies of designing these interfaces involve balancing function and user experience while ensuring that a wealth of information about stored genetic materials is readily accessible. As expert custodians navigate the complex landscape of DNA preservation, they require an interface that serves not only as a control panel but also as a comprehensive data dashboard. This dashboard will display real-time metrics of temperature, humidity, radiation levels, and other critical environmental factors that could affect the integrity of the DNA stored within, allowing for instantaneous monitoring and proactive intervention when deviations occur.

Central to this interface is an AI-driven analytics engine capable of processing vast amounts of data generated from the vaults' environmental sensors. By leveraging machine learning algorithms, the system can analyze historical environmental data to predict potential fluctuations and adjust preservation parameters dynamically. For instance, if a sensor detects a temperature rise above the predefined threshold, the interactive interface could automatically activate cryogenic cooling systems while notifying operational guardians through visual alerts. Such intelligent automation minimizes human error and maximizes the chances of maintaining optimal preservation conditions.

Moreover, the interface could employ virtual and augmented reality capabilities, providing custodians with immersive experiences that take them inside the vaults. By visually representing the DNA storage environment, custodians could navigate through layers of genetic information, receiving informative prompts about individual samples and their historical contexts. This engaging, three-dimensional interaction would not only enhance user understanding but also foster emotional connections with the organisms they are protecting. Drawing attention to the unique attributes of each species—its role in ecosystems and evolutionary lineage—can galvanize deeper commitment among custodians engaged in this vital mission.

Another integral component of the interactive interface is the ability to facilitate collaborative efforts across multiple locations, essential as humanity establishes a global network of cosmic repositories. By connecting various DNA vaults through a centralized communication platform, the custodians can share findings, experiences, and data instantaneously across vast distances—whether they are overseeing a vault on Earth or one situated on Mars. This interconnectedness allows for collaborative decision-making, leveraging the shared expertise of global biologists, ecologists, and technologists. Web-based platforms will enable remote diagnostics and troubleshooting, ensuring custodians can address issues swiftly, regardless of their physical locations.

To further promote inclusivity and empowerment, training modules could be integrated into the interface, allowing new guardians to simulate monitoring and management practices. These interactive lessons could simulate various scenarios, such as emergencies arising from equipment failure or shifts in environmental conditions, preparing custodians to respond effectively when faced with real challenges. Gamification techniques may also be employed to engage and excite users, fostering a strong sense of stewardship and collective responsibility for preserving life in the cosmos.

Security plays a vital role in the design of these interactive interfaces, given the importance of safeguarding both genetic information and the overarching mission. Enhancements such as multi-factor authentication and blockchain-based records would protect access to sensitive genetic data, ensuring only authorized personnel can make changes. Transparency in access logs also nurtures a culture of accountability, where actions within the interface are meticulously documented and verifiable.

In summary, the interactive interfaces for monitoring DNA vaults represent a convergence of technology, biology, and stewardship, essential to the future of cosmic preservation. As custodians become more adept at navigating the complexities of genetic material conservation, these interfaces will empower them with the information, tools, and community they require to safeguard life's intricate tapestries across the universe. Through the fusion of advanced technologies, engagement strategies, and security measures, humanity will not only protect our biological heritage but also affirm its commitment to the continuity of life among the stars. With each interaction, we write a new chapter in the story of preservation—one that ensures the legacy of Earth's biodiversity can flourish in the face of cosmic challenges ahead.

6. Logistics of Space Storage

6.1. Transportation of Fragile Genetic Material

Transportation of fragile genetic material across terrestrial and extraterrestrial environments plays a crucial role in our mission to preserve Earth's biodiversity through interstellar DNA vaults. As we contemplate the logistics of storing genetic material in space, it is essential to consider the delicate nature of DNA, the potential for degradation, and the need for optimal transport conditions. This subchapter will explore the technical, logistical, and security dimensions of ensuring that fragile genetic samples are preserved during the transportation process, noting the importance of interdisciplinary collaboration in this endeavor.

The initial step in the transportation of fragile genetic material involves careful planning and preparation. Samples must be collected, processed, and contained in a manner that minimizes the risk of contamination or damage. High-quality storage containers designed specifically for genetic samples must be utilized, ensuring that these materials are maintained in a stable environment that mitigates factors such as temperature fluctuations, moisture exposure, and physical stress during transit. The choice of transport medium is paramount; cryogenic storage solutions, such as liquid nitrogen or specialized cold packs, can help maintain the integrity of DNA during transport.

Material choice extends to the development of advanced packaging systems that use insulated containers crafted with materials offering thermal protection and radiation shielding. These should be lightweight yet robust, enabling them to endure the rigors of launch, space travel, and potential landings on celestial bodies. Adapting existing biobanking materials to a space-friendly standard will integrate scientific knowledge with engineering innovation—a necessity for the successful transport of genetic material beyond our home planet.

Mitigating physical stress during transport is another critical consideration. Vibration, acceleration, and deceleration are inherent in rocket launches, and these forces can compromise the integrity of fragile biological samples. To combat potential damage from these forces, custom-engineered shock-absorbing systems—such as internal padding and vibration-dampening mechanisms—can be implemented within packages. Employing validated transportation routes and procedures that adhere to best practices in biocompatibility can also be integral to preserving sensitive genetic materials.

The external environment during transport matters as well. While the journey to space is often well-planned, unexpected delays may occur due to weather, logistics, or mechanical failures. Incorporating advanced monitoring technologies inside the containers to track environmental conditions—such as temperature, humidity, and radiation exposure—offers an additional layer of assurance. Data from these sensors can be transmitted back to custodians in real time, alerting them to any deviations from set parameters and allowing for swift corrective actions.

Upon reaching the destination—whether it be a space station, lunar outpost, Martian habitat, or an interstellar vault—efficient protocols must be in place for unloading and transferring the genetic material from transport containers to storage facilities. This involves ensuring sterile handling and carefully maintaining optimal conditions to prevent contamination, physical damage, or temperature fluctuations. Training personnel in the best practices for handling these samples is essential to uphold the integrity of the genetic materials.

Logistic considerations also extend to monitoring chain-of-custody documentation, ensuring strict adherence to bioethics and legal frameworks during transportation. This includes keeping meticulous records throughout the transport phase—documenting the origins of the samples, their handling protocols, and conditions en route. Maintaining detailed transparency serves to protect the intellectual property rights associated with these biological materials, fostering trust among international collaborators.

Collaboration with space agencies and various aerospace partners becomes essential in addressing the logistical complexities of transporting genetic materials. Engaging organizations such as NASA, ESA, and private aerospace companies brings together expertise in spacecraft design, launch procedures, and environmental handling, facilitating robust transport solutions that adhere to safety and reliability standards.

In addition to partnerships, continued research into emerging technologies can support the evolution of transport methods for genetic materials as our ambitions grow. Innovations in robotics, automation, and AI can streamline loading and unloading processes while mastering data handling applications that assess and predict optimal transportation scenarios.

In conclusion, the transportation of fragile genetic material constitutes a multifaceted challenge that necessitates meticulous planning, innovative engineering, and collaboration across various fields of expertise. By addressing storage, transport protocols, environmental monitoring, and chain-of-custody requirements, we can ensure that precious genetic samples endure their journey into space unscathed, safeguarding the genetic blueprints of Earth's biological legacy for future interstellar challenges. Together, these efforts will underpin our commitment to cosmic conservation, embodying the principles of stewardship that guide what lies ahead as we seek to preserve life's essence among the stars.

6.2. Minimizing Energy Consumption for Sustainability

In the context of advancing our cosmic endeavor to safeguard the genetic heritage of Earth, minimizing energy consumption for sustainability represents a critical aspect of environmental stewardship. As humanity endeavors to establish DNA vaults among the stars, a conscientious approach to energy utilization will not only serve to protect our planet's biodiversity but also create sustainable systems capable of functioning in the relentless conditions of outer space.

This subchapter will explore strategies and technologies aimed at minimizing energy consumption while maintaining the efficacy and integrity of the DNA preservation processes.

To begin with, it is vital to assess energy consumption patterns in the design and operation of DNA vaults. Traditional preservation methods, particularly those employing cryogenic techniques, rely heavily on constant energy supply to maintain ultra-low temperatures necessary for DNA integrity. The environmental impact of such high energy demands necessitates innovation, urging us to identify energy-efficient alternatives that can function effectively under the constraints of space travel. The development of technologies that optimize energy efficiency will be crucial in reducing our ecological footprint and increasing the sustainability of our cosmic initiatives.

One avenue for minimizing energy consumption lies in the integration of renewable energy sources. Solar power, in particular, emerges as a frontrunner for energy supply in space habitats. The placement of photovoltaic panels on the surfaces of DNA vaults—as well as on spacecraft en route to interstellar locations—can harness sunlight for energy generation. Space-based solar panels could provide a continuous energy supply without the deleterious effects associated with fossil fuels. Leveraging the advantages of solar energy not only minimizes dependency on non-renewable sources but also promotes the notion of sustainable living in space.

In addition to solar power, another promising option is the utilization of nuclear energy. Compact nuclear reactors or radioisotope thermo-electric generators (RTGs) can supply consistent and reliable power, offering robustness in environments where solar energy may be limited or variable. The exploration of advanced nuclear technologies could provide the energy densities necessary for prolonged missions and the maintenance of cryogenic systems essential for DNA preservation.

Emphasizing energy-efficient design principles during the construction of DNA vaults holds great promise. Optimizing the architectural layout to enhance thermal insulation will reduce energy expenditure significantly. Utilizing advanced materials with high thermal resistance can prevent heat exchange, ensuring that the vaults maintain stable conditions with minimal energy input. Innovations such as vacuum insulation panels or aerogels can provide lightweight solutions that bolster energy efficiency without adding substantial weight to the overall structure.

Moreover, employing passive energy systems—designed to take advantage of surrounding environmental conditions—can further contribute to sustainability efforts. These systems could integrate concepts such as heat reclamation or natural ventilation, where minor fluctuations in temperature are utilized to balance energy needs. In space, utilizing thermal gradients generated by solar exposure or the spacecraft's own heat could help regulate the overall energy consumption of the DNA vaults.

The role of technological advancement in energy management cannot be understated. Implementing smart energy systems—equipped with sensors and artificial intelligence—can optimize energy use and reduce wastage. These systems could monitor environmental conditions and apply machine learning algorithms to predict energy demand based on historical data, adjusting energy supply dynamically to align with real-time requirements. Such adaptability would not only conserve energy but also foster greater resilience in energy management practices.

Furthermore, the overall architecture of transportation should also be considered in this context. Streamlined designs that minimize drag and optimize weight will naturally translate into reduced energy consumption during launches and in-space travel. Transporting DNA samples in lightweight, energy-efficient containers using advanced aerospace engineering principles can leverage significant gains in energy savings during transit to the vaults.

In tandem with establishing energy-minimizing strategies, adopting a culture of sustainability within the broader frameworks of cosmic preservation must be prioritized. Educational initiatives that empha-size the importance of energy-efficient practices can help nurture future generations of guardians who are mindful of sustainability. This cultural shift will engender a collective responsibility toward energy stewardship, ensuring that all aspects of cosmic preservation are aligned with ecological awareness.

Ultimately, minimizing energy consumption for sustainability within the realm of cosmic DNA preservation rests on the intersection of re-newable energy adoption, innovative design principles, technological advancements, and a cultural commitment to ecological responsibil-ity. As humanity embarks on its cosmic journey, establishing efficient energy systems for the preservation of life will not only secure Earth's biological heritage but also position us as conscientious stewards of life among the stars. Armed with these strategies, we can confidently enter a future where the essence of biodiversity is protected and celebrated, ensuring its legacy amid the cosmos for generations yet to come.

6.3. Creating Space-ready Containers

Creating space-ready containers for the preservation of DNA within the vast expanse of the cosmos is a multifaceted endeavor that neces-sitates advanced engineering, a deep understanding of biological materials, stringent safety protocols, and innovative design practices. As humanity opens new frontiers in space exploration, the imperative to safeguard the genetic blueprints of life transcends mere conve-nience—emphasizing the need to develop containers that are resilient, adaptive, and capable of ensuring the integrity of DNA under the harshest conditions imaginable.

At the core of designing these containers is an understanding of the properties of DNA itself. Deoxyribonucleic acid is sensitive to environmental factors such as temperature, radiation, and humidity. Therefore, any space-ready container must be crafted with materials that provide a protective barrier against these deleterious influences. Advanced polymers or composites that can withstand extreme fluc-tuations in temperature, whether scorching heat or intense cold, may be utilized. The materials must not only insulate but also possess the mechanical integrity to endure the rigors of launch and transport, avoiding deformation or breach during the various stages of a mission.

Cryogenic preservation of DNA necessitates that these containers can sustain ultra-low temperatures, often below −80 degrees Celsius, for extended periods. To achieve this, innovative thermal insulation technologies must be harnessed. Vacuum insulation, which provides superior thermal resistance by eliminating convective heat transfer, would be instrumental in maintaining the cold required for DNA integrity. The containers might also be lined with phase change materials that can absorb or release heat as needed, further stabilizing the internal environment.

Apart from thermal considerations, radiation shielding is a critical factor. Cosmic radiation poses significant risks to biological materials; exposure can lead to DNA strand breaks and mutations, jeopardizing the long-term viability of stored samples. To combat this, the containers could be constructed with materials that offer effective radiation attenuation, such as polyethylene or specialized organosilicate glasses. These designs may incorporate a multi-layered approach: an outer layer that absorbs radiation, followed by additional layers acting as thermal insulation and structural support.

Another essential element of design is the integration of advanced monitoring systems within the containers. Real-time data on temperature, humidity, and radiation levels should be continuously relayed to custodians. Incorporation of nanotechnology, such as nanosensors, can greatly enhance monitoring capabilities, enabling the detection of any fluctuations that could compromise the integrity of the DNA samples. Furthermore, these smart sensors should be designed to alert custodians in real-time to any deviations from the established optimal preservation conditions, allowing for immediate corrective actions.

The containers must also account for biosecurity measures to prevent contamination. The design could include multiple seals and sterilization barriers to ensure that the genetic material remains pure and uncontaminated throughout its journey. Utilizing UV sterilization techniques prior to storage can ensure the internal environment is free of unwanted microorganisms. Additionally, protocols must be developed for safely accessing the containers, allowing for retrieval and analysis without compromising the system's integrity.

Ultimately, the design of these space-ready containers should adopt a modular approach that allows for scalability and adaptation. Different containers may be necessary for diverse types of DNA samples—be it plant, animal, or microbial. Modular designs can facilitate seamless integration into various missions, accommodating the specific preservation needs of each organism while also allowing for easier repair or upgrade as technology evolves.

Collaboration among experts in fields ranging from material science, aerospace engineering, biological conservation, and bioethics will be essential in this endeavor. Such interdisciplinary partnerships enable a holistic approach to designing containers that not only fulfill functional requirements but also align with broader principles of ecological stewardship and sustainability.

Furthermore, as we look toward the future, we must consider how these containers could facilitate future reintroduction of the preserved genetic material into suitable celestial environments. Designing them with features that allow for easy extraction and possibly the cultivation of stored organisms in controlled conditions could pave the way for new ecosystems on distant planets.

In conclusion, the challenge of creating space-ready containers for DNA preservation demands cutting-edge technology, rigorous scientific principles, and a commitment to the ethical implications of our preservation efforts. As we seek to ensure the genetic continuity of Earth's biodiversity among the stars, we are not only safeguarding life but also crafting a legacy that embodies our responsibility as custodians of the intricate tapestry of existence. By innovatively addressing the complexity of this endeavor, we fortify our mission to protect life against an uncertain cosmic future, ensuring that the essence of Earth's biodiversity endures and thrives across the universe.

6.4. Collaboration with Space Agencies

As humanity seeks to expand its understanding of the cosmos and safeguard the genetic blueprints of life, collaboration with space agencies emerges as a pivotal element in realizing these ambitious goals. Working alongside established organizations such as NASA, ESA, and their international counterparts, this partnership not only enhances our technological capabilities but also strengthens the ethical framework underpinning our cosmic ambitions. The successful design, implementation, and management of interstellar DNA vaults require a convergence of expertise from various scientific disciplines, making collaboration essential for fostering innovation while navigating unique challenges.

The nature of such partnerships begins with shared objectives: to protect Earth's genetic diversity, facilitate the exploration of new environments, and ensure the long-term survival of life beyond our home planet. Creating platforms for cooperation among space agencies allows for a pooling of resources, ideas, and technologies that can be catalyzed towards initiating and maintaining DNA vault projects. This is particularly important as we design and develop storage strategies capable of withstanding the harsh conditions of space, which include cosmic radiation, extreme temperatures, and the vacuum of space itself.

Building on the existing frameworks of international space collaboration, a nuanced approach to communication arises. Regular workshops, conferences, and symposiums can be organized to facilitate the exchange of knowledge and strategic planning. Through these gatherings, researchers, engineers, and policymakers can foster discussions around both scientific breakthroughs and the ethical implications associated with genetic preservation. Such exchanges pave the way for a comprehensive understanding of how best to utilize genetic materials across different environmental contexts, while simultaneously reinforcing our collective commitment to responsible stewardship.

The collaborative relationship with space agencies extends to developing cutting-edge technologies necessary for the transportation, storage, and monitoring of DNA samples. As the challenge of preserving fragile genetic material in space arises, projects may include the design and testing of advanced cryogenic systems, vacuum-sealed containers, and robust transportation protocols—all rooted in aerospace engineering principles. Engaging engineers and scientists from diverse backgrounds ensures that the vaults are not only functional but also represent the best practices in various areas of expertise.

One area where collaboration becomes essential is in the exploration of potential off-world storage locations. Space agencies are equipped with advanced knowledge and technological resources to conduct planetary surveys, assess geological stability, and evaluate environmental dynamics across celestial bodies. By working together, we can identify optimal sites for DNA vaults that are accessible, secure, and equipped to foster future ecological restoration efforts. For example, research might focus on lunar or Martian landscapes, carefully considering factors such as temperature, radiation levels, and the potential to establish self-sustaining habitats.

Furthermore, the collaboration extends beyond technical expertise to encompass a shared vision of ethical practices in cosmic conservation. As we contemplate the implications of genetic manipulation and DNA storage, establishing ethical guidelines and frameworks becomes paramount. Space agencies can provide guidance in protocols regarding the responsible use of technology and the potential impacts of introducing Earth-based organisms into extraterrestrial environments. Collective discussions should also address the moral obligations we hold as stewards of biodiversity and empower nations and communities to partake in this essential dialogue.

In addition, funding opportunities arise through collaboration with space agencies, providing vital resources for research initiatives, technological innovations, and public outreach efforts. Joint proposals for grants or financially-backed programs can amplify our endeavors around cosmic preservation, ensuring we have the means to develop and execute our plans effectively. Establishing partnerships with universities and research institutions can further enrich these efforts, creating a vibrant ecosystem of research and development that actively engages the next generation of scientists.

Public engagement also plays a significant role in this collaborative landscape. Leveraging the outreach capabilities of space agencies can help disseminate information about the importance of biodiversity conservation and the ramifications of exploring life beyond Earth. Formal programs can be initiated to educate communities on the significance of preserving genetic heritage while inspiring a sense of connection to the cosmic narrative. By engaging the public through educational initiatives, creative storytelling, and multimedia platforms, we forge a united front that celebrates our shared responsibility to protect life among the stars.

Ultimately, collaboration with space agencies embodies the spirit of innovation, responsibility, and foresight that defines humanity's journey into the cosmos. By pooling resources, expertise, and ethical frameworks, we can not only advance our understanding of life but also construct a framework where the genetic treasures of Earth are safeguarded against the uncertainties of the universe. In this collective pursuit, we sow the seeds of hope for a future where life may flourish, transcending boundaries and lighting the way for generations yet unborn, ready to explore new worlds among the stars while honoring the rich tapestry of life from which they arise.

6.5. Ensuring Security in Outer Space

In the futuristic pursuit of interstellar exploration, ensuring security in outer space emerges as a critical component of the broader mission to safeguard the genetic legacy of life on Earth. As humanity steps boldly into the cosmos, navigating the unforgiving celestial environment necessitates a robust framework to protect these invaluable genetic materials stored within DNA vaults. This framework not only encompasses physical security measures but also extends to safe-guarding against cosmic threats, unauthorized access, and potential contamination or degradation of samples during transit and storage.

The physical security of DNA vaults in space begins with the careful selection of locations and structures capable of withstanding both natural and human-made hazards. Selecting potential sites for these vaults involves assessing their geological stability and vulnerability to environmental conditions. The preliminary analysis should consider areas on celestial bodies such as the Moon or Mars that are least prone to seismic activities or extreme temperature fluctuations. Built architectures must utilize advanced insulating and radiation-shield-ing materials to provide additional layers of protection, ensuring the DNA remains viable over extended periods.

Developing a defense system against external cosmic hazards repre-sents another critical aspect of securing DNA vaults. Cosmic radiation and micrometeoroid showers pose substantial threats to biological samples; therefore, employing multi-layered shielding strategies will play a key role. Vaults could be designed with a combination of materials such as polyethylene for radiation absorption and structural composites that can withstand impacts. Reinforced shields, equipped with sensors to detect changes in radiation levels, can alert custodians to potential breaches and initiate protocols to secure the vault.

Furthermore, establishing security protocols for the access and han-dling of DNA vaults is vital. This includes deploying automated systems with biometric authentication, such as retinal scans or finger-print recognition, to ensure that only authorized personnel can enter sensitive areas. The automation of sample retrieval and handling pro-cedures can reduce human error while maintaining strict control over access to genetic materials. Utilizing AI-driven technologies allows for real-time monitoring of vault conditions and rapid response to any security breaches that may occur.

Incorporating data security measures is equally important. Genetic data housed within these vaults necessitates rigorous cybersecurity protocols to prevent unauthorized access or tampering. Utilizing encryption technologies to secure data transmission and employing decentralized blockchain systems for record-keeping can enhance the integrity of genetic information, ensuring that a verifiable chain of custody is maintained.

The responsibilities of custodians extend beyond mere protection; they also encompass the ethical obligation to preserve the dignity of life contained within these vaults. Training programs should be implemented that emphasize the profound significance of genetic preservation, instilling a culture of respect among the guardians tasked with this monumental mission. Awareness of ethical implications surrounding genetic manipulation and reintroduction into extraterrestrial environments should also form a cornerstone of custodial training, guiding decision-making processes that align with humanity's broader stewardship responsibilities.

Additionally, collaboration among international space agencies is crucial in establishing comprehensive security protocols. Shared information regarding threats, best practices, and scientific advancements can strengthen the defenses surrounding these vaults, improving responses to potential issues that arise both on Earth and in space. Joint exercises and simulations can help custodians prepare for emergencies such as meteor strikes, equipment malfunctions, or security breaches.

As we consider the elements underpinning security in outer space, the concept of sustainability cannot be overlooked. Ensuring that DNA vaults remain functional over extended periods, without relying purely on Earth-based resources, is essential for long-term success. This can involve equipping vaults with self-sustaining ecosystems, reusing resources, and employing technologies that optimize energy consumption. This sustainability lens enhances security not only from a biological standpoint but also from the perspective of resource management, ensuring that vaults can operate autonomously without frequent resupply missions.

Ultimately, ensuring security in outer space forms a multifaceted strategy that requires integration across technological domains, ethical frameworks, and interdisciplinary collaboration. By embracing a holistic view of security—addressing physical threats, data integrity, ethical considerations, and sustainability—humanity can forge ahead confidently into the cosmos. With a firm commitment to safeguarding the genetic essence of life, we illuminate the pathway towards a future where humanity not only traverses the stars but does so with a profound sense of responsibility toward the intricate tapestry of life we aim to preserve. The journey to the stars is not merely a physical exploration, but rather a moral expedition to ensure and celebrate the continuity of life across the universe.

7. Exploring Potential Locations in the Universe

7.1. Cataloging Celestial Bodies

In our relentless quest to understand the universe and ensure the survival of life beyond Earth, cataloging celestial bodies has emerged as a cornerstone of our interstellar conservation efforts. This meticulous process involves not merely listing the myriad of planets, moons, and asteroids harbored in the cosmos but also systematically structuring information about their environments, compositions, and potential for harboring life. As humanity eyes the vastness of space for possible homes away from Earth, this endeavor takes on added significance, shaping future missions and the stewardship of our biological legacy.

Cataloging celestial bodies begins with the identification and characterization of the objects that populate our solar system and beyond. Telescopes, both ground-based and space-based, serve as our primary instruments in this quest. Groundbreaking observatories, utilizing advanced imaging techniques and spectrometry, allow astronomers to discern the subtle features of distant planets. The recent advancements in space telescope technology, such as the James Webb Space Telescope, have revolutionized our capacity to peer deeper into the cosmos and gather detailed data about exoplanets and their atmospheric compositions.

Once identified, the next imperative is to classify these celestial bodies based on their physical and chemical properties. Earth-like characteristics, such as the presence of liquid water, essential elements for life, and suitable atmospheric conditions, are monitored carefully, helping researchers prioritize locations for future exploration or the establishment of DNA vaults. Planning missions to examine these promising sites relies on a rich catalog of gathered information—one that encompasses geological, climatic, and potential biological factors.

The process of cataloging extends beyond merely naming celestial objects; it is about creating a comprehensive database that integrates multi-faceted scientific data. Properties like temperature ranges, gravity, radiation levels, and surface composition become critical data points in determining the suitability of a celestial body for hosting life or preserving genetic material. This necessitates the use of sophisticated data management systems that can aggregate diverse datasets from various missions, ensuring seamless access for researchers and conservationists.

Moreover, the process is not limited to our solar neighborhood. As humanity scales its explorational capabilities, understanding distant exoplanets in different star systems becomes essential. Rapid advancements in detection techniques, such as the transit method and direct imaging, yield an abundance of data about exoplanet characteristics. Every body cataloged merits examination concerning its potential to support life or the preservation of life forms adapted to its unique conditions.

A critical aspect of cataloging celestial bodies lies in evaluating their environments concerning potential threats. Cosmic radiation is pervasive across space and poses a significant danger to biological materials. Cataloging efforts incorporate data concerning radiation levels on different celestial bodies, assessing their capacity to shield genetic materials during storage and ensuring optimal conditions for their survival. Understanding these risk factors equips humanity to make informed decisions about site selection and vault design for DNA preservation.

Stability and accessibility constitute another layer of importance in the cataloging process. An ideal site for a DNA vault would not only be shielded from cosmic threats but also ensure relative ease of access for future missions. Assessing the gravitational dynamics, geological stability, and surface characteristics of celestial bodies aids in identifying those most suited for human or robotic exploration. The logistics of launching spacecraft, conducting landings, and establishing long-term outposts become intertwined with the cataloging, requiring a holistic approach to ensure successful implementation.

As researchers catalog celestial bodies, they must also remain vigilant about discovering uncharted territories. The expansive nature of the universe beckons adventurers to explore, yet many celestial objects remain hidden or undiscovered. Cataloging efforts should include data from surveys of less-explored regions, utilizing innovative observational strategies and a blend of ground-based and space-based technologies to reveal potential new sites of interest.

In conclusion, effective cataloging of celestial bodies serves as the backbone of humanity's celestial stewardship and conservation efforts. By methodically compiling and analyzing data on various bodies throughout the universe, researchers and conservationists can not only inform future missions and identification of suitable locations for DNA preservation but also reinforce our commitment to protect life in all its forms. This ambitious endeavor reflects our innate curiosity and responsibility to secure life's continuity—not just for our planet, but for the universe at large. As we refine our celestial catalogs, we lay the groundwork for a future rich with possibilities— a future where life can find new expression across the stars.

7.2. Evaluating Exoplanets for Climate Favorability

Evaluating exoplanets for climate favorability is a critical component in the effort to ensure the sustainability of life as we seek to extend our ecological stewardship beyond Earth. With thousands of exoplanets discovered in recent years, our understanding of these distant worlds has vastly improved, revealing a broad array of conditions that govern their climates. In the pursuit of safeguarding Earth's biodiversity, it becomes imperative to identify and assess exoplanets that possess climate characteristics conducive to the establishment of life—or at least, the possibility of future life.

The evaluation process begins with an understanding of what defines a climate favorable for life. This typically involves factors such as temperature, atmospheric composition, surface pressure, and the presence of liquid water, which are essential for life as we know it. The habitable zone, or Goldilocks zone, around a star—where conditions are neither too hot nor too cold—serves as a useful framework for identifying potentially viable exoplanets. However, recent studies suggest that habitability can extend beyond traditional boundaries defined strictly by distance from a star. Including the effects of atmospheric greenhouse gases, magnetic fields, and geological activity adds layers of complexity to this evaluation.

The quest for exoplanets suitable for potential life begins with sophisticated telescopic observations and remote sensing technologies. Instruments like the Kepler Space Telescope and the Transiting Exoplanet Survey Satellite (TESS) have revolutionized our ability to detect exoplanets and gather data about their sizes and orbits. These spacecraft use various methods, such as the transit method, which measures the dimming of a star as a planet passes in front of it. This detection is followed by the pursuit of spectroscopy, where light from the star that passes through a planet's atmosphere can reveal its chemical composition, helping us assess its ability to support life.

The next critical step is to analyze the atmospheres of these exoplanets to determine if they contain essential gases, such as oxygen, carbon dioxide, nitrogen, and methane. The presence of an atmosphere is crucial not only for sustaining pressure but also for protecting potential life from harmful ultraviolet (UV) radiation. Understanding how an atmosphere interacts with its planet's surface and the surrounding stellar radiation is instrumental in gauging climate stability. Computational models can simulate these interactions, providing insights into what climate conditions might be maintained over geological timescales.

Climate models play a significant role in this evaluation process, helping scientists simulate and predict weather patterns and climate behaviors. These models incorporate factors such as solar radiation, surface temperature, ocean dynamics, and atmospheric composition to provide a holistic understanding of climate systems on exoplanets. Utilizing both one-dimensional and three-dimensional models allows researchers to explore diverse climatic scenarios and assess long-term stability under various conditions, including stellar evolution.

In conjunction with climate modeling, the physical geography of exoplanets must also be taken into account. Factors such as landmass distribution, ocean currents, and geological formations can influence regional and global climates, creating microclimates that could be hospitable for life. For instance, mountainous regions may trap moisture, sustaining localized ecosystems, while vast oceans can regulate temperature and weather patterns. Understanding how these elements interplay provides crucial context for evaluating the overall climate favorability of exoplanets.

We must also consider the potential for climate change on these distant worlds. Just as Earth's climate has evolved through natural cycles and anthropogenic influences, exoplanets may face similar challenges that affect their habitability. Ongoing monitoring of exoplanets will be essential to detect any fluctuations or variations that might jeopardize their sustained habitability.

In the evaluation process, the ethical implications of potential colonization or terraforming cannot be understated. The responsibility we hold as guardians of life extends beyond our planet; we must engage with the idea of environmental stewardship in the context of exoplanets. As we identify potential worlds as candidates for future exploration or habitation, we must weigh the moral obligations associated with altering another planet's climate or environment, ensuring that our actions do not repeat the ecological missteps made on Earth.

As humanity advances in its aspirations to explore and potentially inhabit other worlds, the evaluation of exoplanets for climate favorability reflects our commitment to preserving life. By employing interdisciplinary approaches that blend astrophysics, climate science, and bioethics, we can ensure that our cosmic endeavors maintain the essence of ecological integrity. The assessments made today will shape our understanding of life in the universe and align with the principles of stewardship that guide our journey into the unknown.

In conclusion, the evaluation of exoplanets for climate favorability encompasses a multifaceted exploration of planetary environments and underscores the importance of responsible stewardship as we seek to extend the continuity of life beyond Earth. Through rigorous scientific inquiry and ethical considerations, we can illuminate pathways for future generations, ensuring that the stories of life, in all its forms, continue to resonate throughout the cosmos.

7.3. Stability and Accessibility in the Galactic Neighborhood

In the pursuit of safeguarding life's genetic legacy, understanding the dynamics of stability and accessibility in the galactic neighborhood is essential, as it serves as the bedrock for effective cosmic preservation efforts. This section addresses how celestial factors influence the potential for preserving and reintroducing Earth's biological diversity into the broader universe, exploring the delicate balance necessary to ensure that life can flourish in potentially habitable environments beyond our planet.

The concept of stability in a galactic sense encompasses a variety of elements, including gravitational dynamics, cosmic radiation levels, and the geological characteristics of celestial bodies. The gravitational stability of a host planet or moon is paramount when considering the establishment of DNA vaults or habitats designed for the preservation of life. Bodies within stable orbits around their stars tend to possess the necessary conditions conducive to maintaining climates that can support life. This stability allows for the development of ecologies where organisms can thrive, ensuring that any genetic material stored in DNA vaults can be successfully revived and reintroduced into such environments in the future.

Accessibility, on the other hand, pertains to the logistical feasibility of reaching these celestial bodies and establishing sustainable habitats. The ability to connect selected sites in the galaxy with efficient transportation routes is crucial. This may involve determining optimal pathways across the solar system, balancing fuel consumption, travel times, and ensuring safe landings on diverse terrains. Furthermore, when envisioning interstellar travel, the implications of prolonged distances must be managed effectively. Establishing refueling stations or staging grounds on stable celestial bodies may augment accessibility by providing interim support for missions aimed at reaching more distant storage sites.

An influential factor in both stability and accessibility is the presence of resources. Identifying celestial bodies rich in water—either in liquid form or as ice—holds enormous potential for sustainable bases of operation. Water is not only critical for human life but can also serve as a vital resource for creating oxygen and fuel, essential for supporting life inside DNA vaults and facilitating travel. Bodies such as Europa and Enceladus, with their subsurface oceans, emerge as strong candidates for further exploration, potentially serving as gateways into the cosmos while providing vital resources for preserving life.

Cosmic radiation poses one of the significant challenges in maintaining a stable environment for life, as it has the potential to disrupt biological systems by causing DNA damage. Understanding the radiation exposure that various celestial bodies experience from their respective stars and galactic environments is essential for identifying suitable sites for vaults and habitats. Analyzing cosmic radiation maps generated from space missions can provide insights into which locations offer relative protection, allowing for informed decisions regarding where best to establish preservation efforts.

Moreover, cultivating ecosystems on celestial bodies introduces the necessity for ecological stability, or the ability for organisms to adapt and thrive in their new environments. Developing an understanding of how life has evolved and adapted on Earth aids scientists in selecting organisms with elevated resilience traits—those capable of withstanding the challenging conditions present in extraterrestrial atmospheres. Selecting such organisms for preservation in DNA vaults ensures that future interstellar initiatives can prioritize the reestablishment of diverse ecosystems designed for longevity.

Another layer of complexity is introduced when considering public interest and involvement. Cultivating a sense of global citizenship fosters a communal responsibility tied to cosmic stewardship, amplifying efforts aimed at safeguarding life within the galactic neighborhood. Engaging the public in discussions surrounding potential locations and considerations for biological preservation can empower collective action, garner support for research initiatives, and promote understanding of the ethical obligations we hold regarding life both on Earth and beyond.

In conclusion, the stability and accessibility of potential sites within the galactic neighborhood are intricately woven into the ambition to ensure life's continuity across the cosmos. By embracing interdisciplinary collaboration among scientists, engineers, ethicists, and the public, humanity can develop a comprehensive framework for preserving genetic diversity. This may not only illuminate the intricacies of cosmic existence but also ignite a sense of shared purpose as we endeavor to become custodians of life among the stars, ensuring that future generations benefit from the beauty and diversity of the biological treasures contained within our DNA vaults. As we chart the unexplored territories of our galaxy, the commitment to stability and accessibility will guide our efforts, cementing our responsibility as guardians of life across the universe.

7.4. Navigating Cosmic Radiation Zones

Navigating cosmic radiation zones is a complex yet essential component of humanity's endeavor to safeguard the genetic legacy of life across interstellar expanses. As we venture beyond the familiar confines of Earth and look to establish DNA vaults in outer space, understanding how to effectively navigate regions of intense cosmic radiation becomes paramount. Cosmic radiation poses significant threats to both human health and biological materials, including DNA. Thus, a comprehensive understanding of how to traverse these zones safely is key to our mission of preserving life and ensuring its continuity among the stars.

The first step in navigating cosmic radiation zones involves understanding the different types of radiation that permeate space environments. Cosmic radiation consists primarily of high-energy protons and heavier nuclei that come from sources such as supernova explosions, the sun, and even galactic cosmic rays from other galaxies. This radiation can render genetic material damaged or altered, posing a risk to the integrity of DNA stored in vaults or biological systems placed in these regions. Prolonged exposure can lead to detrimental effects, including potential mutations, and is therefore a crucial consideration for any mission planning to travel through or establish habitats in cosmos-laden areas.

One of the pivotal strategies for safe navigation through cosmic radiation zones is the application of shielding technologies. By incorporating advanced materials into spacecraft and habitat designs, we can mitigate the harmful effects of cosmic radiation on biological materials and human occupants. Traditional materials such as aluminum or polyethylene have been used in spacecraft structures, but their effectiveness can be significantly enhanced through innovative approaches, including multi-layered designs and the addition of hydrogen-rich materials. Hydrogen is particularly effective at absorbing and reducing high-energy protons' impacts, thus reducing radiation levels within protected areas.

Additionally, the use of active shielding technologies is an emerging concept gaining traction in the realm of space engineering. These systems employ magnetic or electrostatic fields generated by superconducting magnets to deflect charged particles away from a designated area, creating a protective bubble around habitats or transport vehicles. Such technologies not only provide a robust defense against radiation but can also be adapted dynamically according to real-time radiation levels detected by onboard monitoring systems.

Another critical aspect of navigating cosmic radiation zones revolves around timing and trajectory planning. Space missions can significantly benefit from strategic timing that considers solar activity cycles, especially those related to solar flares and coronal mass ejections, which amplify radiation hazards. Missions aimed at traversing high-radiation zones should leverage predictive models based on solar weather forecasts, ensuring optimal launch windows that minimize exposure risks.

In addition to timing, mission planners must carefully evaluate the trajectories of spacecraft to avoid unnecessarily longer routes through high-radiation regions. Utilizing computational models to simulate cosmic radiation exposure along various flight paths allows for the selection of safer routes. By implementing adaptive routing software, missions can dynamically alter their courses in response to encountered radiation levels, ensuring that contaminants and hazards are minimized. This strategy is particularly pertinent for longer flights, where extended exposure can accumulate risks.

Training for astronauts and personnel involved in interstellar voyages must also account for navigating cosmic radiation hazards. Preflight educational programs should include thorough training on radiation awareness and safety protocols. Understanding the biological implications of radiation exposure and familiarity with emergency procedures in the event of unexpected radiation surges will equip astronauts with the knowledge to respond proactively to shifting conditions. This holistic preparation ensures not only the safety of crew members but also reinforces the security of biological assets in their care.

Monitoring radiation levels becomes a fundamental aspect of navigating cosmic radiation zones. Continuous data collection through onboard sensors allows for real-time radiation tracking, providing insights into changes that may occur during transit. These systems would play a vital role in assessing the effectiveness of implemented shielding technologies and adapting operational procedures accordingly. The data gathered can also contribute to the larger body of knowledge surrounding cosmic radiation, informing future mission designs and defensive strategies.

Moreover, collaboration with space agencies and institutions specialized in radiation physics will fortify our navigation capabilities. Working together can foster advancements in detection technologies, research into novel shielding materials, and the development of globally accepted protocols for crew safety. By establishing a shared network of expertise and resources, the navigation of cosmic radiation zones can be approached as a collective endeavor.

In conclusion, navigating cosmic radiation zones is integral to humanity's mission of preserving life as we journey into the vast expanses of the universe. By integrating advanced shielding technologies, strategic mission planning, and robust monitoring systems, we prepare ourselves to confront the challenges posed by cosmic radiation. As we safeguard life among the stars, understanding and addressing these hazards become vital responsibilities of both scientific inquiry and ethical stewardship. The pursuit of safety amid cosmic uncertainty not only highlights our commitment to protect biological legacies but also positions humanity as vigilant guardians of life's diversity across the universe.

7.5. Spotting Uncharted Territories

Spotting uncharted territories in the cosmos represents an exhilarating frontier, brimming with potential for discovery, innovation, and the safeguarding of life's legacy. As humanity stands on the threshold of interstellar exploration, the quest to identify and understand the vastness of our universe takes on new urgency—especially in the context of creating DNA vaults that will preserve the genetic blueprints of Earth's biological diversity. This endeavor requires more than just aspiration; it demands a significant investment in scientific inquiry, advanced technologies, and collaboration across multiple disciplines.

The journey begins with astronomical surveys and the diligent identification of celestial bodies. With an array of telescopes, both Earth-based and space-borne, astronomers can gather crucial data about distant planets, moons, and astral phenomena. Instruments such as the Hubble Space Telescope and the recently deployed James Webb Space Telescope possess the ability to detect the faintest signals from afar, enabling researchers to catalog exoplanets and assess their properties. The goal is to pinpoint which of these celestial bodies might serve as viable locations for future habitats and genetic preservation.

To truly gauge the potential of these uncharted territories, scientists must consider a multitude of factors, including distance from their host stars, chemical compositions, atmospheric conditions, and potential for liquid water. The identification of planets situated within their star's habitable zone—the region where temperatures allow for liquid water to exist—becomes pivotal. However, the definitions of habitability have expanded beyond these conventional parameters, and research now explores environments long thought inhospitable, such as icy moons and extreme landscapes where life might adapt in unexpected ways.

Understanding the geological and climatic characteristics of these bodies is essential. Mapping out terrain features, identifying geological activity, and detecting the presence of essential building blocks for life—such as organic molecules—enhance our understanding of the viability of potential candidates. Projects that analyze the spectra of light emitted by distant bodies can reveal the composition of their atmospheres, making it possible to detect vital gases that indicate the potential for life, such as oxygen and methane.

In addition to monitoring our solar system, exploring the broader galactic neighborhood opens the door to further opportunities. The search for potentially habitable exoplanets involves examining their distances from Earth and the feasibility of future missions. Researchers devise mission profiles that consider current technological limitations and conceptualize strategies for transporting humans and equipment to these new environments. Considerations might include targeting nearby systems like Alpha Centauri, or focusing on exoplanets in the Kepler data set that exhibit promising signatures for habitability.

Technological innovation plays a pivotal role in both the observation of celestial bodies and the subsequent exploration of these uncharted territories. Advances in robotics, AI, and machine learning systems enhance our ability to analyze data more efficiently and identify promising locations for exploration. Drones or rovers can support the analysis of potential landing sites, collecting real-time geological data and determining sample viability for future missions. Collaborations between engineers, biologists, and scientists today sharpen our understanding of how best to navigate these landscapes when the time comes for human exploration and habitation.

The importance of engaging the public in understanding these explorations cannot be overstated. Awareness, interest, and investment in space exploration and preservation have significantly grown in recent years. Planetary organizations must prioritize educational initiatives that invite people to participate in discussions about the significance of identifying new frontiers. By cultivating a culture of curiosity and responsibility, budding scientists, students, and enthusiasts can contribute to spotting uncharted territories through citizen science initiatives, public observatories, and educational outreach programs.

Moreover, the ethical implications of cosmic exploration and genetic preservation urge us to approach the task of spotting uncharted territories with caution and reflection. The rapid technological advancements must align with a shared commitment to responsibility in safeguarding interstellar ecosystems. Philosophical discussions around the implications of human intervention in extraterrestrial environments invite deeper inquiries about our role as custodians of life. By considering how our actions might not only affect other forms of life but also alter the trajectory of evolution, we can ensure a future anchored in ecological integrity.

Ultimately, spotting uncharted territories in the cosmos is a quest interwoven with wonder and responsibility. Fostering a comprehensive understanding of distant worlds and their potential for supporting life requires the integration of astrological and ethical dimensions into our exploration efforts. As we identify and examine the various possibilities that lie beyond our home planet, we forge a pathway toward not just securing humanity's legacy but also understanding our place in the vast tapestry of life in the universe. The ongoing journey pushes the boundaries of our knowledge and imagination, beckoning future generations to join in the cosmic dance of exploration, preservation, and awe.

8. Guardians of the Cosmic Libraries

8.1. Roles and Responsibilities of the Custodians

The role of custodians in the preservation of life beyond Earth is both profound and complex, as these individuals or teams bear the immense responsibility of safeguarding the genetic blueprints of Earth's biological diversity within the proposed interstellar DNA vaults. Their duties span various domains, emphasizing not only the scientific and technical aspects but also philosophical and ethical considerations that arise when dealing with the continuum of life in the universe.

At the core of a custodian's responsibilities is the active management of the DNA vaults. This includes meticulous monitoring of environmental conditions such as temperature, humidity, and radiation levels to ensure the integrity of the stored genetic material. Implementing advanced technology solutions, including automated monitoring systems equipped with sensors that gather real-time data, becomes essential in preserving DNA for extended periods. In this capacity, custodians must be well-versed in interpreting this data, understanding what deviations may indicate and how they can be addressed promptly to avoid compromising the samples.

Additionally, custodians play a pivotal role in sample collection and maintenance. This involves adhering to strict protocols to prevent contamination and degradation, ensuring that all practices align with ethical guidelines for biodiversity conservation. The training necessary for custodians encompasses not only technical skills but also knowledge of the biological and ecological significance of each genetic sample they handle. They must appreciate that every organism and its genetic footprint contribute to the broader ecological tapestry, highlighting the intricate interdependencies that characterize our planet's biodiversity.

Custodians also have educational and outreach responsibilities. Engaging with the public, stakeholders, and future generations becomes a vital aspect of their work, as they utilize their platforms to raise awareness about the importance of genetic preservation. This may involve participating in community events, contributing to discussions on biodiversity conservation, and advocating for greater recognition of the implications of cosmic preservation efforts. Through effective communication strategies, custodians can foster a culture that values ecological responsibility and inspires individuals to partake in conservation initiatives—whether on Earth or beyond.

In the context of interstellar exploration, custodians face unique challenges. As humanity prepares to send genetic materials into space, understanding the conditions the vaults will encounter is critical. This awareness will shape how custodians approach the operation of these facilities, as they adapt to the unpredictable nature of space environments. They must strategize on risk management, monitoring for cosmic hazards such as radiation exposure or microgravity effects on stored samples, and devising protocols for safe retrieval and potential reintroduction of organisms into extraterrestrial habitats.

A key facet of the custodians' role is also collaboration—working alongside scientists, engineers, ethicists, and space agencies to advance the mission of cosmic preservation. They must engage in continuous learning, staying updated on technological advancements and biological research developments that could influence best practices in genetic preservation. This cooperation can lead to the establishment of standardized protocols and frameworks, enhancing the efficacy and reliability of preservation efforts across different contexts.

Furthermore, custodians must grapple with ethical dilemmas that arise from the manipulation and preservation of life. Questions around ownership, the rights of biological materials, and the potential consequences of reintroducing organisms to environments where they have not existed for eons necessitate profound reflection and discussion within the custodial community. Engaging in ethical dialogues and frameworks helps ensure that their work aligns with humanity's broader commitment to stewardship.

As custodians look to the future, preparing the next generation of cosmic guardians becomes necessary. Establishing comprehensive training programs that combine scientific education with practical skills equips aspiring custodians with the knowledge to navigate the complexities of conservation. Equally, fostering a culture of universal stewardship—where individuals recognize their responsibility towards all forms of life—promotes a holistic view of interstellar preservation efforts.

In summary, the roles and responsibilities of custodians encompass a wide array of functions that reflect the intricate nature of preserving life in the cosmos. From managing vault environments and ensuring sample integrity to engaging with the public, collaborating across disciplines, and addressing ethical considerations, custodians serve as the guardians of genetic legacies. Their work will not only shape the future of biodiversity preservation but also resonate as a commitment to sustaining connections between life on Earth and the potential for thriving ecosystems across the universe. By embracing these roles with a sense of duty and aspiration, custodians illuminate a path where the essence of life endures, regardless of the challenges posed by time and space.

8.2. Preparing the Next Generation of Cosmic Guardians

Preparing the Next Generation of Cosmic Guardians involves a multi-faceted approach that encompasses training programs, cultural integration, ethical considerations, and the development of a mindset that acknowledges the profound responsibility humanity holds as custodians of life across the cosmos. As we expand our efforts to establish DNA vaults in space, fostering a new generation equipped with the necessary skills, values, and knowledge to embrace the complexities of cosmic preservation is crucial for the continued success of this initiative.

One of the foremost steps in preparing the next generation is the establishment of comprehensive training programs focused on various aspects of cosmic guardianship. These programs should incorporate interdisciplinary curricula that encompass biology, biotechnology, space sciences, ethics, environmental stewardship, and engineering. By marrying these fields, aspiring cosmic guardians will gain a holistic understanding of the challenges and opportunities they will face in preserving life in the universe.

Practical training is essential for instilling the necessary skills to work directly with biological samples, advanced technologies, and research methodologies. Laboratory simulations, hands-on workshops, and field experiments centered around genetic preservation will help reinforce theoretical knowledge. Furthermore, internships with space agencies, research institutions, or private companies engaged in bioengineering, conservation efforts, and space exploration provide valuable real-world experience. This direct exposure cultivates expertise and enables participants to appreciate the functioning of these preservation systems, thus preparing them for the challenges of future missions.

Simulated training exercises are also vital as they help test decision-making abilities in high-stakes scenarios. As potential challenges in cosmic preservation can be unpredictable, scenarios involving unexpected environmental changes, equipment failures, or even biosecurity breaches can facilitate preparation for swift and effective responses. Utilizing virtual reality technologies that create immersive environments simulating space conditions will enable guardians to practice operational protocols while also engaging them emotionally —fostering a sense of investment and responsibility towards the organisms they will protect.

A significant aspect of preparing the next generation is creating a culture of universal stewardship. Education programs should emphasize the philosophical dimensions of cosmic guardianship, instilling a mindset anchored in ethical considerations. Participants must understand the broader implications of their role in cosmic preservation —not only safeguarding the essence of life but also addressing moral questions surrounding genetic manipulation, biodiversity, and ecological integrity. Engaging in discussions around the ethics of introducing Earth-based organisms to extraterrestrial environments helps develop critical thinking skills and a sense of accountability. Encouraging participation in ethics seminars, workshops, and conferences allows aspiring guardians to engage in dialogues with ethicists and thought leaders, enhancing their awareness of the responsibilities associated with their future roles.

Collaborative initiatives between educational institutions, research organizations, and space agencies can facilitate outreach programs designed to raise awareness about the importance of preserving biodiversity, both on Earth and in space. Engaging the public through community projects, public lectures, and social media campaigns allows potential guardians to advocate for cosmic conservation while encouraging community involvement in these vital missions. Building connections with diverse stakeholders enriches the learning experience, bridging the gap between scientific inquiry and public understanding.

The ethics of cosmic preservation will also demand that training programs prepare the next generation to navigate legal frameworks, bioethics, and international agreements surrounding genetic data and biological materials. Understanding the regulatory landscape is essential for ensuring compliance with national and international laws governing technologies deployed in space. Aspirants should learn about the legal frameworks surrounding intellectual property rights, data ownership, and the potential implications of genetic manipulation for biodiversity. Providing insights into international treaties related to cosmic preservation fosters an awareness of the framework through which custodians can operate responsibly and ethically.

Moreover, the cultivation of a collaborative spirit among aspiring guardians is essential. Interdisciplinary and international exchange programs allow participants to work alongside individuals from diverse backgrounds, sharing ideas and best practices while developing mutual respect for various perspectives involved in cosmic preservation. Establishing global networks of cosmic guardians fosters a sense of community and shared purpose, reinforcing the notion that stewardship transcends boundaries and fosters collective responsibility.

Lastly, highlighting the importance of mental resilience and adaptability will prepare the next generation to cope with the uncertainties and complexities that lie ahead. Integrating training on psychological well-being and coping strategies helps equip future custodians with tools to navigate the challenges associated with long-duration space missions, environmental stressors, or unforeseen contingencies.

In summary, preparing the next generation of cosmic guardians hinges on establishing comprehensive training programs that blend biotechnological understanding with ethical considerations, practical skill development, and community engagement. Cultivating an ethos of universal stewardship, grounded in awareness of the broader implications of preserving life across the cosmos, is essential for fostering responsible custodianship. By empowering aspiring guardians with the knowledge, skills, and dedication required for interstellar preservation, we lay the foundation for a future where human endeavors in cosmic exploration are rooted in care, respect, and reverence for the intricate web of life that unites us with the universe. Through these concerted efforts, humanity will rise to its task as custodians of life, ensuring that our biological legacy flourishes under the vast tapestry of stars.

8.3. Training Programs and Simulations
Training Programs and Simulations

In the ambitious journey of cosmic preservation, the establishment of robust training programs and advanced simulations is essential for preparing the next generation of custodians tasked with managing DNA vaults in space. As we expand our reach beyond Earth, a comprehensive educational framework is necessary to equip future guardians with the knowledge, skills, and ethical perspectives required for safeguarding the genetic diversity of life across the universe. This subchapter delves into the effective integration of academic knowledge, practical training, and immersive simulations that together form the backbone of our cosmic stewardship initiatives.

At the forefront of any training program is the importance of a multi-disciplinary approach that combines the fields of biology, genetics, space science, engineering, and environmental ethics. Students aspiring to become cosmic custodians must gain a solid understanding of key biological concepts, including the principles of genetic preservation, the intricacies of DNA, and the ecological significance of biodiversity. The perception that life on Earth operates within delicate ecosystems highlights the need for custodians to become knowledgeable about the interconnectedness of life forms, their environments, and the challenges posed by potential extinction threats.

Alongside foundational biological training, it is crucial to impart technical skills related to the operational management of DNA vaults. This includes understanding advanced preservation techniques—such as cryopreservation and vacuum storage—through hands-on laboratory experiences. Creating partnerships with research institutions and biobanks fosters opportunities for students to engage in practical exercises that familiarize them with sample collection, storage procedures, and contamination prevention strategies. Additionally, engaging in collaborative research initiatives allows aspiring guardians to contribute to ongoing projects focused on biodiversity conservation and genetic technology.

Simulations represent a vital component of training, as they provide immersive environments where students can explore complex scenarios they might encounter in their roles. Advanced simulation software can create virtual representations of DNA vaults in space, allowing participants to navigate various operational tasks. Students can engage with lifelike challenges, such as responding to temperature deviations, radiation exposure, or equipment failures. These simulations facilitate rapid learning in decision-making and crisis management while reinforcing the importance of teamwork and communication under pressure.

Further development of these simulations can incorporate elements of artificial intelligence, offering dynamic scenarios that adapt based on participant decisions. As students make choices in managing their virtual vaults, they can witness the consequences of their actions in real time, creating an experiential feedback loop that enhances learning outcomes. Such engaging educational tools bring the challenges and complexities of cosmic preservation to life, deepening participants' understanding and commitment to their future roles.

In addition to technical and operational training, ethical considerations must be woven throughout the educational fabric. As possible custodians of life on a universal scale, students require training in the ethical dimensions associated with preserving genetic material, reintroducing organisms to extraterrestrial environments, and understanding the implications of genetic manipulation. Engaging with ethical frameworks encourages responsible decision-making and prepares students to navigate the moral dilemmas that might arise in their work.

Workshops and seminars led by experts in genetics, bioethics, and conservation can foster robust discussions around the philosophies of stewardship and humanity's responsibilities towards captured life forms. Exploring case studies on contemporary conservation efforts illuminates the ethical challenges faced by scientists today, highlighting the relevance of these considerations for future interstellar projects.

Emphasizing the importance of teamwork and collaboration throughout the training process will also prepare the future custodians to work effectively across various disciplines. Integrating teamwork exercises into training programs—where participants from diverse academic backgrounds collaborate on joint projects—builds essential interpersonal skills and sets the stage for effective communication in the diverse professional landscapes they will encounter in their careers.

To further enhance the training experience, fostering an inclusive culture among custodians that celebrates diversity and encourages innovative ideas will inspire creativity and problem-solving. These efforts can be bolstered by building mentorship programs that connect aspiring guardians with experienced professionals who can offer guidance, support, and opportunities for growth. Establishing a network of mentors and collaborators reinforces the notion that successful stewardship transcends individual efforts, as collective input shapes the future of cosmic conservation.

Ultimately, the integration of comprehensive training programs and immersive simulations creates a strong foundation for developing the next generation of cosmic guardians. By preparing these individuals not only with scientific and technical expertise but also with ethical perspectives and collaborative skills, we lay the groundwork for responsible stewardship and long-term success in safeguarding life beyond our home planet. As we work hand in hand to develop and implement these training initiatives, we honor our commitment to preserving biodiversity for generations to come, ensuring that life can flourish amidst the stars. This collaborative endeavor places humanity at the forefront of cosmic conservation while nurturing a culture dedicated to sustaining the intricate tapestry of life that spans the universe.

8.4. Creating a Culture of Universal Stewardship

Creating a culture of universal stewardship is a transformative aspiration that transcends mere responsibility for the preservation of life; it embodies a profound commitment to understanding our interconnectedness and shared destiny across the cosmos. In the context of "Arks Among The Stars: DNA Vaults and the Preservation of Life," this culture emerges as a guiding principle that informs our approach to safeguarding not just Earth's biodiverse heritage, but also the potential for life beyond our planet. To forge such a culture requires extensive collective efforts, innovative strategies, and a profound philosophical shift in how we perceive our relationship with nature and the universe.

At the heart of cultivating universal stewardship is the recognition that all forms of life are intertwined in a complex web of interdependence, where the fate of one species is inherently linked to the fate of others. This realization calls for a holistic understanding of ecosystems, where every organism—no matter how small or seemingly insignificant—plays a vital role in maintaining ecological balance. As humans embark on the journey of preserving genetic material through cosmic vaults, it is crucial that we acknowledge our entrenched role as caregivers of the Earth and responsible explorers of the universe.

Education serves as a foundational element in creating a culture of stewardship. By integrating concepts of biodiversity and ecological responsibility into educational curricula, we empower future generations to recognize their role as custodians of life. Education must also extend beyond formal institutions, engaging communities through outreach initiatives that promote awareness of ecological interconnections. By nurturing a sense of wonder and reverence for nature, individuals can develop a commitment to protecting not only the genetic legacy of Earth but also the broader ideals of sustainability and resilience that extend to interstellar environments.

Collective action is equally important in fostering universal stewardship. Global collaboration among nations, researchers, and organizations serves to unite diverse perspectives and methodologies aimed at conserving life across the cosmos. International forums and workshops can facilitate exchanges of knowledge, empowering stakeholders to join forces in addressing the pressing challenges of biodiversity loss and ecological degradation. As custodians of genetic diversity, humanity must be willing to pool resources and expertise, fostering inclusive dialogues that enable the development of interdependent strategies for preserving life—the cornerstone of universal stewardship.

This collective mission must also be grounded in ethical principles that reflect our responsibility to both current ecosystems and the generations to come. Alongside scientific endeavors, we must engage in deep contemplations surrounding the ethical implications of preserving genetic materials, manipulating organisms, and potentially introducing life forms into non-Earth environments. A culture of stewardship must encompass a commitment to doing no harm and prioritizing long-term ecological integrity over short-term gains. Robust ethical frameworks serve to guide decision-making processes, facilitating a thoughtful approach in which scientific advancements align with our moral obligations to protect all forms of life.

To propagate this culture of stewardship, storytelling becomes an invaluable tool. By weaving narratives of hope, interconnectedness, and responsibility into the fabric of our communications, we inspire individuals to envision their place within the broader cosmic tapestry. These stories can transcend cultural boundaries, invoking an intrinsic understanding of what it means to be a part of this universe—fostering empathy and a sense of shared purpose. Modern media, art, and literature can amplify these messages, enabling creative expressions of stewardship that resonate with diverse audiences and reinforce our collective commitment to preserving life.

Furthermore, the integration of technology into this stewardship culture is key. Establishing dynamic platforms where individuals and organizations can share data, experiences, and research ensures that knowledge is not siloed but rather collaboratively cultivated. Engaging citizen scientists through digital tools and apps provides opportunities for people to contribute to ecological assessments and data collection, demonstrating that stewardship can be a shared responsibility, transcending traditional roles of scientists and researchers.

Creating a culture of universal stewardship also emphasizes the importance of resilience and adaptability. As humanity advances its cosmic aspirations, it must recognize that change is inevitable, whether through ecological shifts on Earth or in navigating the uncertainties of extraterrestrial environments. Empowering individuals and communities with skills and strategies to adapt to changes fosters resilience on both personal and collective levels, preparing us to face the challenges of conservation in a rapidly evolving universe.

In conclusion, fostering a culture of universal stewardship demands concerted efforts across education, collaboration, ethics, storytelling, technology, and resilience. It empowers individuals to recognize their roles as guardians of life, crafting a profound commitment to preserving genetic diversity and ensuring the continuity of life across cosmic frontiers. As humanity embarks on its journey among the stars, this culture will serve as the North Star guiding our exploration, nurturing a deep-seated reverence for the interconnected web of existence that binds all living beings—both on Earth and beyond. By nurturing universal stewardship, we not only safeguard the essence of life but also illuminate the path forward, celebrating our shared responsibility to cherish, protect, and elevate the tapestries of life that grace our universe.

8.5. The Ethics of Cosmic Preservation

In a future where humanity undeniably confronts both cosmic possibilities and ecological responsibilities, the ethics of cosmic preservation present a complex yet vital discourse. As we endeavor to create interstellar DNA vaults that preserve the genetic blueprints of life on Earth, we must grapple with fundamental ethical questions that arise from this uncharted territory. These considerations encompass the moral obligations we hold toward our planet and the life forms inhabiting it, the philosophical implications of manipulating genetic material, and the overarching responsibilities tied to stewardship beyond our atmosphere.

A crucial starting point in this ethical exploration involves recognizing our moral obligations to Earth and the diverse life forms that call it home. As custodians of the planet, we are tasked with protecting the intricate ecosystems and biological diversity that have evolved over billions of years. This responsibility extends to preserving genetic material—not merely for practical resilience against existential threats but also to honor the sanctity of life itself. Each species contributes to a broader ecological tapestry; therefore, our commitment to preserving biodiversity must reflect and respect the interconnectedness that sustains our world.

In contemplating cosmic preservation, we must balance human needs with our cosmic responsibilities. The motivations driving space exploration and the establishment of DNA vaults may include aspirations for knowledge, innovation, and even colonization. However, we must earnestly question the ethics of using other celestial bodies as mere repositories for Earth's genetic material. This comes with an inherent risk of potentially disrupting extraterrestrial ecosystems we may encounter or create. Thus, any human endeavor that seeks to manipulate or alter life beyond Earth must be approached with extreme caution and a sincere commitment to minimizing ecological impact.

The philosophical implications surrounding DNA preservation lead us into deeper waters regarding our understanding of life itself. By preserving genetic material and potentially manipulating genomes, we engage with questions about the essence and inherent value of life. What does it mean to play a role in directing or altering the course of evolution for various species? With the advent of technologies such as CRISPR, we possess unprecedented power to edit genes, but this power imposes an ethical dilemma: How do we establish appropriate boundaries in our interventions while ensuring that our advancements do not result in unforeseen consequences?

Assessing the long-term benefits and risks associated with cosmic preservation becomes imperative. As we contemplate the advantages of safeguarding genetic diversity against possible extinction events—be they environmental disasters or cosmic calamities—we must weigh these ventures against the potential risks of manipulating genetic materials or introducing species into environments outside their natural habitats. Could well-intentioned interventions yield harmful unintended consequences that disrupt ecological balances or lead to the extinction of native lifeforms? Reflection on these questions is essential as we ponder the potential extinction of non-terrestrial life forms and the historical precedents of such actions throughout Earth's ecological evolution.

An international consensus on cosmic heritage must serve as an ethical foundation for these endeavors. As space exploration becomes increasingly collaborative, the dialogue surrounding genetic preservation needs to extend beyond national borders. A global framework is essential for establishing ethical standards guiding the preservation, manipulation, and potential utilization of life forms and genetic materials in the cosmos. The establishment of treaties akin to those already negotiated for terrestrial biodiversity—such as the Convention on Biological Diversity—could serve as a model, fostering cooperative efforts toward the shared goal of protecting life throughout the universe.

In summary, the ethics of cosmic preservation introduce a compelling narrative that intertwines scientific aspiration with moral responsibility. As humanity embarks on a journey to secure the genetic legacies of life across the cosmos, engaging with these ethical considerations catalyzes profound dialogue about our roles, responsibilities, and the intrinsic value of life. For the custodians of cosmic biodiversity, it is not merely a mission; it is an ethical commitment that requires respect for life, careful stewardship, and vigilant reflection. It is through this lens of ethics that we can aspire to create a future in which the flourishing of life—both on Earth and among the stars—remains our guiding ambition.

9. Ethical Considerations in Cosmic Conservation

9.1. Moral Obligations to the Earth and Beyond

Moral Obligations to the Earth and Beyond

In the emerging realm of interstellar exploration, humanity faces profound moral obligations that extend not only to our home planet but also to the vast universe that lies beyond. As we embark on the ambitious journey of safeguarding the very essence of life—preserving the genetic blueprints of diverse species within DNA vaults among the stars—we must grapple with the ethical imperatives that accompany such endeavors.

At its core, the moral obligation to Earth compels us to act as stewards of the ecosystems that sustain life. The intricate web of interactions within these ecosystems demonstrates the interdependence of species and their environments. As custodians of life, we must ensure that our actions do not endanger the delicate balance that sustains biodiversity. This stewardship requires an understanding that every organism, no matter how small or seemingly inconsequential, plays a vital role in maintaining ecological health.

This obligation extends to preserving the genetic diversity that underpins the resilience of ecosystems. With rising threats from climate change, habitat destruction, and pollution, numerous species face extinction. The ethical imperative to protect the genetic material of endangered species is rooted in the understanding that preserving diversity enhances the adaptability of life itself, making it crucial to our survival as a species. It is therefore incumbent upon us to capture and protect this genetic heritage not only for its intrinsic value but also for the future viability of life on Earth.

As we consider our responsibilities in the cosmic context, we confront the challenge of preserving life across the universe. This endeavor demands that we reflect on how we approach preservation. The desire to colonize or exploit other celestial bodies must be tempered with caution and respect for potential ecosystems we may encounter. Introducing terrestrial organisms into new environments raises questions about ecological disruption, and we must engage deeply with the ethical implications of such actions.

To approach interstellar biodiversity with integrity, our moral framework must take into account the potential consequences of our decisions. An awareness of unintended setbacks must guide the practices we implement in cosmic preservation. We have witnessed historical precedents on Earth where the introduction of non-native species has resulted in devastating impacts on local ecosystems. The lessons learned from these experiences emphasize the importance of a thoughtful and considerate approach as we explore the possibilities of life among the stars.

In navigating the cosmos, we are reminded of the intricate connections that link us to the universe itself. Our moral obligations extend beyond the preservation of Earth's biodiversity; they encompass a broader view of cosmic custodianship. This means recognizing that the universe is not an empty void awaiting human presence but a rich tapestry of existence that is deserving of respect. Every star, planet, and celestial body must be seen as part of a greater ecological system, one that we have a responsibility to protect rather than exploit.

Facilitating global conversations around these ethical obligations becomes pivotal in shaping our responsibilities. Engaging diverse voices—scientists, ethicists, Indigenous leaders, and policymakers—in discussions about the implications of cosmic exploration will help cultivate a holistic view of stewardship. By fostering dialogue and consensus, we can establish a shared understanding of our role as guardians of life, ensuring that decisions reflect a commitment to sustainability, respect, and harmony.

As we move toward an uncertain future among the stars, we must urge ourselves to reflect on our moral obligations to this intricate universe. In this undertaking of cosmic preservation, the questions we ask and the values we uphold will ultimately shape our legacy.

Embracing our role as stewards of life on Earth and beyond not only fulfills our ethical duties but also enriches our experiences as explorers, reminding us of the interconnectedness of all existence. Thus, our moral obligations become a guiding beacon illuminating the path toward a future that honors the richness of life and our place within it—both on our home planet and among the galaxies.

9.2. Balancing Human Needs and Cosmic Responsibility

In the quest to balance human needs and cosmic responsibility, we find ourselves at the intersection of pressing existential threats and the vast, uncharted territories of space. Humanity's aspirations to explore and inhabit other worlds hinge upon a profound understanding of our responsibilities to both our planet and the cosmos at large. As we contemplate the creation of interstellar DNA vaults designed to safeguard Earth's genetic legacy, the question emerges: how can we ethically navigate our pursuit of knowledge and survival while respecting the intricate tapestry of life?

The urgency of safeguarding Earth's biodiversity stems from the burgeoning awareness of the numerous existential threats posed by climate change, habitat destruction, and other anthropogenic stresses. Humanity's insatiable appetite for resources has led to the degradation of ecosystems and the premature extinction of countless species. Amid this backdrop, the impetus for establishing DNA vaults becomes not merely a scientific endeavor but a moral imperative—a conscious decision to act as stewards of life, preserving the genetic blueprints of diverse organisms for future generations.

However, as we turn our gaze toward the stars, we must recognize that this responsibility does not diminish; rather, it amplifies. The pursuit of cosmic exploration necessitates a delicate balancing act between expanding humanity's horizons and ensuring that our actions do not lead to the degradation of other potential ecosystems or life forms we might encounter. The ethos of cosmic responsibility compels us to consider the potential ecological consequences of our interventions, whether we are reintroducing Earth-based species into alien environments or harnessing genetic technologies to engineer resilient organisms tailored for extraterrestrial conditions. Each of these actions demands a rigorous ethical framework that weighs the benefits against the potential disruption of existing systems.

One foundational principle is the need for informed consent—not just from the living beings on Earth but from the ecosystems and potential life forms of the cosmos. As we consider introducing genetic material from Earth to other celestial bodies, we must tread lightly, mindful of the ecological consequences of our actions. The introduction of non-native species has historically led to disruptions and extinctions in once-thriving ecosystems; we must learn from these lessons in our cosmic endeavors.

Furthermore, advocacy for a precautionary approach amplifies our moral obligation. The uncertainty surrounding the effects of reintro-ducing genetic material into potential alien ecosystems urges us to prioritize caution, developing contingency plans and viable strategies for management. As custodians, we must create ethical governance frameworks that dictate how DNA vaults are utilized—not simply for the preservation of life, but to safeguard ecological integrity in environments where life may be fragile or where life as we know it might not exist.

The importance of global collaboration cannot be understated. Cos-mic preservation is not limited to any one nation, organization, or set of individuals; it is an endeavor that requires collective action. By fostering partnerships across countries, cultures, and disciplines, we can share knowledge, resources, and best practices, all while promot-ing a culture of inclusivity in our approach to cosmic stewardship. This collaboration should extend to indigenous wisdom and ecolog-ical perspectives, integrating diverse viewpoints that can inform our understanding of life and preserve the integrity of ecosystems.

Moreover, embracing public engagement and education will elevate the discourse surrounding our shared responsibility. Creating a culture of awareness around the implications of our cosmic ambitions fosters a sense of ownership and stewardship among individuals and communities. In doing so, we illuminate the complexity of the challenges we face and inspire collective action to address them. We must carve out spaces for dialogue, not only to inform the public about the significance of preserving genetic diversity but also to engage them in the ethical considerations that accompany our exploration efforts.

In summary, balancing human needs and cosmic responsibility is a monumental task that requires both introspection and collective action. It invites us to consider the moral implications of our pursuits, urging us to define our role as caretakers of a shared ecological legacy. By adopting a cautious yet ambitious approach to cosmic exploration —founded on a respect for existing ecosystems, an understanding of our responsibilities, and a commitment to collaboration—we can ensure that our legacy as guardians transcends the bounds of Earth and stretches across the stars. As we embark on this audacious journey, let us hold fast to the belief that by acting with integrity, we can illuminate a future where life continues to thrive, wherever our explorations may take us.

9.3. The Philosophical Implications of DNA Preservation

The exploration of philosophical implications surrounding DNA preservation touches upon profound questions about humanity's role as custodians not only of Earth's biodiversity but also of life's potential across the cosmos. As we consider the establishment of DNA vaults among the stars, these questions challenge us to examine the ethical, existential, and pragmatic dimensions of safeguarding life as we know it. Engaging with these implications invites a deeper understanding of how our decisions today will shape the legacies of tomorrow.

At the forefront of this discourse lies the ethical responsibility of preserving genetic material. DNA is often viewed as the blueprint of life, encapsulating the history, adaptability, and uniqueness of each organism. Thus, the preservation of DNA transcends a mere technical endeavor; it embodies our moral obligation to honor the intricate web of life that has evolved over billions of years on Earth. The decision to store genetic material for future generations signals a commitment to not just biodiversity preservation but also to an appreciation of the evolutionary dialogues that have shaped life in its myriad forms.

This perspective provokes contemplation regarding the intrinsic value of life itself. What does it mean to prioritize certain species or genetic materials over others? As custodians, we must navigate the challenges of selecting which organisms to preserve, recognizing that all species have their own ecological roles and intrinsic worth. This implies a need for a careful assessment—the intricacies of ecosystems must be respected, and decisions must be made with consideration for the sacrifices inherent in prioritizing certain life forms over others. The philosophy of conservation biology emerges as a necessary guidepost, encouraging an inclusive view that values not only economically significant species but all forms of life, including those that may be less understood or seemingly less critical to ecosystems.

In parallel, the philosophical discussions surrounding the manipulation of genetic material challenge us to confront our place in the continuum of life. The advent of technologies such as CRISPR offers extraordinary capabilities for editing genomes, igniting debates over the implications of directing evolutionary paths. As we engage in genetic preservation and potential manipulation, we must grapple with existential questions: Is it ethically sound to reshape life itself? Do we risk playing a god-like role in directing the legacies of living organisms? The moral ramifications of such choices call for rigorous dialogue that weighs human innovation against the potential disruption of natural processes.

Furthermore, as we prepare to launch DNA vaults among the stars, the implications of translocating life beyond our planet become ever more salient. Should we endeavor to introduce Earth's organisms to extraterrestrial environments? The ethical considerations surrounding such actions necessitate frameworks that address the potential impact on both introduced species and existing extraterrestrial ecosystems. Here, caution should reign, as unanticipated consequences could arise from introducing genetic materials to environments where they have not evolved.

In contemplating the long-term benefits and risks of DNA preservation initiatives, we are reminded that our actions today will echo across time and space. Preserving the genetic legacy of life is not solely a matter of safeguarding biodiversity for future generations; it is also about recognizing the role we play in shaping the possibilities of life. Striking a balance between the pursuit of knowledge, humanistic aspirations, and responsible stewardship is paramount. As custodians, we must ensure that our preservation efforts honor not only the genetic legacies we aim to protect but also the ecosystems within which these legacies thrive.

International consensus on cosmic heritage emerges as a vital point of discussion in this philosophical landscape. The need for cooperative frameworks that celebrate the shared value of biodiversity and genetic preservation across borders is essential as we reach for the stars. In this context, discussions surrounding the ethical and legal frameworks for a shared cosmic heritage gain significance. Treaties that govern the preservation and responsible manipulation of genetic materials must reflect global agreements on the ethical implications of cosmic exploration.

Thus, the philosophical implications of DNA preservation demand a commitment to ethical reflection, an understanding of our responsibilities, and the recognition of our place within a broader ecological narrative. As we forge ahead on our cosmic journey, the insights garnered from these philosophical inquiries will guide us in shaping our choices, reminding us of the interconnectedness of all life and the profound responsibility we carry as custodians of a shared destiny. Ultimately, our ability to engage thoughtfully with these implications will dictate the richness of our legacy—one that endures not just on Earth but in the limitless expanses of the universe, nurturing the precious diversity of life that connects us all.

9.4. Assessing Long-term Benefits and Risks

Assessing long-term benefits and risks in the realm of cosmic preservation is of paramount importance as humanity embarks on ambitious initiatives to establish DNA vaults among the stars. This endeavor represents not only a technical challenge but also a profound moral and philosophical undertaking. As custodians of Earth's genetic heritage, we must navigate the complexities of our aspirations with a clear understanding of the potential advantages and pitfalls that lie ahead.

One of the foremost benefits of establishing DNA vaults in space is the ability to safeguard the genetic material of Earth's biodiversity against existential threats. The increasing frequency of natural disasters, climate change, and anthropogenic pressures present growing risks to countless species. Launching facilities in space to preserve genetic blueprints provides a hedge against catastrophic events that could decimate life on Earth. This preservation effort ensures that, even in the face of extinction, we may have the capability to revive or reintroduce species in future ecosystems, be they on Earth or other celestial bodies.

In addition to safeguarding biodiversity, the long-term storage of genetic material in space opens avenues for scientific research and innovation. The knowledge lost through extinction can be preserved, offering future scientists insights into evolutionary processes, genetics, and ecosystem dynamics. By maintaining access to a wide array of genetic material, researchers may discover solutions to pressing problems, from medical advancements rooted in genetic diversity to biotechnology applications that enhance yields in agriculture. The capacity to analyze and manipulate genetic material from both familiar and alien environments presents a considerable boon for scientific progress.

However, these benefits are contrasted by several long-term risks. One significant concern involves the potential consequences of reintroducing preserved organisms into ecosystems that may have undergone substantial changes. The ecological balance in any environment is delicate; introducing genetically preserved or modified species could disrupt established relationships and lead to unforeseen consequences. The historical precedents of invasive species on Earth serve as cautionary tales, emphasizing the need for thorough ecological assessments and risk evaluations before any reintroduction efforts are undertaken.

Another critical risk pertains to the ethical implications of genetic manipulation and preservation. As humanity gains the ability to edit genetic material with precision, many questions arise surrounding ownership, control, and the extent of intervention in natural processes. Who decides which organisms are preserved and which are not? Should we attempt to resurrect extinct species, and if so, at what cost? Genetic modification raises concerns about unintended side effects, and the moral implications of 'playing God' create a complicated ethical landscape for custodians. Establishing robust ethical frameworks and governance structures is vital to ensure that actions taken in the name of preservation honor both the organisms involved and the ecosystems we've committed to protecting.

As we contemplate the establishment of interstellar DNA vaults, the risks associated with technological failures or breaches of security warrant serious consideration. The integrity of the stored genetic material must be upheld against environmental threats, data loss, or human error. Robust safety protocols, continuous monitoring, and contingency plans are necessary to minimize the likelihood of catastrophic failures that could jeopardize our preservation efforts. Trust in the systems implemented to safeguard life will prove essential, as public confidence will depend on transparency and accountability in our endeavors.

In examining long-term benefits and risks, the aspect of international cooperation must also be highlighted. The collective ventures to preserve life across the cosmos can serve as a unifying force, fostering collaboration among nations, organizations, and individuals. However, the distribution of benefits, technological advancements, and resources must be assessed equitably to mitigate potential tensions or disparities. Cooperative frameworks that encourage shared governance will promote a sense of collective responsibility, ensuring that cosmic preservation efforts align with global ethical standards.

In summary, assessing the long-term benefits and risks associated with cosmic preservation is a critical task as humanity embarks on this grand journey. By understanding the potential advantages—such as safeguarding biodiversity, advancing scientific knowledge, and fostering cooperation—while also recognizing the risks of ecological disruption, ethical implications, and technological failures, we can formulate a comprehensive approach that promotes responsible stewardship. The conscious governance of our preservation initiatives will empower humanity to honor the intricate interplay of life and ensure that our genetic legacy endures for future generations—not only on Earth but also among the stars. In this delicate balancing act, the proactive measures we take today will ultimately dictate the vibrancy of life that flourishes in the cosmic tapestry of tomorrow.

9.5. International Consensus on Cosmic Heritage

In an age where the survival of biodiversity is intertwined with humanity's cosmic aspirations, reaching an international consensus on cosmic heritage emerges as not just necessary, but imperative. This consensus embodies the collective recognition of the significance of preserving life across the cosmos, encapsulating the ethical, cultural, and scientific dimensions of our responsibilities toward both terrestrial and extraterrestrial ecosystems. As we stand on the threshold of interstellar exploration and the establishment of DNA vaults among the stars, it is vital that nations come together to forge agreements that honor our shared commitment to safeguard the genetic legacy of life.

The first step in establishing an international consensus involves fostering dialogue among diverse stakeholders, including governments, scientists, indigenous communities, artists, and ethicists. By creating forums for discussion—such as international conferences and workshops—representatives from various disciplines can share insights, visions, and concerns about cosmic conservation. These interactions are essential for developing a shared understanding of cosmic heritage and the values that underpin our commitment to biodiversity preservation.

One of the core principles that should emerge from these discussions is the recognition of the intrinsic value of life itself. The preservation of genetic diversity transcends national boundaries; it embodies a moral obligation to protect the intricate web of ecological interconnections that sustains existence. Nations must acknowledge that by safeguarding genetic materials from Earth, we are not only protecting the delicate ecosystems we inhabit but also ensuring the potential for diverse forms of life in environments yet to be explored. Establishing agreements that prioritize the intrinsic value of life—both on Earth and beyond—will help unify our efforts toward preserving this heritage.

In parallel, the consensus should explicitly address the ethical dimensions of manipulating and preserving DNA across the cosmos. There must be comprehensive discussions about the implications of genetic modifications, the potential introduction of organisms into extraterrestrial environments, and the moral responsibilities associated with such actions. Developing frameworks that prioritize caution and ethical reflection can guide decisions, ensuring that actions taken with the intent of cosmic preservation uphold ecological integrity and respect for the cosmos as a shared heritage.

A critical area of concern that needs to be highlighted within this consensus is the potential risks involved in cosmic conservation efforts. Discussions should encompass the consequences of introducing Earth-based life forms into alien ecosystems, contemplating both the ecological invasiveness of such actions and the risks of disrupting existing interstellar balances. Agreements must foster ecological assessments that inform decisions on when, where, and how to introduce or revive species, prioritizing preservation based on a deep understanding of ecosystems.

Collectively, nations should also determine protocols to address issues related to ownership rights over genetic materials preserved in DNA vaults. Questions surrounding intellectual property, research data sharing, and equitable access to genetic resources must be carefully navigated to prevent monopolization and ensure the benefits of genetic preservation extend to all of humanity. A consensus on respecting the rights of indigenous peoples, whose knowledge and relationship with local biodiversity infuse valuable perspectives into conservation, should be embedded in these agreements, acknowledging their role as custodians and educators.

Additionally, engendering a spirit of cooperation and partnership is vital for effective cosmic preservation initiatives. Acknowledging the prospective challenges of extended space missions, nations should strive to collaborate on research efforts focused on enhancing our understanding of genetic material preservation. Solutions for shared technology development, monitoring systems, and communication frameworks can lead to a more comprehensive approach to cosmic biodiversity.

Public engagement plays a crucial role in establishing an international consensus on cosmic heritage. Actions to promote awareness of the ethical and ecological issues surrounding cosmic preservation must prioritize diverse narratives, fostering connections between scientific communities and civil society. By involving the public in dialogues and outreach efforts, we can cultivate a broader understanding of the importance of preserving genetic diversity, inspiring collective action and ensuring that all voices are represented in the cosmic stewardship conversation.

In conclusion, reaching an international consensus on cosmic heritage represents a pivotal milestone in humanity's journey toward safeguarding life across the cosmos. Through collaboration, dialogue, and ethical reflection, we can forge a shared vision that prioritizes the intrinsic value of life, addresses potential risks, and recognizes the importance of equitable access to genetic resources. Such consensus will guide our cosmic conservation efforts, ensuring that as we venture into the stars, we do so as guardians of life's rich genetic legacy —prepared to celebrate and protect the diverse forms of existence that may flourish in the uncharted territories ahead. This endeavor promises to enrich not only our legacy on Earth but also the prospects of life in the vast expanse of the universe.

10. The Role of Robotics in Space Exploration

10.1. Automated Arks: The Future of Self-sustained Repositories

Automated arks represent the cutting edge of self-sustained repositories, advancing humankind's ambitions to preserve the genetic blueprints of Earth's biodiversity as we explore the cosmos. These automated systems are particularly essential in an era where the urgency of ecological conservation on Earth aligns with cosmic aspirations for exploration and colonization. The promise that these automated arks hold lies not only in their ability to securely store DNA but also in their potential to actively manage the complexities of biological preservation, monitor environmental conditions, and facilitate research—all without continuous human oversight.

A cornerstone of the automated ark's design is the integration of advanced robotics and artificial intelligence. By employing sophisticated algorithms, these systems can efficiently control environmental parameters, ensuring that genetic materials are stored under optimal conditions. This involves harmonic regulation of temperature, humidity, and radiation levels, all of which can threaten the integrity of DNA. With a fully automated system, the potential for human error diminishes, ensuring that the delicate balance required for preservation is maintained consistently over long periods.

The self-sustaining capabilities of these automated arks extend beyond monitoring. Incorporating renewable energy sources like solar panels ensures that the systems can operate autonomously, even in remote cosmic locations. This independence is crucial in environments where resupply missions may take years, or where human intervention is not feasible. Intelligent design also allows the arks to utilize energy-efficient technologies, enabling them to adapt to fluctuating environmental conditions without compromising their core functions.

In addition to energy efficiency, automated arks must establish seamless communication networks, both internally and with Earth. This will facilitate data sharing, enabling custodians to monitor the status of vaults in real-time, receiving alerts if conditions deviate from the established thresholds. This interconnectivity enhances the capability to manage vaults hundreds of thousands of miles away, allowing for timely interventions should an issue arise. Establishing these communication links ensures that the knowledge and responsiveness of human custodians are never far from the automated systems they oversee.

Moreover, automated arks will need to engage in self-repair and maintenance. As with any technology, wear and tear will inevitably occur. The integration of self-repair mechanisms, informed by AI-driven analytics, allows these vaults to recognize when components are malfunctioning and either repair themselves or alert human custodians to the issues. This facet of design not only minimizes operational risks but also improves reliability, ensuring the long-term sustainability of the system.

Beyond preservation, automated arks also have the potential to serve as research laboratories. Equipped with advanced analytic tools, these vaults can enable DNA sequencing, organism revival attempts, and genetic manipulation directly on-site. This capability allows for rapid experimentation in extraterrestrial environments, increasing our understanding of genetic resilience in space while minimizing the need to transport organisms back to Earth. The vaults could serve as laboratories for future studies into how genetic material behaves under alien environmental conditions, potentially revealing new insights into adaptation and evolution.

However, as we march toward the future of automated arks, ethical considerations must remain at the forefront of our ambitions. Questions about ownership of genetic material, responsibility for potential interspecies interactions, and the westward-toward nature of our endeavors require careful deliberation. Transparency in decision-making about what life forms to preserve and the mechanisms by which we engage with extraterrestrial ecosystems becomes essential as we push the boundaries of possibility.

Furthermore, the relationship between humans and machines emerges as an essential focus in understanding the philosophy of custodianship. The collaboration between humans and technology must be designed to enhance our unique perspectives while capitalizing on the efficiency and capabilities of machines. This balance can promote a more profound understanding of our responsibilities, as technology augments our current limitations and expands our reach into the cosmos.

In conclusion, automated arks symbolize the convergence of advanced technology and ecological responsibility, ultimately providing the infrastructure necessary for preserving life's diversity across the universe. These sophisticated repositories will not only help safeguard Earth's genetic resources but also empower future custodians to pioneer new paths of exploration and discovery. The vision of automated arks invites humanity to rise to its challenge of cosmic stewardship, illuminating opportunities to protect life in all its forms —no matter where it may flourish in the vastness of space. Through innovation and ethical reflection, we can ensure the essence of life continues to thrive in the unparalleled expanse of the cosmos.

10.2. The Precise Collaboration Between Man and Machine

The precise collaboration between man and machine represents a paradigm shift in how we approach the preservation of life in the cosmos. As humanity embarks on ambitious endeavors to create interstellar DNA vaults, the synergy between human expertise and advanced robotic systems becomes essential to navigating the complexities of cosmic stewardship. This collaboration not only augments our capabilities but also transforms our understanding of custodianship in the deep expanse of space.

Central to this collaboration is the integration of advanced robotics into the operational framework of DNA vaults. These automated systems play a critical role in the reliable handling, storage, and monitoring of genetic materials. Robotics can reduce the risks associated with human error, ensuring that fragile samples are managed under optimal conditions. For instance, robots equipped with precision instruments can consistently maintain cryogenic temperatures or construct controlled environments that mimic the ideal conditions for DNA preservation. Such consistent performance is particularly vital in space, where environmental factors may oscillate dramatically and human presence may not always be feasible.

The capabilities of these advanced robotic systems extend beyond mere mechanical functions. AI-powered algorithms embedded within these machines can analyze vast sets of data in real-time, monitoring the health of stored genetic materials and predicting potential issues before they arise. For example, these systems can detect even the slightest deviations in temperature or humidity, enabling rapid corrective actions before any damage occurs. This form of predictive analytics enhances the vault's resilience and reliability, allowing for more proactive management of genetic legacies.

Furthermore, as custodians of life, human operators become essential collaborators with these automated systems. Their expertise in biological sciences, genetics, and ecological conservation allows them to guide the operation of robotic systems meaningfully. Human judgment remains indispensable in decision-making processes regarding which genetic materials to preserve, thereby ensuring that ethical considerations are always at the forefront. The partnership between man and machine is symbiotic; while machines enhance precision and efficiency, human custodians bring context, insight, and ethical reflection to the operational landscape.

The collaboration between man and machine can also extend to data management and bioinformatics. The vast amounts of genetic information that will be generated and preserved in DNA vaults necessitate sophisticated data analysis capabilities. Robotics equipped with AI-driven data processing algorithms can categorize, analyze, and visualize genomic data, facilitating accessibility for human researchers. This dynamic interplay transforms how we understand genetic diversity and resilience on both terrestrial and extraterrestrial levels. By leveraging the combined strengths of human intellect and machine processing power, scientists can draw more nuanced insights from the genetic materials they preserve.

Additionally, advancements in communication technologies and interfaces further empower this collaboration. The development of intuitive user interfaces allows human operators to engage seamlessly with robotic systems, monitoring operations remotely and overseeing the vault's conditions in real-time. Through virtual or augmented reality technologies, custodians can be transported into simulated environments where they can interact with the robotic systems, overseeing the vault's contents while extending their operational reach. These interfaces facilitate transparency and highlight how machines can operate as extensions of human agency within the broader framework of stewardship.

Nevertheless, as we capitalize on this collaboration, we must also address the ethical considerations that emerge from our reliance on automated systems. Issues such as data security, unauthorized access, and algorithmic biases must be systematically evaluated. Establishing protocols for accountability ensures that human oversight is preserved, even in an age of increasing automation. The way we design and implement these systems must reflect a commitment to ethical stewardship, ensuring that technology serves our responsibility to respect and protect the biodiversity we aim to preserve.

Moreover, preparing future generations of custodians necessitates training programs that encompass both biological expertise and technical knowledge. Emerging custodians must be equipped not only to understand the complexities of life on Earth but also to engage with the technological tools that will be at their disposal. Fostering an interdisciplinary educational approach that encompasses biology, robotics, data management, and ethics cultivates a new cadre of guardians who can navigate the evolving landscape of cosmic preservation.

In summary, the precise collaboration between man and machine is paramount in our efforts to establish DNA vaults among the stars and safeguard the genetic legacy of life. This synergy enhances our capabilities, augments the precision of operations, and deepens our understanding of stewardship in the cosmos. As we innovate our approaches to preserving biodiversity, we must remain rooted in ethical principles and ensure that these technological advancements empower humanity to act responsibly as custodians of life. The future of cosmic preservation resides in our ability to harness this collaboration, illuminating a path where humanity's legacy endures across the universe, transcending the challenges posed by time, space, and beyond.

10.3. Unmanned Missions for Continuous Monitoring

Unmanned missions have become an integral part of our efforts to monitor and preserve the genetic diversity of life as humanity reaches out into the cosmos. These automated systems offer a practical solution for continuous monitoring of DNA vaults designed for long-term preservation of Earth's biodiversity. Given the vast distances and relatively inhospitable environments of outer space, unmanned missions provide a means to ensure that our genetic legacies remain intact without the need for constant human presence in challenging conditions.

The advantages of deploying unmanned missions are multifaceted, beginning with their capacity to operate autonomously for extended periods. In environments where resupply missions may take years, relying on automated systems mitigates the need for human crews to endure prolonged exposure to the rigors of space travel. These robotic systems can be designed to function independently—detailing, observing, and managing the conditions of DNA vaults while relaying real-time data back to Earth. This capability facilitates efficient data collection, allowing for proactive maintenance and adjustments in response to environmental changes impacting the genetic material stored within the vaults.

To maximize their effectiveness, unmanned missions can be equipped with an array of advanced sensors and monitoring technologies. Integrating environmental data collection systems enables unmanned vehicles to continuously assess parameters such as temperature, humidity, cosmic radiation levels, and even the health of biological samples. Using predictive algorithms, these systems can analyze the gathered data to forecast potential threats to the integrity of the genetic material and make necessary adjustments, all without human intervention. This commitment to ongoing observance ensures that custodianship remains vigilant even in the absence of human oversight.

Moreover, unmanned missions can harness the potential of artificial intelligence (AI) and machine learning technologies to enhance their operational capabilities. These advancements allow for the collection, processing, and analysis of vast amounts of data, which can be integrated into a central database of genetic information. AI techniques can reveal patterns, correlations, and predictions that help inform future decisions about the preservation strategies employed in the vaults. Ultimately, through evolving algorithms, these automated systems can continuously improve their functionality, adapting to new challenges as they arise.

The scope of unmanned missions extends beyond mere monitoring. They can be used for the collection and preparation of genetic material, ensuring samples are viable for long-term preservation. Robotic arms, equipped with precise manipulators, can retrieve and handle genetic material without risking contamination, while sophisticated laboratory-grade systems can conduct preparations such as cryopreservation in situ. This ability to process samples in the field adds value to their utility, allowing for swift action as new organisms are discovered or selected for preservation.

In addition to monitoring tasks, unmanned missions possess the potential to facilitate communication between DNA vaults and Earth-based management systems. This capability is paramount as it nurtures transparency and fosters collaboration, ensuring that key stakeholders are equipped with real-time data for strategic decisions. The establishment of a robust communication framework, relying on both satellite and deep-space transmission technologies, enables the safeguarding of genetic materials to transcend the limitations of distance—creating a lifeline that connects custodians with their repositories across the vastness of space.

However, with the deployment of unmanned missions, ethical considerations come into play. The potential for automated systems to operate autonomously prompts discussions regarding accountability, oversight, and responsibility for decision-making processes. As custodians of life, we must grapple with questions concerning the balance of human judgment and automated operations, ensuring that ethical principles are applied across all interventions in cosmic preservation.

The use of unmanned systems also raises inquiries into the impact of technology on our understanding of stewardship. How do we ensure that reliance on automation does not diminish our connection to the ecosystems we aim to protect? Striking a balance between leveraging cutting-edge technologies and maintaining an intimate understanding of the life forms we seek to preserve will be essential as we engage with unanswered questions surrounding both autonomy and interdependence.

Additionally, preparing the next generation of custodians should incorporate the intricacies of unmanned missions, weaving in both the promise and challenges of automated systems. Training programs should equip future guardians with the knowledge to manage these technologies, instilling not only technical expertise but also ethical considerations surrounding the deployment of robotic systems.

In conclusion, unmanned missions for continuous monitoring represent a vital enhancement in our cosmic preservation efforts. By integrating advanced monitoring capabilities, real-time data analysis, and autonomous operations, these systems create a framework for safeguarding genetic materials as humanity ventures forth into the cosmos. As we embrace the potential of automation, we must remain mindful of our ethical responsibilities as custodians, ensuring that our technological aspirations remain firmly anchored in a commitment to protecting the intricate web of life—both on Earth and among the stars. Through thoughtful deployment of unmanned missions, we illuminate a path toward a future where life's legacies are not only preserved but thrive across the vast expanses of the universe.

10.4. Robotic Languages and Communication Interfaces

In our journey into the cosmos, the development of robotic languages and communication interfaces becomes a pivotal aspect of how humanity interacts with machines and systems designed for the preservation of life across vast distances. As we design automated DNA vaults and other systems for cosmic preservation, creating effective communication methods between humans, machines, and the environments they monitor will be essential to ensuring reliability and efficacy in safeguarding nature's genetic diversity.

Robotic systems in space will often operate in environments where human presence is either limited or non-existent. This necessitates sophisticated communication interfaces that enable seamless interaction with these automated systems. These interfaces must not only facilitate the transfer of information but also ensure that humans can understand and interpret the data being monitored and managed. The development of a standardized robotic language can provide a framework for these communications, allowing both robotic systems and human operators to exchange instructions, data, and alerts efficiently.

The language of robotic systems could embody a set of protocols that incorporate sensor readings, operational commands, environmental data, and status updates into a coherent dialogue. Such a language must be multi-layered, able to convey basic messages while also supporting complex instructions that may involve nuanced decision-making processes. For instance, a robotic vault monitoring system might utilize a modular grammar that allows it to synthesize data regarding temperature and humidity levels, combined with real-time alerts about potential risks like radiation exposure.

Interpreting this data requires advanced algorithms capable of translating sensor outputs into actionable information for human custodians. The challenge lies not only in conveying raw data but in representing that data in a way that is meaningful and comprehensible. Incorporating visual representations, such as graphs or alerts that use color codes, could enhance human understanding of the systems' statuses, ensuring that custodians can act swiftly in response to alerts.

Moreover, artificial intelligence (AI) can play a transformative role in enhancing the capabilities of communication interfaces. AI systems could learn from previous interactions, adapting to the preferences and communication styles of individual operators. This would simplify the decision-making process, allowing human custodians to focus on strategic interventions rather than becoming overwhelmed by raw data. Over time, AI could abstract complex information into easily digestible formats, making the interaction between humans and robotic systems much more intuitive.

The versatility of communication interfaces extends to accommodating diverse cultural and linguistic backgrounds, as international collaboration in cosmic preservation will likely necessitate a universal robotic language. Ensuring that communication systems can be translated into various spoken and written languages supports inclusivity, allowing custodians from different countries and cultures to thrive in their shared role of cosmic stewardship.

As we explore the frontiers of robotic languages and communication interfaces, we also must consider the ethical implications tied to their use. Questions regarding accountability, oversight, and trust in automated systems arise as humans increasingly rely on machines to execute critical conservation tasks. Ensuring transparency in how systems communicate, process data, and reach decisions is imperative for fostering confidence in these technologies.

Additionally, integrating feedback loops into communication interfaces promotes continuous improvement in system performance. Operators must have the ability to provide input into system behaviors, facilitating a two-way dialogue where experiences shape future interactions. This connection empowers custodians to refine how they engage with robotic systems, ensuring that evolving needs and ethical considerations are met.

In summary, the development of robotic languages and communication interfaces represents a profound leap forward in how we approach cosmic preservation. Establishing clear, efficient, and ethical communication methods between humans and machines is essential for ensuring that automated systems effectively fulfill their purpose —safeguarding the genetic legacies of life across vast distances. As these systems evolve and adapt, they will become indispensable allies in our pursuit of knowledge and stewardship, illuminating the path forward as humanity embarks on its cosmic journey of exploration and conservation.

10.5. Exploration Beyond Mirrors: Holographic Projections in Space

Exploration beyond the known confines of Earth's biosphere beckons us to consider the innovative uses of holographic projections in space —an area filled with unbounded potential in the quest for cosmic preservation. As humanity dreams of creating interstellar DNA vaults to safeguard the genetic legacy of life, the role of holography emerges as a captivating fusion of technology, art, and science that could enhance our understanding and management of biological resources. By harnessing the principles of light manipulation, holographic technology may serve as a vital tool for visualization, monitoring, and even communication among diverse cosmic endeavors.

Holographic projections offer the ability to create three-dimensional representations of complex data sets, enabling custodians to visualize intricate relationships and patterns that might otherwise remain hidden in conventional two-dimensional charts or graphs. The multifaceted nature of biological data—encompassing genetic sequences, metadata, ecological interactions, and environmental variables—demands robust methods for analysis and interpretation; holography provides a compelling, immersive approach to facilitate this understanding.

Imagine a scenario where custodians of interstellar DNA vaults can project holographic visualizations of genetic materials in real time. By manipulating light to create detailed three-dimensional renderings of DNA strands, proteins, and even entire organisms, custodians would obtain a visceral understanding of the structural intricacies that characterize life. Holography not only enhances educational outreach, but it also empowers decision-making processes, allowing custodians to assess genetic material for viability and integrity from a vantage point that transcends traditional viewing limitations.

Beyond visualization, holographic projections can serve as real-time monitoring systems within DNA vaults. Integrated into the environmental monitoring equipment, holography could convey immediate status updates regarding the internal conditions of the vaults while providing operators with the capacity to interact with holographic interfaces. For instance, custodians could explore simulated vault environments, analyzing status markers and making adjustments through intuitive gestures. This engagement with data represents a paradigm shift in our relationship with technology, creating bridges between human intuition and machine logic that foster a deeper understanding of complex biological systems.

Moreover, holography has the potential to facilitate remote collaboration among multinational teams of custodians and scientists. During missions where human presence may be limited or impossible, holographic communication interfaces could enable teams from around the world to engage dynamically in ongoing data analysis and operational management. These interactions would serve to democratize knowledge and expertise, fostering collective decision-making that honors the diverse perspectives encapsulated in global stewardship initiatives.

The implications of holographic technology extend beyond mere preservation; they also capture the rich narratives of life's potential and evolution. By utilizing holography, custodians could visualize interactions among species and varying genetic traits, showcasing the intricate dance of interdependence that defines ecological systems. This visual storytelling invites a culture of awareness and respect for biodiversity, inspiring generations to embrace their roles as stewards of life, both on Earth and within the cosmos.

On the frontier of artistic expression, holographic projections also allow for the fertile interplay between science and creativity. Artists could harness these technologies to transcend their canvas, bringing life to visual interpretations of cosmic preservation. Holographic experiences in exhibitions could invite audiences to engage emotionally with the stories of endangered species, the significance of genetic diversity, and visions of future ecosystems. Art and science, intertwined through holography, have the potential to inspire empathy and connection, forging bonds that unite citizens toward the shared goal of preserving the richness of existence.

However, the integration of holographic technology into cosmic preservation raises ethical considerations that must not be overlooked. As the capability to manipulate the perception of reality becomes increasingly sophisticated, custodians and policymakers must ensure that these tools are deployed responsibly and transparently. The narratives constructed through holography should seek to inform and engage rather than manipulate perceptions. An ethical commitment to delivering accurate representations of ecological realities and the interdependence of life will enhance the credibility of conservation efforts.

In conclusion, exploration beyond mirrors through holographic projections emerges as a potent approach to cosmic preservation. By harnessing the transformative power of these technologies, humanity can visualize the delicate intricacies of life, create immersive monitoring systems, and engage in collaborative efforts to safeguard genetic legacies as we journey among the stars. The interplay of art, science, and technology will not only enrich our understanding of biodiversity but also empower us to boldly venture into the universe as responsible custodians. Through the lens of holography, the stories of life's resilience and potential unfold, igniting a collective commitment to preserving these narratives for generations yet to come.

11. Bioethics and Legalities of Cosmic Gene Preservation

11.1. Legal Framework for DNA Vaults

The preservation of life through DNA vaults in space necessitates establishing a comprehensive legal and ethical framework to navigate the complex interplay of scientific innovation, societal needs, and cosmic responsibilities. Understanding and addressing the legalities surrounding DNA vaults, intellectual rights, and international treaties ensure that humanity remains accountable and ethical stewards of life as we transition into an era of cosmic exploration.

The legal framework for DNA vaults must incorporate multiple aspects that govern the preservation and utilization of genetic materials. The framework must establish protocols for the collection, storage, and use of genetic information—ensuring compliance with both existing laws on Earth and the unique challenges presented by outer space. This legal structure will facilitate smooth operations and clarify custodial responsibilities, thus ensuring that the vaults preserve life without fear of legal repercussions. It will also delineate the roles of various stakeholders involved, from scientists to governmental agencies and private entities, creating clarity in shared responsibilities and objectives.

Intellectual rights of biological materials are a critical aspect of the legal framework. As genetic materials, including DNA sequences, represent not only scientific data but also the unique heritage of species, ownership must be defined clearly. Discussions surrounding who holds the rights to DNA—whether derived from Earth or beyond—will shape the nature of genetic research and conservation efforts. Clear guidelines will foster responsible practices, avoiding monopolization while ensuring equitable access for researchers and organizations involved in preserving biodiversity.

Patents and trademarks for genetic data present another layer of intricacy in the legalities surrounding cosmic preservation. The potential for patenting genetic sequences or engineered organisms raises ethical dilemmas about ownership and commercialization. Striking a balance between incentivizing innovation through intellectual property rights and maintaining the principle of shared access to genetic materials will require thoughtful legal considerations. As humanity ventures into new territories, it must tread carefully, ensuring that policies align with ethical stewardship principles while promoting scientific progress.

Safeguarding genetic diversity also poses significant legal challenges. With the fundamental goal of preserving Earth's biological heritage, laws must underscore the importance of maintaining genetic integrity and promoting ecological resilience. Provisions in the legal framework should address potential risks and consequences, including how to manage instances of genetic alterations or reinsertion into ecosystems, thus ensuring that decisions made today do not lead to unintended hazards for future generations.

International treaties and cosmic laws are critical in providing a cohesive framework governing cosmic preservation. As exploration efforts extend beyond national borders, establishing agreements that acknowledge shared responsibilities and promote collaborative approaches becomes essential. Treaties could guide how countries protect cosmic heritage while underscoring the necessity for transparency and shared governance—ensuring that conservation efforts are equitably integrated into global actions.

While laws and legal frameworks establish order and responsibility, the ethical considerations woven throughout these discussions form the moral backbone of cosmic preservation. Engaging philosophers, ethicists, and various stakeholders will promote a rich dialogue that addresses the ethical ramifications tied to genetic preservation, manipulation, and potential reintegration into other ecosystems. At the heart of these conversations is an emphasis on respect for life and responsibility towards ecological balance, fostering a culture of stewardship that embraces the interdependence of life on Earth and beyond.

In conclusion, the legal and ethical considerations surrounding DNA vaults in space encapsulate a critical aspect of our journey into the cosmos. By establishing robust legal frameworks, recognizing intellectual rights, and fostering international cooperation, humanity can ensure that our cosmic preservation efforts align with our ethical responsibilities. This commitment to legality and ethics strengthens our role as guardians of life, guiding our aspirations to explore the universe while honoring the intricate threads that connect all living beings. Engaging deeply in these discussions will ultimately solidify our legacy as accountable stewards, preserving biodiversity and nurturing life amid the stars.

11.2. Intellectual Rights of Biological Materials

As humanity forges its path into the cosmos, one of the most pressing issues we face is the preservation of life across the vast expanses of space, particularly in the form of biological materials encapsulated in DNA. With this profound responsibility comes the necessity of understanding and defining the intellectual rights associated with these vital genetic repositories. The subchapter on this topic delves into the intricacies inherent in the ownership, usage, and legal framework surrounding biological materials, presenting a multifaceted exploration of ethical principles that guide our cosmic stewardship.

Understanding the intellectual rights of biological materials in the context of cosmic preservation begins with the definition of terms and the delineation of ownership. Genetic materials, particularly those sourced from endangered species or organisms of significant ecological value, raise important questions about who holds the rights to these biological resources. The complexities are further heightened when considering genetic materials stored in DNA vaults in space: who owns the genetic blueprints contained in these vaults? Is it the nation that originally collected the samples, the scientific community, or perhaps even the organisms themselves?

From a legal perspective, existing frameworks relating to biodiversity and genetic resources can be instructive. International agreements such as the Convention on Biological Diversity (CBD) establish guidelines for the fair and equitable sharing of benefits arising from the utilization of genetic resources. For cosmic vaults, these principles should be adapted; as genetic samples are preserved in extraterrestrial environments, a comprehensive legal framework must be developed to secure rights while fostering international collaboration and ethical stewardship.

The role of patents and trademarks further complicates the landscape of ownership and intellectual rights of biological materials. The ability to patent genetic sequences and engineered organisms introduces an intersection of commercial interests and conservation ethics. On one hand, patenting can incentivize research and innovation, facilitating advancements in genetics and biotechnology. Conversely, it raises concerns about monopolization and access; the commodification of genetic resources may prevent equitable access for researchers and communities dedicated to preserving biodiversity. Finding a balanced solution that fosters scientific growth while promoting the equitable utilization of genetic materials is paramount, and requires ongoing discussions among scientists, policy makers, and ethicists worldwide.

Safeguarding genetic diversity through legal frameworks requires careful structuring to account for potential risks involved in manipulating genetic resources. As advances in gene editing technologies such as CRISPR open new avenues for research and innovation, concerns arise regarding the implications of altering the genetic makeup of organisms intended for preservation or reinstatement. Who bears responsibility for unintended consequences resulting from genetic modifications? Establishing clear accountability measures is essential to ensure that actions taken with the intent of cosmic preservation align with ethical considerations and ecological integrity.

An international consensus on the rights associated with biological materials must extend beyond ownership, addressing legalities around the movement of genetic resources across borders. As humanity collectively embraces its stewardship role for genetic diversity, shared agreements regarding the transport, storage, and use of these materials will create mutual trust and responsibility. Countries must engage in dialogues that foster cooperation in preserving knowledge, resources, and their inherent rights tied to cosmic conservation.

In addition to the legal and ethical implications, there is a compelling need to consider the cultural significance of biological materials. Many cultures view particular species as integral to their heritage, spirituality, or identity, and therefore, the preservation of genetic resources should honor these narratives. Inclusive frameworks that respect indigenous knowledge and incorporate traditional conservation practices will enhance our cosmic preservation efforts, ensuring that the voices of diverse communities are heard and valued.

As the dialogue around intellectual rights of biological materials evolves, technological advancements will inevitably play a significant role. Innovations in blockchain technology, for instance, could enable the secure tracking of genetic resources, ensuring accountability and transparency in their handling. This technological approach aligns with contemporary discussions around data ownership, governance, and equitable access, establishing a more reliable and diverse framework for cosmic preservation.

In summary, the intellectual rights of biological materials are a complex tapestry woven from legal, ethical, ecological, and cultural threads. As humanity embarks on its interstellar journey to safeguard life through DNA vaults, the established frameworks governing ownership, patents, and legalities must reflect our commitment to responsible stewardship. Striking a balance between innovation and equity will be crucial as we seek to protect and honor the profound diversity of life in the universe. By fostering meaningful discussions among diverse stakeholders, we pave the way for a future where the preservation of genetic legacies is affirmed as a collective endeavor— a celebration of life itself, bound together across the cosmos.

11.3. Patents and Trademarks for Genetic Data

Patents and trademarks play a crucial role in the complex landscape of genetic data ownership and preservation, particularly as humanity embarks on interstellar initiatives aimed at safeguarding Earth's biodiversity in DNA vaults located among the stars. The establishment of a legal framework governing intellectual property rights is essential for navigating the myriad ethical, scientific, and commercial questions related to genetic material and biotechnology.

At the core of discussions about patents and trademarks in this context is the invention and ownership of biological data. As genetic material, particularly DNA sequences, serves as the fundamental blueprint for life, the potential to patent these sequences presents both opportunities and challenges. On the one hand, patents offer a mechanism for protecting innovative treatments and biotechnological advancements resulting from genetic research, providing inventors and organizations incentives to invest in this essential work. However, they also introduce ethical questions about the commodification of life itself. Is it just to claim ownership of strands of DNA that belong to living organisms? Can we ethically monetize the genetic code of endangered species or organisms that have yet to be discovered?

In considering the implications of patents on genetic data, we must also reflect on their accessibility and the potential for monopolization. If certain entities control patents for critical genetic sequences, they may restrict access to these resources for researchers, conservationists, and organizations dedicated to biodiversity preservation. Legal frameworks must ensure that intellectual property rights do not hinder scientific research and equitable sharing of genetic resources. By contextually framing patents within an ethical understanding of stewardship, we can design systems that promote innovation while safeguarding the public interest.

Trademarks also come into play when considering the identification of genetic material and its derived products. The need for clear labeling and identification of genetically modified organisms (GMOs) and biotechnology-derived products brings forth discussions on public health, consumer rights, and ecological integrity. Trademarks can help consumers make informed decisions, and they hold the potential to shape public perceptions on the safety and sustainability of products derived from genetic research.

Legal challenges arise in determining eligibility for patents and trademarks across international borders, particularly as nations vary significantly in their legal frameworks governing biogenetics. Establishing international treaties that standardize practices in genetic data ownership and usage is necessary to foster collaboration and prevent conflicts that may arise from territorial disputes over genetic resources. The Convention on Biological Diversity serves as an excellent example of a widely accepted treaty focused on conserving biodiversity and establishing equitable sharing of genetic resources. Nonetheless, expanding upon these frameworks specifically for genetic data in the context of space and cosmic preservation is necessary for global efforts.

Additionally, ethical implications surrounding the ownership of genetic data must be closely scrutinized. Proposed policies should reflect a commitment to social equity and justice, ensuring that access to genetic resources, particularly for Indigenous communities who may have longstanding connections to certain species, is respected and protected. Initiatives that engage different cultural perspectives can lead to a more inclusive framework for genetic data governance, acknowledging that living organisms embody rich ecological and cultural significances.

As we consider the potential future of cosmic preservation, establishing clear guidelines for the patenting and trademarking of genetic materials becomes increasingly vital. Discussions should encompass not just the mechanics of legal frameworks but also the implications of their implementation. Questions regarding the sustainability of life forms we seek to preserve in space, potential impacts on ecosystems, and the values embedded in genetic resources must remain at the forefront of policy discussions.

In summary, the governance of patents and trademarks for genetic data within the cosmic conservation landscape encapsulates a rich interplay between ethical considerations, scientific responsibilities, and legal frameworks. Striking a balance between fostering innovation in genetic research and ensuring equitable access to genetic resources is essential to both the preservation of life on Earth and the continued exploration of the universe. As we navigate the complexities of intellectual property rights, we must remain committed to the principles of stewardship, awareness, and respect for all living forms as we endeavor to become responsible guardians of life—both on our home planet and beyond.

11.4. Safeguarding Genetic Diversity: Legal Challenges

Safeguarding genetic diversity through effective legal frameworks presents a series of nuanced challenges requiring cooperation, foresight, and an ethical commitment across political, scientific, and social spheres. As humanity forges into the cosmos, creating DNA vaults that house the genetic legacy of Earth's biodiversity, the intersections of law, ethics, and conservation must be navigated with care.

One of the primary legal challenges is the establishment of jurisdiction over genetic materials. As nations and organizations venture into space, the question of ownership must be addressed: Who holds the rights to the genetic materials preserved within these vaults? This is complicated by the fact that genetic samples often originate from various geographic and ecological contexts. Effective legal structures must clarify that the origin of these materials does not diminish their intrinsic value.

Furthermore, the patenting of genetic material raises additional concerns. The intricate strands of DNA encode not just biological information but also cultural identity and historical significance. The ability for entities to patent genetic sequences leads to questions around the commodification of life itself, which in many cultures is considered sacred. Legal frameworks must ensure that the preservation of genetic data is treated with respect, promoting equitable access to resources without permitting monopolies over life-sustaining materials.

As legal systems grapple with the implications of conducting genetic preservation across borders, international treaties emerge as crucial elements in fostering cooperation and establishing shared responsibilities. Treaties such as the Convention on Biological Diversity help articulate principles for protecting biodiversity but must be adapted to address the extra-terrestrial context. Establishing universally accepted guidelines surrounding genetic material, akin to existing interstate treaties, will cultivate a shared commitment for preserving cosmic biodiversity.

Regulations must also contemplate the ethical considerations inherent in manipulating genetic data and species. With the rise of advanced genetic technologies such as CRISPR, the capacity for humans to reshape life introduces significant responsibilities. While the drive to deploy these technologies may coincide with the pursuit of knowledge and discovery, we must ensure that such actions remain grounded in ethical considerations—honoring the intrinsic value and dignity of all organisms. This necessitates collaborative dialogues between legal scholars, ethicists, and conservationists to construct frameworks that balance those ethical imperatives with the scientific ambitions of our interstellar aspirations.

As the risks associated with introducing Earth-based organisms to extraterrestrial environments loom, establishing precautionary measures becomes imperative. Clear guidelines around the introduction of modified or preserved species into non-Earth systems are essential to protect both the existing ecosystems and the genetic materials intended for preservation. Such protocols should incorporate ecological impact assessments, considering the potential effects on local ecosystems prior to any decisions being made.

Moreover, navigating the complexities of cross-border genetic material transfer necessitates policy development around data security and ownership rights. This includes equitable mechanisms for sharing data that ensure participating nations and organizations are treated fairly. The rise of digital platforms for genetic data management invites the need for data stewardship laws that address how genetic information should be shared, utilized, and protected, enabling a collaborative approach to cosmic preservation.

In conclusion, safeguarding genetic diversity through legal frameworks presents ethical challenges that encompass ownership, the role of patents, international cooperation, and ecological responsibility. As humanity embarks on its ambitious journey beyond Earth, establishing comprehensive, adaptive legal guidelines will empower us to act as responsible custodians of life. By nurturing collaboration and dialogue across diverse perspectives, we ensure that the knowledge and richness of life on Earth is heralded into the cosmos as a legacy —one that respects not only the genetic material but also the life it represents, fostering a deep, abiding commitment to cosmic stewardship. Through careful legal and ethical consideration, we can embrace the challenges of cosmic preservation, illuminating a future where life —both on Earth and beyond—can continue to thrive.

11.5. International Treaties and Cosmic Laws

International treaties and cosmic laws are crucial instruments for humanity's efforts in preserving life as we extend our reach into the cosmos. As the establishment of DNA vaults among the stars becomes an increasingly viable aspiration, the need for a well-defined international legal framework to govern such initiatives grows paramount. These laws and treaties will not only clarify responsibilities and ownership but also ensure sustainable practices that respect the ecological intricacies of both Earth and extraterrestrial environments.

At the heart of this legal framework is the concept of cosmic heritage, which necessitates the protection of genetic resources not just as individual entities, but as part of a larger, interconnected biological tapestry. International treaties, akin to those already established for environmental protection and biodiversity conservation on Earth, must be crafted to ensure that the knowledge, rights, and responsibilities associated with cosmic preservation are equitably shared among nations and peoples. Such agreements could apply ethical precedents that acknowledge the intrinsic value of biodiversity, underlining humanity's obligation to protect and preserve life in all its forms, whether within our atmosphere or beyond.

Key considerations within these treaties should include the rights of sovereign nations over genetic resources collected within their territories, as well as clear guidelines for the sharing and utilization of genetic materials across international borders. This is particularly relevant as samples may be transported to DNA vaults in outer space. Equity in benefit-sharing is paramount; collaborative research initiatives and joint conservation efforts should be facilitated, ensuring that all nations have a role in the stewardship of genetic diversity.

Furthermore, the legal framework must address the ethical implications of genetic manipulation and the potential consequences of introducing organisms into non-Earth ecosystems. The treaties should establish precautionary principles that mandate thorough ecological assessments before any genetic materials are released into new environments. Understanding historical precedents of biological intrusions and their environmental consequences underscores the necessity of these safeguards.

Central to the discussion of international treaties is the recognition of indigenous rights and traditional knowledge. Many societies around the globe have deep cultural connections to the genetic resources found in their environments. These communities must have a say in how their biological resources are used, and their knowledge should be respected and integrated into cosmic conservation efforts. Establishing protocols that acknowledge and protect indigenous interests not only enhances the legitimacy of preservation initiatives but also fosters a holistic approach to biodiversity conservation.

As we advance into space exploration, the establishment of international governance structures is vital. Creating global councils or forums dedicated to discussing the implications of cosmic preservation fosters inclusive dialogues. These platforms should aim to reconcile diverse perspectives among various stakeholders—from scientists and policymakers to indigenous representatives and civil society. By encouraging collaborative discussions, we can aspire to develop consensus around shared goals, ethical standards, and responsibilities.

The implementation of legally binding agreements, alongside voluntary codes of conduct, presents a balanced approach that addresses both immediate needs and long-term aspirations for cosmic conservation. By adopting an adaptable legal framework, nations can support each other in preparing for the challenges of the cosmos while remaining responsive to emerging scientific developments and ecological realities.

In conclusion, international treaties and cosmic laws represent essential frameworks for ensuring the responsible preservation of life's diversity across the universe. By acknowledging the interdependence of all life forms and instituting ethical guidelines, we can create comprehensive legal systems that support the interconnectedness of ecosystems—both terrestrial and extraterrestrial. These treaties will position humanity not merely as explorers but as conscientious stewards of cosmic biodiversity, committed to ensuring that the legacy of life flourishes amid the stars. As we navigate the uncharted territories of space, fostering international collaboration through legal frameworks will pave the way for a future in which all life and knowledge are revered and protected across the cosmos.

12. The Influence of Astronomy on Ecosystem Understanding

12.1. Correlating Stellar Phenomena with Biological Cycles

The relationship between cosmic phenomena and biological cycles is an area of growing interest, particularly as humanity expands its reach into the cosmos and seeks to preserve the genetic legacies of life on Earth. This intricate correlation raises fascinating questions about the ways in which celestial events influence terrestrial ecosystems and, by extension, our efforts in cosmic preservation. As we stand at the threshold of interstellar exploration, probing the links between the cosmos and the biological sciences opens new horizons for understanding life itself.

To begin, it is vital to establish a foundational understanding of biological cycles on Earth. Life is not static; it is influenced by a multitude of factors, many of which are directly shaped by astronomical phenomena. The cycles of life—including growth, reproduction, and death—are often tightly aligned with environmental cues that can be traced back to celestial events. For instance, the changing positions of the Earth in its orbit around the sun result in seasonal variations that dictate patterns of plant blooming, animal migration, and breeding cycles. These seasonal shifts are intrinsically linked to the solar cycle and the amount of light and heat that the Earth receives, demonstrating that life on our planet is inextricably connected to cosmic rhythms.

One of the most significant astronomical factors impacting biological cycles is the moon's gravitational influence. Tides, driven by the moon's pull, have far-reaching effects on marine ecosystems, shaping everything from breeding behaviors in coastal species to the dynamics of food webs. Some organisms, such as certain species of coral, time their spawning events to lunar cycles, releasing gametes into the water based on the moon's phase. Understanding such connections is crucial as we consider not only the preservation of genetic diversity on Earth but also the potential transplantation of such species into extraterrestrial environments, where these astronomical influences may differ dramatically.

The interplay between solar activity and terrestrial climates also warrants examination. Solar cycles, characterized by variations in solar output and magnetic activity, influence Earth's climate patterns, which, in turn, affect biological responses. Periods of heightened solar activity can lead to increased temperatures, altered precipitation patterns, and shifts in ecological dynamics. These disruptions can have cascading effects on the timing of biological events, such as flowering or migration, ultimately impacting species' survival and reproductive success. Therefore, understanding these solar influences is essential for predicting how life may respond to changes that could arise in other celestial contexts.

As humanity embarks on cosmic preservation efforts, particularly through the establishment of DNA vaults intended to safeguard genetic diversity, we must acknowledge that any introduced life forms will exist under different celestial conditions. It is imperative to investigate how variations in light, radiation, gravity, and atmospheric composition might affect the biological cycles of Earth's species if they were reintroduced to extraterrestrial environments. What may thrive in one context might falter in another; thus, our methods must include extensive research into the biological adaptability of preserved species.

Astrobiology, the study of life in the universe, plays a vital role in this inquiry, expanding our horizons to contemplate the myriad forms life could take in other celestial realms. By understanding how life adapts to varying conditions across Earth, scientists can draw parallels and hypothesize about potential extraterrestrial ecosystems and the biological cycles that might prevail there. The discoveries within our own solar system, particularly on Mars and the icy moons of Jupiter and Saturn, deepen our comprehension of life's resilience in the face of extreme conditions.

The connections between celestial phenomena and biological cycles compel us to adopt an integrated approach to cosmic preservation. This requires interdisciplinary collaboration between astronomers, ecologists, geneticists, and ethicists as we explore the implications of introducing or reviving life beyond Earth. A clear understanding of how stellar events influence terrestrial systems will allow us to inform decisions about species selection, habitat design, and monitoring protocols—all crucial facets of our efforts in cosmic conservation.

Moreover, as we work to establish a framework for such preservation initiatives, considerations about the ethical implications of our actions come to the forefront. The potential for unintended consequences in manipulating genetic material, especially when considering the long-term impacts on ecosystems in which they may be introduced, must be rigorously evaluated. We must acknowledge that our responsibility as custodians extends beyond preservation; it encompasses a profound commitment to ecological integrity and respect for the interconnected web of life we aim to protect.

In conclusion, correlating stellar phenomena with biological cycles is a rich landscape for inquiry that reveals the profound interconnectedness of life on Earth and the cosmos at large. Enhancing our understanding of these relationships will greatly inform our cosmic preservation initiatives as we seek to safeguard life's genetic heritage against the uncertainties of the future. Through rigorous research and interdisciplinary dialogue, we can cultivate a vision of stewardship that not only acknowledges the complexities of biological systems but also honors the intrinsic value of life throughout the universe. The journey into that which is beyond our reach becomes not merely an exploration of the stars, but a celebration of the resilience that defines life itself.

12.2. The Cosmic Calendar: Events and Impacts

The vast timeline of existence stretches out before us, not just in geological terms but as an expansive cosmic calendar—each tick marking the momentous events that shape the universe and, by extension, life itself. To understand the correspondence between cosmic events and the subsequent impacts on Earth and other celestial bodies is both a scientific and philosophical endeavor. As humanity strives to protect life through the establishment of DNA vaults, we must appreciate how cosmic phenomena interweave with biological cycles, influencing evolutionary trajectories and the vitality of ecosystems.

The cosmic calendar begins with the Big Bang, an event nearly 13.8 billion years ago that initiated the expansion of the universe. This monumental occurrence set in motion the processes that would create the stars that birthed galaxies and the planets within them. Cosmic events such as supernovae, gamma-ray bursts, and the formation of massive celestial bodies are punctuated throughout this timeline —each contributing to chemistry's rich tapestry. It is through the remnants of these cosmic events that essential chemical elements were forged, elements that would become the building blocks of life as we know it. Carbon, nitrogen, oxygen, and others synthesized in the stellar crucibles provided the essential materials for organic molecules, laying the groundwork for life's emergence.

As stars and planets form and evolve, they carry with them a history of such cosmic events that influence local conditions. For Earth's development, our location within the solar system establishes unique advantages; the stable light of the sun nurtures solar cycles that regulate seasons and climate, profoundly impacting biological rhythms. The interplay between these celestial events and terrestrial life is evident in the cyclical patterns of reproduction, migration, and growth observed in various species—a reflection of life adapted to its cosmic surroundings.

Yet, it is not merely the light emanating from stars that directs biological outcomes; cataclysmic events like asteroid impacts profoundly reshape life on Earth. These historical punctuations are embedded in our evolution, with events such as the extinction of the dinosaurs altering biodiversity's trajectory. The relationship between cosmic occurrences and biological consequences is thus a continuous dialogue where each influence resonates throughout the ages.

Looking forward, we come to the central question of how cosmic events impact our conservation efforts as we venture into space. The establishment of DNA vaults necessitates a thorough understanding of celestial influences when selecting locations for preservation. The potentiality of this preservation taps into cosmic timelines, recognizing that the environments we introduce Earth-based life into may undergo changes due to solar activity, cosmic radiation, and other stellar phenomena. The trust in our ability to navigate these challenges lies not only in the advancement of technologies and methods but also in a profound understanding of our role as stewards of life in an ever-evolving cosmic landscape.

Moreover, these explorations prompt reflections on the ethical implications of our actions. How do we assess the long-term impacts of introducing forms of life to extraterrestrial environments? Which ancient traits should be preserved as we seek to ensure species adapt and thrive? As we construct narratives around cosmic preservation, we must tread carefully within this landscape, ensuring decisions are informed by science, ethics, and the understanding of interdependencies that define ecosystems both on Earth and beyond.

In summary, the cosmic calendar encapsulates the events that shape not only our universe but also the life that persists within it. By appreciating the interconnection between cosmic phenomena and biological cycles, humanity can approach the establishment of DNA vaults with insight—recognizing that our stewardship must honor the intricate balances of life that have evolved over billions of years. By embarking on this mission with respect for the cosmic influences that interlace with terrestrial life, we can ensure that the legacy of biodiversity transcends the boundaries of time and space, thriving in the awe-inspiring expanse of the universe.

12.3. Studying Cosmic Influences on Terrestrial Climates

Studying cosmic influences on terrestrial climates is an expansive inquiry that interweaves astrophysics, climatology, biology, and conservation. As humanity seeks to safeguard life's diverse genetic blueprints within DNA vaults positioned against the backdrop of the universe, understanding the interactions between celestial phenomena and terrestrial environments becomes crucial. Establishing a nuanced comprehension of how cosmic factors shape climatic conditions on Earth empowers us to enhance the resilience of biological systems amid changing climates—whether they arise from historical astrophysical events or ongoing anthropogenic impacts.

Central to studying cosmic influences on terrestrial climates is the recognition that Earth exists within a dynamic solar system, where the interplay of solar output, gravitational interactions, and cosmic events shapes the planet's climatic rhythms. Solar cycles, characterized by variations in solar radiation due to sunspot activity, have demonstrable effects on Earth's climate patterns, including the modulation of temperature and atmospheric circulation. As the sun emits energy, fluctuations in solar activity can induce shifts in weather phenomena, influencing everything from monsoon cycles to drought occurrences. By systematically studying these correlations, researchers can begin to unravel the broader implications of cosmic events on climate stability.

Equally important are cosmic radiation's effects, which permeate Earth's upper atmosphere and interact with its magnetic field. The inflow of cosmic rays can influence cloud formation, terrestrial radiation levels, and even greenhouse gas concentrations through complex physical processes. Understanding how cosmic radiation impacts Earth's climatic systems enhances our knowledge of potential feedback mechanisms and informs conservation strategies aimed at maintaining biodiversity as climate dynamics evolve.

The historical events of cosmic significance—such as asteroid impacts —furnish critical insights into how terrestrial climates can be abruptly altered. The iconic event believed to have contributed to the extinction of the dinosaurs, around 66 million years ago, exemplifies how celestial catastrophes can foster drastic climate shifts. This event culminated in cooling periods due to the substantial particulate matter released into the atmosphere, obscuring sunlight and interfering with photosynthesis on a massive scale. Investigating these past occurrences equips scientists with valuable data on the resilience and adaptability of biological systems.

A key area of interest is how ongoing climate change, exacerbated by human actions, interacts with cosmic influences. The anthropogenic release of greenhouse gases has already led to a marked warming of the atmosphere, raising questions about how these changes might interplay with cosmic cycles. For instance, understanding the resilience of Earth's ecosystems in a warming world requires contemplating how altered conditions may intersect with solar cycles, storm patterns, or cosmic radiation exposure.

As we study cosmic influences on terrestrial climates, the implications extend beyond mere scientific curiosity; they prompt ethical considerations regarding our stewardship of life. A deeper understanding of these correlations invites us to reflect on our role as guardians, charged with protecting the biodiversity that has adapted to centuries of climatic variations. The preservation of genetic diversity in DNA vaults is not solely a matter of archiving material; it embodies a commitment to ecological integrity amidst the dynamic interplay of terrestrial and cosmic influences.

Furthermore, there lies an opportunity for interdisciplinary collaboration among scientists, policymakers, and conservationists to address climate-related challenges through a comprehensive lens. Such collaboration may lead to innovative strategies for mitigating climate impacts—strategies informed not only by terrestrial observations but also by the recognition of cosmic factors that shape our planet.

In conclusion, studying cosmic influences on terrestrial climates enriches our understanding of the complexities that define ecological balance and resilience. By embracing the interconnections between celestial events and climate dynamics, we can fortify our commitment to cosmic preservation through the establishment of DNA vaults while also fostering a sense of responsibility towards the intricate web of life that exists on Earth. The quest for knowledge stands as a bridge, illuminating the pathways through which human actions can harmonize with the continuous rhythmic dance of the cosmos, ensuring that the legacy of life endures through the ages—both in the familiar embrace of our home planet and the uncharted realms that lie ahead.

12.4. Astrobiology: Life in the Martian Context and Beyond

Astrobiology has emerged as a field of tremendous interest and significance in the context of our exploration and understanding of life beyond Earth, particularly in the Martian context and beyond. As humanity prepares to launch into the cosmos, the study of astrobiology serves not only to inform us about the potentiality of life on other planets but also to shape our ethical responsibilities as custodians of life—a dynamic that reverberates throughout cosmic preservation efforts.

Mars has long captured the imagination of scientists and the public alike as a prime candidate for astrobiological exploration. With its similarities to Earth, including polar caps, seasonal weather patterns, and evidence of ancient rivers and lakes, Mars presents intriguing possibilities for the existence of past or even present life forms. The discovery of liquid water, or its historical presence, is a significant indicator that Mars meets some of the fundamental criteria needed to support life.

Astrobiological investigations on Mars focus on understanding the conditions under which life might have existed or could potentially exist today. The presence of microbial life is a primary consideration —organisms that have adapted to extreme conditions on Earth offer insights into potential Martian counterparts. Extreme environments, such as hydrothermal vents, acidic lakes, and polar ice caps, reveal the adaptability of microorganisms that survive in seemingly inhospitable conditions. This adaptability exemplifies the resilience of life and informs our astrobiological models as we explore it in extraterrestrial contexts.

Beyond Mars, the search for life extends throughout our solar system and into exoplanets found in distant star systems. The methods used in investigating these bodies evolve concurrently with advancements in technology and knowledge. As robotic missions land on Mars and other celestial bodies, astrobiologists examine soil samples, climate data, and radiative processes to better understand how life may interact with its environment. Data collected through remote sensing, spectroscopy, and in situ analyses contribute to a warehouse of knowledge that will assist researchers in determining the habitability of other worlds.

In studying the potential for life and the existing Martian ecosystem, ethical considerations are paramount. The premise of colonizing or terraforming Mars cannot be entertained without acknowledging the possibility of indigenous Martian life, however primitive it might be. It becomes imperative that any exploration efforts respect potential ecosystems and avoid contamination. This ethical framework must invoke a consciousness of our responsibilities as explorers and custodians, ensuring that we do not replicate historical precedents on Earth, where the introduction of non-native species has disrupted ecosystems.

In parallel, the lessons learned from Mars inform us about the implications of atmosphere, radiation environment, and resource availability that stand as essential primitives for biological existence. The Martian atmosphere—thin and composed predominantly of carbon dioxide—poses formidable challenges for life as we know it. Furthermore, elevated radiation levels due to the lack of a protective magnetic field pose a risk to future biological organisms intended for preservation in vaults or potential colonization efforts. These factors compel us to reconsider our approaches as we strive to establish DNA vaults that might one day safeguard snippets of life either for restoration on Mars or elsewhere.

As we extend our search for life beyond Mars, galaxies filled with exoplanets await examination. The study of these distant worlds evokes wondrous possibility; astrobiology holds the potential to unveil life forms profoundly different from our terrestrial understanding. Understanding the patterns of cosmic evolution—from stellar formation influencing planetary development to the conditions that allow for life to flourish—will catalyze scientific pursuits that push boundaries for preservation.

Importantly, the intersection of astrobiology and technology plays a significant role in our exploration of potential life beyond Earth. The innovations in genetic analysis and biotechnology bolster our ability to assess genetic diversity and adaptability in terrestrial organisms, providing insights into potential modifications or preservation strategies for reintroducing life into environments where it once thrived.

As astrobiology evolves alongside human ambitions in the realm of space exploration, ethical imperatives shape our responsibilities. Understanding that preserving genetic material is both a practical aim and a moral obligation emphasizes our interconnectedness within the cosmic continuum. Every organism—weave through time—holds the stories of its adaptation and survival, deserving of respect and preservation.

In conclusion, astrobiology serves as a critical tool in our quest to explore life beyond Earth. With Mars as a focal point and the exploration of distant exoplanets on the horizon, the insights gained from studying these environments shape our understanding of life's potential beyond our planet. As we navigate this new frontier, the ethical considerations, responsibilities, and innovations inherent in astrobiology will define our role as custodians of life—impacting our choices as we protect our rich biological heritage and extend our reach into the cosmos. Through these explorations, we not only illuminate the potential for life in the universe but also honor our responsibility to foster and preserve it, not only for our time but for generations yet to emerge among the stars.

12.5. Understanding Cosmic Evolution and Biodiversity

In our exploration of cosmic evolution and its impact on biodiversity, we must consider the intricate tapestry of the universe that influences life on Earth and potentially on other planets. The journey of cosmic evolution represents billions of years of stellar events, chemical processes, and planetary formation that have shaped the emergence of life in profound ways. Understanding this journey is essential for comprehending the multifaceted realities of biodiversity, particularly as we endeavor to establish DNA vaults that preserve the genetic legacies of Earth's organisms against potential existential threats.

The cosmic narrative begins with the birth of the universe, marked by the Big Bang, which set in motion the expansion and cooling of energy and matter. Over time, gravitational forces resulted in the formation of stars, galaxies, and planets. It is within the cores of stars that the fundamental building blocks of life—elements like carbon, nitrogen, and oxygen—are created through nuclear fusion. These elements are eventually dispersed into space through supernova explosions, enriching the interstellar medium and providing the raw materials for planet formation and the genesis of life.

As planets form and evolve, they engage dynamically with their cosmic environments, and these interactions can significantly influence the trajectory of biological evolution. For example, a planet's distance from its star, its atmospheric composition, and geological activities determine its climate and environmental conditions. Earth, positioned in the so-called "Goldilocks zone," possesses a range of temperatures that allow for the presence of liquid water, essential for life as we know it. The climatic changes induced by celestial mechanics—such as axial tilt or orbital variations—affect seasonal patterns and influence evolutionary pressures on organisms inhabiting the planet.

Examining how cosmic events have shaped biological diversity allows us to draw parallels between the cosmic context of Earth and the potential for life on other planets. Mars, for instance, offers a tantalizing glimpse into planetary history; while it may appear desolate now, evidence suggests it once hosted flowing water and possibly microbial life. As we explore Martian terrains, there is a possibility of uncovering fossils or genetic remnants that may illuminate our understanding of life's adaptability and resilience under varying astronomical conditions.

This knowledge becomes ever more significant as we pursue the establishment of DNA vaults designed to safeguard Earth's biodiversity. Understanding the interplay between cosmic factors and biological cycles will inform the selection of organisms to preserve, ensuring that those chosen for preservation possess traits that enhance resilience in potential extraterrestrial environments. The vaults themselves may incorporate insights from astrobiology to optimize conditions for what future reintroduction endeavors may look like, particularly in planning for environments where biological parameters differ from those on Earth.

The exoplanet hunt, propelled by advancements in astronomical technology, opens new avenues for understanding cosmic evolution beyond our solar system. The search for potentially habitable planets in other star systems raises questions about how varying celestial conditions could give rise to unique forms of life. By studying the chemical and physical parameters of these newfound worlds, scientists can infer the qualities that may support or inhibit the emergence of biological systems. Knowledge gained from this exploration fuels the greater narrative of life across the universe, pushing the boundaries of how we define and understand adaptability.

As we consider the implications of cosmic evolution on biodiversity, ethical considerations also emerge. The recognition that life is an extraordinary product of cosmic processes calls upon us to approach conservation efforts with reverence and mindfulness. This perspective informs our responsibilities to protect not only the genetic legacies encapsulated in vaults but also the living systems on Earth that are interconnected with these cosmic narratives. Each life form, having evolved through the inexorable pull of cosmic influences, is deserving of respect as we engage in our quest to preserve these genetic treasures.

In conclusion, understanding cosmic evolution and its relationship with biodiversity unlocks a profound appreciation for both the interconnectedness of life on Earth and the potential for life beyond our planet. As we forge ahead in our cosmic preservation endeavors, this knowledge will guide our choices, strategies, and ethical considerations, ensuring that our responsibility as custodians reflects the wisdom cultivated through an awareness of the cosmos. By honoring this relationship, we can contribute to a narrative where life's resilience flourishes, extending our commitment beyond the confines of Earth and into the endless expanse of the universe.

13. Blending Science Fiction with Scientific Prospects

13.1. Inspirations from Fictional Tales

In examining the inspirations from fictional tales, we find a treasure trove of narratives that have shaped human perceptions of the cosmos and our place within it. Throughout history, fiction has served as a lens through which we understand the complexities and possibilities of life beyond Earth. It has encouraged society to dream big and sparked the imaginations of generations, pushing the boundaries of science and instilling a sense of cosmic curiosity.

From the early works of classic authors like H.G. Wells and Jules Verne to modern epics like those created by Arthur C. Clarke, science fiction has played a pivotal role in exploring themes of interstellar travel, genetic manipulation, and the preservation of life. In Wells' "The War of the Worlds," readers are confronted with the idea of humanity facing existential threats from extraterrestrial invaders, a theme that resonates with contemporary discussions surrounding biodiversity preservation and the need to safeguard life against cosmic challenges. Here, the invasion serves as an allegory for humanity's susceptibility to existential risks, prompting reflections on our responsibilities to protect life on Earth.

Likewise, Clarke's "Rendezvous with Rama" introduces readers to a mysterious alien spacecraft that presents opportunities for exploration, learning, and understanding the unknown. The narrative encapsulates the desire for discovery and the journey into the immeasurable cosmos, reaffirming the idea that our quest for knowledge often lies intertwined with the fate of life itself. Such tales encourage readers to ponder what lies beyond our planet and reflect on the potential for discovering life—whether it serves to enhance our understanding of biology or poses new ethical dilemmas when interacting with unfamiliar organisms.

Moreover, contemporary works, such as "The Martian" by Andy Weir, contribute a fresh perspective on humanity's relationship with other worlds, emphasizing themes of ingenuity, resilience, and survival. Weir's protagonist, Mark Watney, embodies the human spirit as he learns to adapt to a foreign environment while relying on scientific principles to navigate the harsh realities of life on Mars. This narrative thrusts forward the idea of establishing sustainable habitats and highlights our obligation to think ahead about the possibilities of preserving life on other worlds.

The speculative nature inherent in fictional narratives promotes the imagination of genetically modified organisms, artificially created life forms, and the ethical consequences of manipulating genetics. In works like "Do Androids Dream of Electric Sheep?" by Philip K. Dick, readers grapple with questions surrounding authenticity, consciousness, and the definition of life itself. These tales challenge our existing notions of ecosystems, urging us to contemplate not only the preservation of biological legacy but also the evolution of life in response to scientific advancements.

While fiction broadens our horizons and stirs our imaginative faculties, it is essential to distinguish between such narratives and the realities of scientific feasibility. The creative license afforded to authors permits for fantastical elements that may not hold true upon closer examination. For instance, while the concept of synthetic life forms and advanced artificial intelligence may inspire many, the practical applications and ethical considerations surrounding these technologies remain complex. The delicate balance of genetic manipulation and its consequences necessitates rigorous scrutiny if we are to responsibly pursue these paths in the realms of science and preservation.

At the same time, while science fiction offers a canvas for dreaming of the future, it is paramount to remain rooted in the principles of feasibility and ethics when actualizing these visions. The narratives may inspire technological advancements, but they should be tempered with reflections on ecological systems, evolutionary biology, and the moral imperatives that underscore our stewardship of life. These stories can illuminate pathways for conservation if they are approached with the understanding that our actions—as dreamers and doers—hold real-life consequences for our world and any potential worlds we explore or inhabit.

In this context, the convergence of fiction and scientific aspirations reveals a rich narrative promising growth, exploration, and stewardship. As we blend the imaginative with the feasible, we empower ourselves to navigate the challenges of preserving life among the cosmos, gleaning insights from our history, reflections, and narratives that will guide us into the future.

13.2. Distinguishing Fiction from Feasibility

Distinguishing fiction from feasibility is a critical endeavor as humanity forges its path into the realm of cosmic preservation. The leap from fantastical narratives that populate science fiction to tangible, actionable plans for creating interstellar DNA vaults requires a careful examination of what's possible with current technology and what remains within the realm of theoretical exploration. While fictional tales inspire us to envision futures filled with advanced civilizations and interstellar habitats, it is essential to ground these dreams in the realities of today's scientific understanding and technological limitations.

Science fiction has long served as a playground for imaginative exploration, allowing writers to construct worlds where anything seems achievable. From vast space-faring arks to genetically engineered organisms adapted for extraterrestrial environments, the narratives crafted in these stories captivate the human mind and spark curiosity about life beyond our planet. Yet, while they provide inspiration, these tales often gloss over the complexities and challenges involved in turning dreams into reality.

To distinguish fiction from feasibility, we must first understand the often tenuous connection between speculative technologies portrayed in literature and the actual scientific principles underlying them. For instance, the idea of terraforming Mars to create a habitable environment for humans captures the public's imagination, yet the practical application of such a concept remains laden with insurmountable challenges. These include not only the vast resources and technologies required to manipulate an entire planetary ecosystem but also the ethical implications tied to altering a foreign world. Academic and scientific discourse must temper the excitement of fictional narratives, focusing instead on the biological and ecological realities of existing life forms and their responses to environmental changes.

Moreover, we must be aware of the limitations of current technology. Genetic editing tools like CRISPR hold remarkable promise for altering the DNA of existing organisms, but these technologies are still in the early stages of development and understanding. The complexities involved in genome editing, the potential for unintended consequences, and the moral obligations associated with such interventions necessitate cautious deliberation. Here, the question of whether we should act on the creations of fictional tales or the principles of ethical science looms large.

Feasibility assessments are further complicated by the unpredictability of future advancements. While science fiction often paints a picture of instant technological solutions, the reality is that progress is iterative and prone to setbacks. What may seem achievable in one era may require decades of research, development, and testing before it becomes practical. The bold endeavors of today can yield unforeseen results or hurdles we cannot yet predict. Cultivating a realistic mindset about the timeline of technological development is essential in separating speculative fiction from the actionable tasks of creating sustainable systems for life preservation.

It is equally vital to engage with the philosophical implications that accompany our attempts to bring fictional technologies into existence. As we explore the possibilities of genetic manipulation and the creation of interstellar habitats, critical ethical questions emerge: What responsibilities do we hold as we shape life and ecosystems? Should we prioritize the preservation of specific genetic materials, and if so, which species or traits deserve our attention? These inquiries require careful reflection and dialogue among scientists, ethicists, and the broader public in order to foster well-informed approaches to cosmic preservation.

While fiction can serve as an incubator for ideas and explorations, the transition to feasible solutions necessitates rigorous scientific inquiry. Making distinctions between visionary storytelling and real-world challenges involves ongoing discussions, interdisciplinary collaboration, and tireless research. These forms of inquiry must embrace uncertainty and recognize that while our imagination can push the boundaries, reality serves to ground our aspirations in the interconnected web of life we aim to protect.

In conclusion, distinguishing fiction from feasibility is vital as humanity embarks on the profound journey of cosmic preservation. By critically analyzing the technologies and ethical considerations that arise from speculative narratives, we can forge a path grounded in scientific reality while fostering the creativity and imagination that drive our exploration. With an understanding of our limitations and responsibilities, we can navigate the complexities of preserving life's genetic legacy across the universe, ensuring our initiatives reflect a commitment to sustainability and ethical stewardship as we reach for the stars.

13.3. The Realities and Limitations of Fictional Technologies

The exploration of fictional technologies, particularly in the context of cosmic preservation, brings forth a fascinating interplay between imagination and reality. In the pursuit of safeguarding the genetic legacy of life both on Earth and potentially in extraterrestrial environments, we encounter a broad spectrum of envisioned technologies, many of which are rooted in the speculative realms of literature and film. While these imaginative narratives often capture our aspirations for the future, they also underscore the significant limitations inherent in translating fiction into feasible scientific practices.

Fictional technologies serve as powerful catalysts for inspiring innovation, prompting scientists, engineers, and dreamers alike to ponder possibilities that extend beyond current capabilities. From space-faring ships powered by advanced propulsion systems to sophisticated genetic modification techniques that promise to enhance the resilience of species, the narratives constructed in fictional works often challenge us to rethink the boundaries of our existing technological landscapes. The interplay of advancements in biotechnology and space exploration reflects the ideas seeded by these fictions, pushing the boundaries of our imaginations into the domain of scientific inquiry.

However, as we progress from inspiration to implementation, we are frequently met with the harsh starkness of reality. Scientific pursuits are bound by the laws of physics, the limitations of current technologies, and ethical considerations that govern our actions. While fictional technologies may present dazzling solutions for cosmic preservation, they often neglect the complexities and intricate challenges involved in bringing such visions to life. The optimism of narratives, where advanced civilizations flourish in perfect harmony with nature and harness resources seamlessly, contrasts sharply with the grounded realities faced in designing sustainable and ethically sound systems.

A prime example of this dichotomy lies in the portrayal of artificial intelligence within fictional narratives. In many tales, autonomous systems effortlessly manage multifaceted environments, displaying unparalleled efficiency and intelligence. Yet, the truth of existing AI technology, while progressing rapidly, remains far from the sentient beings depicted in fiction. The challenges of safety, security, and ethical concerns in AI development complicate our trust in these technologies, necessitating rigorous protocols and oversight that fictional tales often gloss over.

Moreover, the manipulation of genetics holds significant promise for addressing existential threats, as highlighted in numerous science fiction plots. The ability to genetically engineer organisms for cosmic environments excites the imagination. However, the potential risks and unintended consequences associated with genetic modifications cannot be overlooked. Regulatory hurdles, ethical questions about ownership and consent, and the ecological impacts of introducing modified organisms into untamed environments weigh heavily on the feasibility of such endeavors, urging introspection and careful scrutiny.

Additionally, the urge to replicate fantastic technologies from fiction can lead to impractical expectations and misaligned priorities in scientific research. While the allure of such innovations captivates our collective imagination, it is imperative to remain committed to a systematic and evidence-based approach to cosmic preservation. The gap between envisioned technologies and achievable solutions serves as a reminder that while aspiration can fuel scientific inquiry, careful analysis and ethical evaluation must guide our advancements.

As we navigate the complexity of distinguishing fiction from feasibility in the realm of cosmic preservation, it is essential to remain open to innovative thinking while embracing a comprehensive understanding of our limitations. The challenges of translating fictional ideas into tangible actions call for interdisciplinary collaboration, where scientists, ethicists, artists, and the public can come together to explore potential solutions, share insights, and address the ethical ambiguities associated with cosmic stewardship.

In summary, while fictional technologies ignite the flames of curiosity and exploration, their translation into real-world applications necessitates a critical examination of feasible practices and ethical responsibilities. The intersection of creativity and science necessitates a nuanced approach that values imaginative hope while remaining anchored in pragmatism. The journey ahead in cosmic preservation is not merely about the technologies we create but the thoughtful consideration we apply in navigating the path toward sustainability and ethical stewardship across the universe. By blending our aspirations with grounded realities, we can shape a legacy that celebrates the richness of life, both here on Earth and beyond.

13.4. Dreamers of the Cosmic Future

Dreamers of the Cosmic Future

As we stand on the precipice of a new era in humanity's relationship with the cosmos, it becomes imperative to reflect on the visionaries and dreamers who have shaped our understanding of the universe and our place within it. The notion of reaching for the stars and preserving life amidst the vast expanse of the cosmos is not merely a scientific ambition; it embodies a deep-seated desire for exploration, discovery, and continuity. The dream of a cosmic future, one where humanity evolves beyond its terrestrial bounds while safeguarding the genetic legacy of life on Earth, requires the collective imagination and contributions of countless individuals from diverse fields.

The archetype of the dreamer is woven into the fabric of human history, manifesting through the stories, thoughts, and actions of those who dared to envision worlds beyond their own. From ancient astronomers gazing at the night sky, captivated by the brilliance of stars, to modern scientists employing cutting-edge technology to explore the depths of the universe, the dreamer has always played a vital role in realizing the possibilities that lay ahead. The vision of DNA vaults in space, designed to secure the genetic blueprints of Earth's biodiversity, symbolizes the aspirations of dreamers who seek not just survival, but thriving amid the cosmic tapestry of existence.

As humanity embarks on its cosmic adventure, we must recognize the contributions of literary and artistic figures who have imagined the cosmos in ways that resonate with our own aspirations. Authors like Isaac Asimov, Ursula K. Le Guin, and Arthur C. Clarke have stoked the fires of curiosity through their thought-provoking works that explore the ethical implications of space travel and the interconnectedness of life. These narratives challenge us to envision a future where humanity works harmoniously with the ecosystems around us, examining the delicate balance between progress and preservation.

The technological advancements inspired by these dreamers serve as the foundation for our endeavors today. The concept of DNA preservation in space, while rooted in scientific principles, draws upon imaginative projections of what is possible. The merging of scientific exploration and visionary thinking brings forth a boundless potential to unlock the mysteries of both life and the cosmos. As we write the next chapters of this cosmic journey, the aspiration to enable life to flourish beyond our home planet becomes a collective objective, fueled by the dreams of those who came before us.

Collaboration stands as a cornerstone in ensuring the realization of these cosmic ambitions. As we articulate the concept of universal stewardship, one that recognizes our responsibility toward Earth's biodiversity and potential extraterrestrial ecosystems, we must engage decision-makers, scientists, ethicists, and artists in meaningful dialogues that reflect a shared vision. The synthesis of ideas from varying disciplines can harmonize scientific innovation with ethical considerations, positioning humanity as custodians of life across the cosmos.

Additionally, the dream of a cosmic future calls us to reflect on the unfolding stories that will shape human history as we broaden our horizons. The generational legacy we create today will imprint upon the minds of tomorrow's dreamers—those who will inherit responsibility for stewardship among the stars. By cultivating a culture that values exploration, cooperation, and respect for all forms of life, we empower future generations to carry forth a torch of hope, illuminating the pathways of cosmic preservation.

However, with this vision comes a moral imperative. It is crucial that as we expand our reach, we acknowledge the deep ethical considerations associated with cosmic preservation. Great care must be taken to ensure that our aspirations do not supersede our commitment to respect and protect the intricate web of life that sustains us. The act of dreaming—while a powerful catalyst for innovation—must be tempered by wisdom and humility, ensuring that we preserve not only our genetic legacies but also the very essence of existence that binds us all together.

In conclusion, the dreamers of the cosmic future embody the spirit of exploration, imagination, and responsibility. As we delve deeper into the possibilities of safeguarding life among the stars, we must draw upon the narratives, visions, and ethical principles that inspire us. The journey toward a sustainable and harmonious coexistence in the cosmos is one that we embark on together, weaving a rich tapestry of life that spans beyond Earth and into the uncharted realms of space. Through collaboration, reflection, and a steadfast commitment to stewardship, we can realize the boundless potential that life offers —both on our planet and in the cosmos, ensuring that the essence of existence thrives amidst the wonders of the universe.

13.5. Literature Influencing Scientific Progress

Literature has long served as a wellspring of inspiration for scientific progress, igniting the imaginations of thinkers, scientists, and explorers alike. This intricate interplay between storytelling and innovation has reached a crescendo in the context of cosmic preservation, where narratives function not only as a means of exploring ideas but also as a vital catalyst for advancing scientific inquiry and technological development. Fictional narratives find their resonance in contemporary scientific ambitions, inviting us to envision futures where humanity secures the genetic blueprints of life within interstellar DNA vaults, preserving our biodiversity in the face of cosmic uncertainties.

Throughout history, literary works have charted the blueprint for scientific exploration. From the captivating tales of Jules Verne, who envisioned underwater and lunar adventures, to the contemplative musings of Isaac Asimov, whose foundation of robotics spurred technological development, these works fostered curiosity and propelled real-world advancements. Such narratives often implant the seeds of inquiry in society, inspiring innovators to push beyond perceived limits and explore the fringes of possibility.

In the realm of cosmic preservation, literature offers us vivid portraits of what it means to be custodians of life. H.G. Wells' "The Time Machine" and Ray Bradbury's "The Martian Chronicles" present compelling explorations of humanity's relationship with nature and the consequences of technological advancement. They caution us about the potential pitfalls of disregarding ecological balance and emphasize the moral responsibility embedded in our explorations of the cosmos. These themes resonate deeply within the frameworks we establish for preserving genetic diversity, urging us to confront the ethical dilemmas intrinsic to our quests.

The fascination with extraterrestrial life forms and the mysteries of other worlds serves as a motivating force for scientific endeavor. As we contemplate the establishment of DNA vaults endowed with the genetic legacy of Earth, the imaginative realms presented in literature provide insights into potential adaptations of life within alien environments. Works like Philip K. Dick's "Do Androids Dream of Electric Sheep?" challenge our understanding of what constitutes life. They provoke introspection about the implications of genetic manipulation and artificial life, setting a foundation for philosophical exploration at the crossroads of ethics and technology.

Moreover, literature promotes a culture of inquiry that transcends traditional scientific boundaries. Collaborative storytelling invites interdisciplinary dialogues, where artists, scientists, and ethicists converge to explore the narratives that shape human understanding of life. Such dialogues create platforms for discussing how we might address the pressing questions tied to cosmic preservation—from the implications of genetic engineering to the moral responsibilities associated with engaging in extraterrestrial ecosystems. By blending art and science, we build bridges that nurture creativity and foster holistic thinking, crucial in navigating the complexities of cosmic challenges.

Our current age is characterized by the rapid acceleration of technological advancements, yet the cautionary tales relayed through literature remind us of the precedents already set by human endeavors to manipulate nature. "Frankenstein" by Mary Shelley serves as a timeless narrative warning of the consequences of unchecked ambition. This cautionary tale aligns closely with our intentions to preserve biodiversity through the establishment of interstellar DNA vaults, urging us to place ethics at the forefront of our work. The responsibility to protect life from the potential ramifications of our scientific pursuits propels us to reflect on the possible futures we can create—or destroy—through our actions.

In sum, the literature that has shaped humanity's view of the cosmos and our place within it serves as an invaluable resource in guiding scientific progress. As dreamers, scientists, and artists entwine their narratives, we find inspiration in the tales that illuminate ethical considerations, speculative possibilities, and the moral imperatives tied to cosmic stewardship. The stories we tell not only ignite passion within the scientific community but also instill a sense of shared responsibility among all individuals as we journey ahead. As we endeavor to create DNA vaults to preserve the essence of life among the stars, we must stay attuned to the timeless narratives that beckon us toward a future defined by care, respect, and reverence for the intricate web of life we hold dear.

By drawing upon the influence of literature that inspires scientific progress, we lay the groundwork for a responsible and visionary approach to cosmic preservation—one where we honor life's diversity while exploring the endless possibilities that await us among the stars.

14. Global Collaborations and Universal Peace

14.1. Bringing Nations Together for Cosmic Endeavors

Bringing nations together for cosmic endeavors represents an essential vision for the future, where collaboration transcends borders and fosters collective responsibility in the pursuit of cosmic preservation. As humanity transitions into an era of interstellar exploration, the need for united efforts to safeguard Earth's genetic diversity amid the uncertainties of space becomes increasingly apparent. This subchapter considers the foundations, mechanisms, and imperatives of fostering global cooperation in cosmic initiatives.

Historically, significant advancements in exploration have stemmed from collaborative efforts among nations. The International Space Station serves as a prime example, where diverse space agencies work together to conduct scientific research and foster international goodwill. Such models can be adapted to cosmic preservation, as the establishment of DNA vaults designed to safeguard Earth's biodiversity necessitates input from a wide array of countries and cultural perspectives. A unified commitment toward cosmic preservation lies at the intersection of environmental sustainability, scientific inquiry, and ethical stewardship, encouraging nations to come together for a common cause.

Embarking on this journey requires that nations recognize the interdependence tied to the preservation of life—not just for their own populations, but for future generations and the ecosystems that rely on cooperation across ecological balances. By establishing mutual agreements that celebrate the shared responsibility of protecting genetic diversity, nations can lay the groundwork for joint fulfilment of cosmic responsibilities. Treaties addressing the safeguarding of life in outer space may act as guiding frameworks that ensure equitable distribution of resources and benefits resulting from these cosmic endeavors.

Global workshops and conferences focusing on cosmic stewardship can serve as platforms for knowledge sharing, providing opportunities for scientists, policymakers, and citizens alike to engage in meaningful discussions. These gatherings can facilitate the exchange of best practices, innovative strategies, and technological advancements vital for cosmic preservation. By fostering a spirit of collaboration, such platforms could strengthen relationships among nations while aligning efforts toward achieving common objectives.

Establishing international committees and councils dedicated to cosmic preservation represents another vital mechanism to unite efforts. These bodies could oversee the strategic direction of preservation initiatives, ensuring that ethical considerations remain central to ongoing projects. By creating frameworks for cooperation among scientists and researchers from various countries, these committees can foster partnerships that promote the progressive sharing of knowledge and resources, navigating the legal frameworks that regulate cosmic stewardship.

The sharing of technological advancements across borders is instrumental in propelling global progress in cosmic preservation. Nations with established space programs can collaborate with emerging space-faring nations to facilitate knowledge transfer and ensure that cutting-edge technologies are accessible to all. By promoting joint research and development initiatives, countries can coalesce around shared objectives, cultivating a culture of innovation that transcends national interests.

Furthermore, humanity's united front against cosmic catastrophes is increasingly essential as the threats posed by asteroids, cosmic radiation, and other hazards loom large. Collaborative efforts in monitoring, risk assessment, and emergency preparedness can be facilitated through international partnerships. Establishing protocols to identify and respond to cosmic threats, and sharing the responsibility of safeguarding life beyond Earth, reinforces the notion that cosmic preservation is a shared endeavor.

In fostering a spirit of collaboration and union, it is crucial to recognize the cultural dimensions that enrich our cosmic endeavors. Diverse cultures bring varying perspectives and philosophies to the understanding of life, the cosmos, and our responsibilities to both. Embracing these differences allows for a more holistic approach to cosmic preservation, engendering an appreciation for the interconnectedness of all living beings and encouraging a dialogue that extends beyond scientific discourse.

In conclusion, bringing nations together for cosmic endeavors epitomizes humanity's collective commitment to safeguarding life's genetic legacy across the cosmos. By establishing international frameworks, facilitating knowledge sharing, and nurturing collaboration through workshops and committees, we foster a spirit of cooperation that reflects a deeper understanding of our responsibilities toward both our planet and the vast universe beyond. As nations work hand in hand to navigate cosmic challenges, they lay the foundation for a sustainable and harmonious future—one where the preservation of biodiversity is not merely an aspiration but a shared commitment, illuminating the path toward a future rich in possibilities and discoveries across the stars.

14.2. Global Workshops and Conferences on Cosmic Stewardship

Global workshops and conferences on cosmic stewardship play an essential role in advancing humanity's commitment to preserving the genetic blueprints of life throughout the universe. As we face unprecedented existential threats to biodiversity on Earth, these international convenings serve as platforms for collaboration, knowledge sharing, and the establishment of ethical frameworks that will underscore our stewardship of life in outer space. The imperative of organizing such gatherings arises from the realization that cosmic conservation is not solely a task for scientists, policymakers, or ethicists; it calls for a collective involvement from various stakeholders across disciplines and geographies.

At the heart of these workshops is the dissemination of information about ongoing cosmic preservation efforts and the lessons learned from ecological initiatives on Earth. These conferences create opportunities for scientists to present their research, share innovative methodologies, and discuss the implications of their findings for the broader goals of cosmic stewardship. By bringing together experts from fields ranging from astrobiology to environmental ethics, these gatherings encourage the cross-pollination of ideas, fostering critical conversations surrounding the preservation and protection of life across different celestial environments.

In addition to showcasing scientific advancements, these workshops aim to highlight the ethical considerations integral to cosmic stewardship. Discussions around the implications of genetic manipulation, the introduction of Earth-based organisms to Martian or lunar ecosystems, and the preservation of biodiversity through space-oriented initiatives are vital subjects enriching the dialogue. These conversations can lead to the establishment of international norms regarding the ethical treatment of life forms, ensuring that actions aimed at cosmic preservation do not exploit or endanger existing ecosystems —whether terrestrial or extraterrestrial.

Global workshops can also serve as incubators for innovative solutions to the pressing challenges of cosmic stewardship. By encouraging collaborative brainstorming sessions, participants can tackle issues such as maintaining optimal preservation conditions in DNA vaults, advancing long-term monitoring techniques, and establishing frameworks for international cooperation in cosmic preservation efforts. Collective efforts may yield actionable strategies, generating tangible pathways toward realizing inclusive and equitable approaches to preserving biological diversity.

Public engagement remains a core component of these workshops, aiming to raise awareness of the cosmic preservation mission beyond the confines of the scientific community. National and international outreach initiatives can bolster public understanding of the significance of safeguarding genetic diversity, inspiring citizens to connect with broader efforts aimed at life preservation. Incorporating educational programs tailored for school-aged children can cultivate an early appreciation for conservation, encouraging the next generation to envision themselves as custodians of life's legacies.

Collaboration with various organizations and institutions amplifies the reach and impact of these workshops. Partnerships with space agencies, universities, conservation organizations, and non-profits can cultivate a community that shares and validates common goals. Engagement with indigenous communities further enriches the dialogue; their deep-seated knowledge of ecological principles can inform our stewardship responsibilities. This inclusive perspective can fortify ethical frameworks, encompassing a broader understanding of the intricate connections between Earth's biodiversity and the cosmos.

As humanity strives toward interstellar exploration and the creation of DNA vaults, the urgency for collective action becomes more pronounced. By convening global workshops and conferences on cosmic stewardship, we create a culture of collaboration where diverse voices are heard and respected. Such gatherings reinforce the understanding that preserving life's genetic legacy is not the responsibility of one nation or organization but the duty of all humankind. By striving towards shared objectives, we can cultivate a sense of unity and planetary commitment to cosmic preservation—a legacy that extends far beyond ourselves and into the annals of existence across the universe.

In conclusion, global workshops and conferences on cosmic stewardship play a transformative role in advancing humanity's comprehension of and commitment to safeguarding life's genetic blueprints. By fostering interdisciplinary collaboration, ethical dialogue, and public engagement, these gatherings promote a unified vision of cosmic preservation that resonates deeply within the hearts and minds of individuals across the globe. As we navigate the complexities of our responsibilities toward life, these workshops serve as the crucibles of knowledge, inspiration, and connection that will help usher in a brighter, more sustainable future for generations to come—as we embrace our role as custodians of life among the stars.

14.3. Establishing International Committees and Councils

Establishing international committees and councils for cosmic preservation is an essential step toward creating a cohesive framework that addresses the myriad challenges associated with safeguarding life's genetic diversity as humanity ventures into the universe. These collaborative entities are designed to bring together nations, organizations, and experts from diverse fields, fostering an atmosphere of cooperation and shared responsibility that transcends geographical and cultural boundaries.

The first key function of international committees and councils is the development of guidelines and best practices for DNA preservation in space. By pooling knowledge and expertise, stakeholders can establish evidence-based protocols that ensure the integrity and viability of genetic material during transportation, storage, and potential reintroduction into extraterrestrial environments. Such guidelines must be adaptable, incorporating insights gleaned from ongoing research and technological advancements, thereby ensuring that the strategies employed remain effective and relevant as circumstances evolve.

In addition to best practices, these international entities are tasked with coordinating research initiatives that address pressing questions surrounding cosmic preservation. By fostering collaborative projects among participating nations and organizations, committees can facilitate knowledge-sharing that accelerates scientific breakthroughs. This collaborative approach not only enhances the scope of research but also allows for pooling of resources and funding, decreasing costs and increasing the impact of cosmic conservation efforts.

Central to the discussions held by these committees and councils is the incorporation of ethical considerations into the framework of cosmic preservation. The complexities tied to genetic manipulation, the introduction of Earth-based life forms into alien ecosystems, and the ownership of genetic data necessitate dialogue among ethicists, scientists, and policymakers. Establishing an ethical code of conduct ensures that decision-making processes reflect a commitment to sustainability, integrity, and respect for all life forms we aim to preserve.

Education and public engagement play a crucial role in the mission of international committees and councils as well. By raising awareness about the importance of cosmic preservation, these organizations can mobilize global support and inspire involvement from communities worldwide. Workshops, conferences, and outreach initiatives provide valuable opportunities for individuals to engage with cosmic conservation efforts, fostering a culture of stewardship that aligns with humanity's expanding aspirations in space.

Furthermore, these committees can serve as platforms for negotiations and agreements among nations regarding the shared responsibility tied to cosmic biodiversity. As the legal frameworks governing extraterrestrial ecosystems continue to evolve, committees can facilitate the establishment of international treaties that codify rights and responsibilities concerning genetic resources. By advocating for the equitable sharing of benefits derived from cosmic exploration and preservation, committees can prevent conflicts and ensure that the wonders of the universe are accessible to all.

Establishing international committees and councils also reinforces the notion that preserving life is a shared endeavor—one that can transcend the divisions that often characterize national interests. By fostering collaboration among diverse nations and cultures, these entities can provide a stabilizing force, ensuring that efforts remain directed toward the collective goal of cosmic stewardship rather than being driven by self-serving interests.

The effectiveness of these committees depends on their ability to adapt to the evolving challenges and opportunities presented by cosmic preservation. As the landscape of scientific discovery and exploration shifts, committees must remain agile, able to pivot their focus and strategies to address emerging threats or advancements.

Continual engagement with the scientific community, policymakers, and the public will ensure that these entities remain at the forefront of cosmic preservation efforts, harnessing collective knowledge and fostering a spirit of innovation.

In summary, establishing international committees and councils for cosmic preservation is a critical step in fostering cooperation, ethical considerations, and public engagement as we embark on our quest to protect Earth's genetic legacy in the cosmos. These entities serve to create frameworks for effective research, promote shared responsibility among nations, and advocate for policies that align with cosmic stewardship ideals. By weaving together the insights of scientists, ethicists, and communities, these committees can illuminate a path forward—one that honors the intricate tapestry of life that spans the universe and commits to safeguarding its continuity for generations to come. Ultimately, the convergence of dedicated efforts through international collaboration will empower humanity to navigate the cosmos with a sense of purpose, preserving the essence of life in the endless expanse beyond our home planet.

14.4. Sharing Technological Advancements for Joint Progress

In an era defined by rapid advancements in technology and an insatiable curiosity for the cosmos, the sharing of technological advancements for joint progress becomes crucial for the sustenance of life. As humanity endeavors to establish DNA vaults among the stars to preserve the genetic blueprints of Earth's biodiversity, international collaboration rooted in technological cooperation is not just beneficial but essential. This subchapter delves into the multifaceted dimensions of such sharing, exploring how technological advancements can be leveraged to foster collaborative cosmic stewardship and address the pressing challenges of genetic preservation.

At the heart of this initiative is the realization that progress in space exploration and biotechnology can have reciprocal benefits. As space agencies, private enterprises, and research institutions work collectively, sharing innovations leads to accelerated development across multiple fields. In the context of DNA vaults, technological sharing could enhance the mechanisms of genetic storage, transportation, and retrieval, significantly improving the reliability and efficiency of these ambitious structures. By bringing together expertise from diverse teams, the robustness of cultural and scientific insights ensures that the vaults themselves become highly adaptive and sustainable entities, capable of responding to challenges posed by their cosmic environments.

In ethical terms, the sharing of technological advancements is a commitment to equity and inclusivity. As nations, organizations, and communities contribute their unique perspectives and innovations, the benefits of collaboration extend to all involved. This creates a framework for mutual support and understanding, fostering a sense of shared responsibility toward cosmic preservation. Countries equipped with less advanced technologies can receive knowledge transfer from those at the forefront of aerospace and genetic research, enabling a broader range of nations to participate in the stewardship of life across the cosmos.

Moreover, collaborations may lead to innovations in monitoring and security systems that enhance the viability of DNA vaults. The integration of AI and machine learning technologies can empower custodians to monitor the conditions vital for the preservation of genetic materials, providing real-time alerts and insights that facilitate decisive interventions and critical decision-making. By sharing software development and engineering innovations, the thresholds for effective monitoring can be elevated, reinforcing the integrity of the vaults.

Structuring platforms for collaboration, such as international workshops, symposiums, and collaborative research initiatives, fortifies this exchange. Envisioning a cosmic community where scientists and policymakers convene regularly to share findings and advancements cultivates an atmosphere of continuous learning and progress. This collaborative spirit can be formalized in treaties or agreements that establish protocols for shared research, funding mechanisms, and technology development agreements that propel cosmic preservation forward.

Beyond the operational aspects of sharing technological advancements lies the cultural dimension. The stories told through art, literature, and media can shape narratives surrounding interstellar preservation, fostering a sense of unity and purpose. The exchange of ideas between artists and scientists creates expansive avenues for imaginative exploration—transforming visions for DNA vaults into compelling stories that resonate within the human spirit. By weaving technological progress into cultural contexts, we can inspire public engagement and ensure that cosmic stewardship captures the imagination of future generations.

As we share advancements, we must remain aware of the ethical implications that permeate the discourse. The potential for unintended consequences stemming from technological sharing prompts us to audit the impact of these innovations. For example, the implications of transported technology—whether it pertains to genetic engineering, AI, or space exploration—demand that all participants maintain a commitment to ethical stewardship. A focus on transparency and accountability in implementing shared technologies ensures that our efforts align with the values of cosmic guardianship.

In conclusion, sharing technological advancements for joint progress encompasses a holistic approach that interweaves ethical considerations, collaborative frameworks, and cultural narratives into the mission of cosmic preservation. When nations and organizations unite in this pursuit, they elevate the prospects of impactful cosmic stewardship that transcends traditional boundaries. Embracing an ethos of cooperation, innovation, and respect for life's diversity will empower humanity to navigate the complexities of preserving genetic legacies amidst the vast cosmos. As we endeavor toward these horizons, the fusion of technology and humanity will prove essential in writing a future that celebrates life—both on Earth and among the stars.

14.5. Humankind's United Front Against Cosmic Catastrophes

The vision of humankind's united front against cosmic catastrophes integrates not only the advancements of science and technology but also a profound commitment to the preservation of life's biodiversity amid the vast and unpredictable realities of the universe. As we stand at a pivotal moment in history, it is essential to recognize that the cosmic threats we face, such as asteroid impacts, solar flares, and radiation exposure, necessitate a collective, coordinated response—one that transcends national boundaries and emphasizes global cooperation.

Cosmic catastrophes have the potential to invoke significant disruptions to life on Earth. The history of our planet is dotted with reminders of past existential threats, including catastrophic asteroid impacts that have led to mass extinctions. For instance, the impact that contributed to the extinction of the dinosaurs illustrates how a single event can reshape the course of biological evolution. The urgency of these realities calls for a proactive approach, leveraging the collective efforts of nations, scientists, and organizations dedicated to mitigating the impacts of future cosmic events.

A united front against cosmic catastrophes involves establishing collaborative protocols for monitoring potential threats. International partnerships between space agencies, universities, and research institutions can create comprehensive monitoring systems that track near-Earth objects (NEOs) and assess their potential impact risks. By sharing data derived from advanced telescopic surveys and radar tracking systems, nations can enhance their capabilities for early detection and response to asteroid threats, ensuring that strategies are in place for both potential impact scenarios and preventative measures.

Moreover, the advancements in planetary defense technologies can be amplified through shared knowledge and resource allocation. Developing innovative approaches, such as kinetic impactors or gravitational tractor systems, to redirect or disrupt incoming asteroids represents an area ripe for international cooperation. Collaborative research initiatives can pool funding and expertise, leading to more efficient and effective methods of protecting life on Earth from cosmic threats.

In addition to immediate responses to astronomical dangers, addressing the long-term challenges posed by solar radiation and space weather becomes paramount. Solar flares, when redirected toward Earth, can disrupt not just natural ecosystems but also modern infrastructure, affecting communication systems, power grids, and satellite operations. By establishing global frameworks for monitoring solar activity and developing advanced warning systems, nations can better predict and prepare for the effects of space weather, safeguarding both our technological systems and the ecological health of our planet.

The prospect of establishing human habitats on celestial bodies also raises considerations about ensuring the safety and resilience of these environments against cosmic tragedies. By implementing protocols that allow for swift evacuation or protection from cosmic radiation and impact events, we can enhance the long-term viability of lunar or Martian outposts. Crafting spaces that emphasize both safety and sustainability promotes a future where human ambition can thrive without compromising the integrity of ecosystems—on Earth and beyond.

Additionally, fostering public awareness and engagement around the importance of proactively addressing cosmic threats is crucial. Educational initiatives and outreach campaigns can inspire a greater understanding of the scientific principles surrounding cosmic phenomena while promoting a collective ethos centered on preservation and cooperation. Cultivating curiosity about the challenges posed by space can draw the younger generation into the discourse, encouraging innovative thinking around solutions while reinforcing our shared responsibilities.

Recognizing that cosmic threats transcend boundaries ignites a spirit of unity among diverse populations. When confronting astronomical hazards, humanity can rise above perceived divisions, whether they are defined by nationality, culture, or ideology. This collaboratively forged front serves as a testament to our shared stakes in the survival of life and the protection of our planet.

In conclusion, the vision of humankind's united front against cosmic catastrophes embodies a commitment to interdisciplinary collaboration, the innovative use of technology, and active public engagement. As we navigate the complexities of preserving life amid the uncertainties of space, this united effort emphasizes our responsibility to future generations—ensuring that the essence of life continues to flourish, even in the face of cosmic challenges. Embracing this shared destiny cultivates a beacon of hope, illuminating our collective path toward a future that honors the interconnectedness of life while boldly embracing the possibilities the cosmos has to offer.

15. Technology Transfer from Space to Earth

15.1. Exploring the Repurposing of Space-bound Innovations

Exploring the repurposing of space-bound innovations provides a fascinating perspective on how technology developed for cosmic exploration can be utilized to address significant challenges on Earth. As humanity embarks on its journey among the stars, we must take into account the widespread potential of these advancements to not only protect life's genetic legacy but also enrich our lives here at home. The evolution of space-related technologies offers innovative solutions that can contribute to sustainable practices, ecological integrity, and improved quality of life.

At the forefront of this exploration is the understanding that many technological breakthroughs achieved during space missions have direct applications on Earth. The development of advanced materials, for instance, has led to lighter and more durable products that can enhance various industries, from construction to transportation. Innovations in building materials designed for lunar habitats have fostered opportunities for improving resilience and efficiency in structures on Earth, resulting in reduced emissions and increased sustainability.

One of the most notable advancements originating from space technologies is the area of water purification systems. NASA's research into environmental control during space missions led to the creation of sophisticated purification systems capable of filtering and recycling water supplies. These systems can effectively eliminate contaminants and provide potable water even in challenging environments. By adapting these technologies for use in developing nations or areas facing water scarcity, we can promote health and well-being while addressing critical resource challenges on Earth.

In the realm of agricultural technologies, space innovations have yielded sophisticated remote monitoring tools that facilitate precision farming practices. Data collected from satellite imagery and drones allows farmers to track crop health, soil moisture levels, and nutrient requirements. This intelligence enables more efficient resource allocation and minimizes the impact of agricultural practices on the environment, introducing agile strategies for food production that boost yield while safeguarding ecosystems.

Repurposing space-bound innovations is not solely confined to technological applications; it extends to our understanding of systems and processes. The nature of life beyond Earth leads researchers to think holistically about ecosystems and their management. Concepts like closed-loop systems, which have been employed in life support systems aboard spacecraft, offer models for sustainable urban planning on Earth. These systems recycle resources and minimize waste, providing a pathway toward circular economies that support financial viability alongside ecological stewardship.

Furthermore, advancements in information technologies exemplified by data processing and communication systems developed for deep-space missions can enhance public health and safety initiatives back on Earth. The use of data analytics to monitor health trends, track disease outbreaks, and support remote healthcare services represents a significant leap forward in predictive analysis and proactive intervention, made possible by leveraging space-derived technologies.

Creating vigorous industries through adaptation of space innovations unfolds new economic opportunities while fostering community resilience. As these advanced technologies enter various sectors—from health to agriculture and material sciences—the creation of robust industries centered around sustainable practices cultivates economic growth and job creation, ultimately empowering communities.

The future of space-derived goods carries exciting implications as advancements continue to emerge. Innovations in propulsion systems, resource extraction, and in-situ resource utilization will not only enhance our capabilities for sustainable space exploration but could also address terrestrial challenges, such as renewable energy sources and resource management. Considering the potential to repurpose technologies designed for the harsh realities of space can galvanize a new wave of exploration rooted in sustainability.

In conclusion, exploring the repurposing of space-bound innovations unveils a realm where cosmic ambitions intersect with the pressing needs of our planet. As humanity reimagines the future of life, the lessons learned from space exploration and technological advancements will shape our sustainable practices on Earth and inform the stewardship of biodiversity on a cosmic scale. By embracing these innovations, we not only safeguard genetic legacies but also illuminate pathways for progress that resonate across the universe, pioneering a future governed by ecological integrity and shared responsibility.

15.2. Notable Developments Influenced by Cosmic Technology

Notable developments influenced by cosmic technology represent a convergence of scientific innovation and altruistic ambitions aimed at preserving life across the universe. As humanity embarks on the grand endeavor of establishing DNA vaults in the cosmos, a myriad of advancements in technology, space exploration, and biology have emerged, equipping us with tools that significantly enhance our capacity to safeguard genetic diversity. These developments not only illuminate pathways for cosmic preservation but also reveal how lessons learned from space exploration can be translated into impactful solutions for challenges faced on Earth.

One fundamental area where cosmic technology has made its mark is in the realm of materials science. The harsh conditions of space demand that any equipment or systems used in extraterrestrial environments are built from advanced materials that can withstand extreme temperatures, radiation, and potential mechanical stresses. The advancements created for spacecraft protection eventually find their way into everyday applications. For example, the development of lightweight, durable materials resistant to wear and tear has significant implications for environmental sustainability, leading to more efficient transportation systems and durable products that reduce waste.

Moreover, data collection and processing technologies developed for space missions have transformed our understanding of Earth's ecosystems. NASA's Earth Observing System (EOS) satellites, which gather insights about climate patterns, land use, and environmental changes, allow scientists to monitor biodiversity from afar. The wealth of data obtained through these systems informs not only scientific research but also policy decisions regarding conservation practices. By establishing protocols for monitoring species distributions and ecosystem health from space, we can undertake proactive measures to protect biodiversity as environmental challenges escalate.

In a similar vein, advancements in robotics and automation, initially focused on space exploration, are being repurposed to enhance conservation efforts on Earth. From the deployment of drones for wildlife monitoring to robotic systems equipped with AI for data analytics, these technologies improve our capacity to study and conserve endangered species while minimizing human impact. The invaluable insights gained through these automated systems allow conservationists to make evidence-based decisions, promoting sustainable practices that resonate across borders.

Additionally, space-bound research on extremophiles—microorganisms that thrive in extreme conditions—has inspired researchers to explore resilience and adaptability in Earth's ecosystems. Understanding how these organisms withstand harsh environments provides insights into developing strategies for conserving threatened species under changing climate conditions. By applying these lessons from biospheres beyond Earth, we can inform the genetic preservation strategies implemented in the cosmic vaults and ensure species retain their resilience in the face of ever-evolving challenges.

Furthermore, the collaborative spirit fostered by international space missions has encouraged a shared commitment to cosmic preservation that transcends national boundaries. As nations work together to share technology, expertise, and resources in our quest to explore the stars, this approach promotes greater understanding and mutual respect for global biodiversity. Space technologies are thus woven into the larger narrative of humanity's responsibility to protect the intricacies of life, linking our extraterrestrial ambitions to our duties to Earth.

As we aspire to safeguard genetic legacies in vaults among the stars, notable developments influenced by cosmic research must also incorporate a keen awareness of sustainability. Technologies designed for extraterrestrial habitats have sparked innovations in closed-loop systems that could be applied to terrestrial conservation efforts. These systems, which recycle resources and minimize waste, can promote sustainable living practices on Earth. By utilizing knowledge gleaned from cosmic initiatives, we can forge pathways that honor both our planetary stewardship and our cosmic aspirations.

In conclusion, the notable developments influenced by cosmic technology offer a rich landscape of opportunities and innovations that interlace the aspirations of cosmic preservation with the pressing challenges of life on Earth. By harnessing advancements in materials science, data collection, robotics, and collaborative efforts, we can improve our understanding of ecosystems, develop resilient strategies for conservation, and establish effective governance frameworks for managing genetic resources. The journey into the cosmos need not occur in isolation; it can serve as a powerful reminder of our collective responsibility to protect and celebrate the diverse forms of life that populate our planet while reaching for the stars. Ultimately, it is this harmonious integration of advancements in technology and ethical stewardship that will shape the future of life preservation across the universe.

15.3. Applying Cosmic Advances to Earth's Problems

The preservation of life and the safeguarding of genetic diversity are not merely earthly concerns but cosmic imperatives. With the advent of interstellar exploration, humanity is tasked with addressing the challenges of cosmic preservation, which can only be achieved through the integration of scientific innovation and collaborative efforts. As we explore the applications of cosmic advancements to Earth's problems—specifically in the realm of preserving life—we uncover the multifaceted synergy that can emerge when we harness technology, ethics, and creative thought.

The journey begins with the recognition that many technologies developed for the exigencies of space exploration can have profound applications on Earth. For instance, space research has led to advancements in water purification techniques that emerged from the challenges of sustainability in extraterrestrial environments. These technologies can be adapted to improve access to clean water in drought-stricken regions, showcasing how cosmic innovation can directly benefit earthly communities.

Further, the study of extremophiles—microorganisms that thrive in the inhospitable conditions of space—provides insights into the resilience and adaptability of life. By understanding how these organisms survive in extreme environments, scientists can develop strategies for conserving Earth's endangered species that require similar survival adaptations. Genetic studies of extremophiles may even inspire new approaches in biotechnology, leading to innovations in agriculture designed to withstand climate stressors.

Space-based data collection has also revolutionized our understanding of environmental changes on Earth. The information gathered through satellite imagery enables conservationists to monitor ecosystems, climate patterns, and biodiversity in real-time. These insights facilitate the development of predictive models that can guide responsible resource management and strategic conservation efforts, allowing us to adapt and respond effectively to the existing challenges facing Earth's ecosystems.

As we consider the potential for applying cosmic advancements to Earth's problems, public-private partnerships emerge as a pivotal strategy. These collaborations can bolster funding and resource allocation for research, development, and implementation of technologies aimed at preserving life. Such alliances will not only enhance innovation but also ensure that advancements in technology are accessible and effectively transitioned for terrestrial use.

Policy frameworks that stimulate technological adoption while prioritizing sustainability are crucial in creating vigorous industries that arise from adaptations made in the context of space research. By investing in green technologies and sustainable practices, we can launch initiatives that tackle pressing environmental challenges while positioning society to thrive economically.

Futuristic perspectives on life preservation underscore how space-derived innovations can redefine our relationships with nature. By promoting self-sustaining ecosystems inspired by space exploration endeavors, we can cultivate practices that minimize waste, enhance energy efficiency, and encourage biodiversity. These strategies may serve as blueprints for expanding conservation efforts both on Earth and in extraterrestrial environments, aligning our responsibilities toward cosmic stewardship.

The implications of such advancements ripple into broader conversations about societal engagement. Public involvement and awareness strategies are essential for fostering a culture that values preservation efforts. By harnessing educational programs, outreach initiatives, and media engagement, we can elevate public understanding of cosmic preservation's significance—spurring collective action toward safeguarding genetic diversity in all its forms.

In conclusion, applying cosmic advancements to Earth's problems not only symbolizes innovation but also embodies a commitment to the ethical stewardship of life. By recognizing the interconnectedness between our planetary responsibilities and cosmic aspirations, we can illuminate a path forward that safeguards the essence of existence across time and space. It is the collaborative spirit—fueled by the convergence of science, technology, art, and ethics—that empowers us to embrace our role as guardians, nurturing genetic diversity both on our home planet and beyond. Through these endeavors, we redefine what it means to preserve life and champion the future of cosmic stewardship.

15.4. Creating Vigorous Industries Through Adaptation

Creating vigorous industries through adaptation to new technological and scientific realities is pivotal for the evolution of humanity's cosmic aspirations. As we embark on monumental projects like establishing DNA vaults in space, the intersection of innovation and economic viability presents an opportunity not only to secure Earth's genetic diversity but to foster sustainable industries at the same time. This subchapter explores the various adaptations necessary for creating dynamic sectors that will thrive as we move toward our celestial ambitions.

The first and foremost step in establishing these vigorous industries is recognizing the potential economic benefits derived from advancements in space research and preservation technologies. The development of sustainable practices in DNA preservation, biotechnology, and materials science will create new markets and job opportunities. Industries focused on genetic engineering, for example, can adapt their technologies for both terrestrial and extraterrestrial applications. These sectors can drive research in resilience-enhancing techniques, enabling organisms to survive harsh environments, thus supporting cosmic preservation initiatives while also addressing local agricultural challenges.

Collaborative ecosystems between private enterprises and public institutions will underpin these adaptive industries. Space agencies, universities, and innovation hubs must foster relationships that empower the development of cutting-edge technologies, such as advanced cryogenic systems and automated environmental monitoring tools. By pooling resources and knowledge, initiatives can emerge that lead to breakthroughs in preservation and sustainability. This collaboration could take the form of research consortia, tax incentives for companies pursuing green technologies, or grants aimed at fostering public-private partnerships that prioritize innovative solutions for cosmic stewardship.

Another core aspect of creating thriving industries will be the educational initiatives targeting the next generation of scientists, engineers, and custodians. Educational institutions can adapt their curricula to incorporate interdisciplinary studies that connect biology, space sciences, ethics, and technological innovation. By providing students with hands-on experiences in scientific research, robotics, and environmental monitoring, we cultivate a knowledgeable workforce ready to tackle the challenges of cosmic preservation.

Immersive training programs and workshops focused on the use of robotic systems for monitoring DNA vaults can engage participants actively and foster skill development. The ability to conduct research into preserving life across celestial environments can inspire students towards careers in conservation science, biotechnology, and space exploration. This investment in human capital becomes foundational in fostering industries that support ongoing cosmic ambitions.

In parallel, adapting existing industries to incorporate space-derived technologies offers another route to establishing vigorous sectors. Established agricultural, pharmaceutical, and materials science industries can learn from the innovations driven by space exploration. Collaboration with space agencies can yield information on resource utilization and sustainability practices borrowed from life support systems designed for space missions. By enriching these sectors with knowledge from their cosmic counterparts, we can reinforce the resilience and sustainability of domestic industries.

The interconnection between space innovations and earthly industries conveys a broader understanding of the importance of adaptability. Each advancement in technology provides opportunities to rethink conventional approaches to production and conservation. For example, the sustainable materials developed for space habitats might inspire new construction practices that reduce waste and minimize energy consumption on Earth. Emphasizing a mindset of adaptability within industries not only encourages creativity but also positions them to respond efficiently to changing market conditions.

Moreover, as we explore the implications of cosmic preservation on economic growth, we must pay close attention to public involvement and awareness. Engaging the public through outreach initiatives and educational programs fosters a sense of community ownership in these efforts. Highlighting the connection between industries and cosmic preservation raises awareness of biodiversity conservation, environmental resilience, and ethical stewardship. When the public understands the importance of these efforts, their support can drive policy change and resource allocation, further strengthening the adaptation of industries to align with cosmic stewardship.

In conclusion, creating vigorous industries through adaptation equips humanity to navigate the complexities of cosmic preservation proactively. As we explore the vastness of space and embark on ambitious initiatives like the establishment of DNA vaults, the interplay between technological advancements, education, public engagement, and collaboration will transform these aspirations into reality. By adapting industries to leverage innovations while emphasizing sustainable practices, we can not only secure Earth's genetic legacy but also cultivate robust sectors that resonate with our cosmic symphony —a future where resilience, ingenuity, and stewardship come together to illuminate a brighter tomorrow. Through these efforts, humanity stands poised to thrive amidst the stars, ensuring that life's diverse legacies continue to flourish across the cosmos.

15.5. Forecasting the Future of Space-Derived Goods

Forecasting the future of space-derived goods is a crucial exercise as humanity embarks on its cosmic journey to preserve and protect life through the establishment of DNA vaults in space. As we aspire to secure the genetic blueprints of Earth's biodiversity against potential threats and cosmic uncertainties, the implications of our initiatives ripple through various sectors—including technology, economics, and ethics. Understanding and anticipating how these developments will unfold over time is essential for shaping a future where the preservation of life intertwines with the advancements in science and technology.

At the forefront of this future lies the advancement of biotechnological practices. As our understanding of genetic manipulation and preservation continues to evolve, we can anticipate that improved methods for storing, editing, and reviving genetic material will emerge. Innovations in cryogenics, vacuum storage, and automated monitoring systems will enable us to maintain the integrity of DNA vaults with greater reliability and efficiency. The application of artificial intelligence may revolutionize how genetic data is managed, allowing for predictive analytics that enhances decision-making concerning species preservation and restoration.

Moreover, as we explore the cosmos and consider potential extraterrestrial habitats, the design of advanced life support systems will take on new significance. We foresee the development of technologies capable of creating closed-loop ecosystems that recycle resources efficiently, mirroring natural processes observed on Earth. This capability not only supports sustainable practices in space but can also be repurposed for solving pressing environmental issues on our home planet. There lies immense potential for demonstrating how innovations derived from cosmic exploration can yield vital benefits for society, reinforcing our commitment to preserving life.

The economic implications of space-derived goods also warrant attention. As industries grow around biotechnology, genetic preservation, and sustainable practices, new markets will emerge, stimulating economic growth. The investments made in technologies developed for cosmic preservation will foster sectors dedicated to environmental resilience, genetic research, and agricultural advancements. As we explore the intersection between biotechnology in space and Earth, we can anticipate integrative approaches leading to innovative practices that prioritize sustainability and equitable distribution of resources.

Public awareness and involvement will play a central role in shaping this future. As we continue to reveal the significance of cosmic preservation to global audiences, efforts must prioritize educational initiatives that inspire curiosity, awareness, and engagement. Engaging communities through outreach programs, workshops, and public exhibits will foster a sense of ownership in conservation efforts. By cultivating a culture that values preservation, individuals may contribute to shaping the policies that govern our interactions with genetic materials, advocating for responsible stewardship of life in the cosmos.

The ethical implications surrounding genetic manipulation, preservation, and the potential introduction of Earth-based life forms to extraterrestrial environments pose ongoing challenges for our cosmic endeavors. As we consider the ethical landscapes surrounding these interactions, we envision frameworks that guide decision-making, ensuring that actions reflect a commitment to respect for all forms of life. By incorporating diverse voices and perspectives—drawing from scientific expertise, indigenous knowledge, and ethical discourse—we can cultivate an approach that honors the intricacies of life and our shared responsibilities as custodians of genetic diversity.

In the coming decades, we anticipate robust international collaboration in cosmic preservation efforts, with countries united by a commitment to exploring the universe responsibly. Establishing agreements centered on shared responsibilities for genetic preservation will help cultivate a sense of global stewardship. Collaborative partnerships among nations, organizations, and institutions will pave the way for innovation and research focused on safeguarding genetic resources, broadening our horizons in both science and relations between peoples.

While the future of space-derived goods presents tremendous promise, we must remain vigilant regarding the inherent uncertainties that come with exploration. By continuously reassessing goals, maintaining ethical dialogues, and adapting to technological advancements, we will cultivate resilience in our approaches, ensuring the preservation of genetic diversity amid the complexities of cosmic landscapes.

In conclusion, forecasting the future of space-derived goods as they relate to cosmic preservation initiatives captures the essence of humanity's evolving relationship with life in the universe. Through technological advancements, economic growth, ethical considerations, and collaborative efforts, we can shape a future marked by harmony and responsibility. It is this vision that will guide us toward making informed choices that honor the interconnected web of life as we traverse the cosmos, ensuring that the genetic richness of Earth thrives even in the most distant reaches of the universe. As we continue this journey, let us remain committed to our role as guardians of life's intricate tapestry, weaving a future where sustainable practices and cosmic aspirations intersect in a beautiful continuum of existence.

16. Public Involvement and Awareness Strategies

16.1. Educational Programs and Outreach Initiatives

Educational programs and outreach initiatives are integral to the success of cosmic preservation efforts, as they bridge the gap between scientific inquiry and public engagement. As humanity embarks on ambitious projects to establish DNA vaults among the stars—repositories designed to safeguard Earth's genetic legacy—educational strategies must ensure that knowledge about cosmic biodiversity is disseminated widely and effectively. By fostering an informed and engaged community, we empower individuals to embrace their roles as custodians of life, lighting the way for collective action toward preserving our planet's rich tapestry of existence.

At the core of effective educational programs is the development of curricula that integrate science, ethics, and technology. Educators should aim to create interdisciplinary frameworks that not only address the biological aspects of conservation but also consider the philosophical and ethical scenarios surrounding genetic preservation in extraterrestrial environments. By nurturing students' critical thinking skills and ethical awareness, we can prepare future generations to confront the complex challenges and dilemmas that arise from cosmic stewardship.

Workshops, seminars, and courses designed to engage students and lifelong learners alike can revolve around topics such as biodiversity, space exploration, and the implications of genetic engineering. Hands-on activities and simulations can further enhance these experiences, allowing participants to engage with the principles of cosmic preservation actively. Additionally, incorporating guest speakers from various disciplines—astronomy, genetics, philosophy, and ecology—enriches the learning experience, exposing students to myriad perspectives on life's interconnectedness.

Outreach initiatives play a pivotal role in raising awareness about cosmic biodiversity beyond academic settings. These initiatives can target public audiences through community events, exhibitions, and public lectures that highlight the significance of protecting genetic diversity. Informative campaigns utilizing creative storytelling, art exhibitions, and multimedia presentations can help demystify scientific concepts related to cosmic preservation, making them accessible and relatable to diverse audiences.

The use of media, both traditional and digital, can amplify these outreach efforts, ensuring that knowledge of cosmic biodiversity resonates with wider audiences. Engaging documentaries, podcasts, and social media campaigns can serve to present the relevance of preserving life across the cosmos. By harnessing the power of visual storytelling, we can capture hearts and minds, fostering a collective commitment to protecting life's genetic legacies.

Interactive exhibits, particularly those designed for museums or science centers, offer opportunities for immersive learning experiences. By utilizing virtual reality technology to simulate the environments of DNA vaults or the potential ecosystems of other planets, visitors can interact with both the scientific concepts and ethical questions embedded in cosmic preservation. These dynamic experiences can cultivate curiosity and inspire participants to engage further with the challenges of biodynamic conservation.

Community-supported projects provide additional avenues for public involvement and collaboration. Engaging local communities in conservation initiatives—such as habitat restoration, species monitoring, or educational outreach—serves not only to enhance understanding but also fosters a sense of ownership and responsibility. Initiatives that emphasize the interconnectedness of local ecosystems with the broader cosmic context encourage communities to see themselves as active participants in the stewardship of life.

Moreover, funding through public-private partnerships represents a critical mechanism for supporting educational programs and outreach initiatives. By establishing relationships between government agencies, corporations, and non-profit organizations, resources can be pooled to expand conservation initiatives, outreach efforts, and educational endeavors. These partnerships foster an atmosphere of shared responsibility, enabling innovation and collaboration that nurture the future of cosmic preservation.

In summary, educational programs and outreach initiatives form the backbone of humanity's exploration into cosmic preservation. By intertwining scientific inquiry, ethical considerations, and public engagement, these strategies empower individuals and communities to become responsible stewards of life across the universe. Through robust educational frameworks, inclusive outreach efforts, and creative collaborations, we light the path toward a future where humanity cherishes and protects the rich diversity of life—not only on Earth but also among the stars. This commitment to preservation ensures that the legacy of Earth's genetic heritage endures amid the vast uncertainties of cosmic existence.

16.2. Leveraging Media for Wider Reach

Leveraging media effectively is a powerful strategy in promoting cosmic preservation and increasing public awareness of the importance of safeguarding Earth's genetic diversity for future generations. As humanity embarks on ambitious projects, such as establishing DNA vaults among the stars, engaging diverse audiences through various media platforms becomes crucial for fostering understanding, collaboration, and advocacy for cosmic conservation. This subchapter delves into the multifaceted approaches of leveraging media to achieve wider reach and inspire collective action toward the preservation of life across the cosmos.

In the age of information, effective media utilization enables custodians of cosmic preservation efforts to share compelling narratives that resonate with the public, educating them about the significance of biodiversity and the potential threats it faces. Social media platforms, in particular, offer unprecedented opportunities to connect with global audiences, share success stories, and mobilize support for conservation initiatives. By crafting engaging content that highlights the marvels of genetic diversity—whether through captivating imagery, informative videos, or poignant narratives—custodians can harness the power of storytelling to foster a sense of connection and responsibility.

Educational campaigns that utilize multimedia presentations can serve to demystify the concepts surrounding DNA preservation and cosmic exploration. Interactive web applications, podcasts, and documentaries can weave together the threads of science, ethics, and culture, illustrating the interconnectedness of these fields in the worldview of cosmic preservation. Collaborating with scientists, educators, and communicators to create informative documentaries can amplify public interest and knowledge about the need to preserve life as we venture into the cosmos.

Furthermore, leveraging media to spotlight individual stories of people involved in cosmic preservation can humanize these endeavors. By sharing personal narratives—whether they be scientists, young activists, or communities undertaking conservation initiatives—media can capture the emotional essence of the mission, encouraging others to see the implications of genetic stewardship in relatable terms. Highlighting these personal connections can invite broader public engagement and foster a collective identification with the vision of preserving life across the universe.

Engaging with art and creative expression expands the reach of media in the realm of cosmic preservation. Collaborative projects that unite scientists and artists can produce inspiring visual narratives that intertwine art, science, and thematic elements of cosmic stewardship. Art installations, visual exhibits, and multimedia performances can evoke emotions that drive people to reflect deeply on their connection to life and the responsibility they hold as stewards of biodiversity. Such expressions challenge audiences to process complex scientific ideas and ethical dilemmas while igniting their imaginations about what the future can hold.

Additionally, hosting virtual conferences and webinars provides an interactive platform for global audiences to engage in discussions surrounding cosmic preservation. These events can feature expert panels, workshops, and Q&A sessions that facilitate direct communication between scientists and the public. By incorporating diverse formats, including visual presentations and interactive discussions, these initiatives enable participants to gain insights into the latest advancements and ethical considerations associated with cosmic preservation.

Strategic collaboration with media outlets and influencers can enhance the visibility and impact of conservation messages. Partnering with journalists, public figures, and artists who emphasize the importance of biodiversity can amplify the narrative, reaching audiences who may not yet be aware of cosmic preservation efforts. Social media campaigns, led by well-known influencers, can further promote awareness and solidarity for conservation initiatives, drawing attention to specific events, projects, or calls to action.

Monitoring the effectiveness of media engagement is vital to understanding what resonates with the public. Metrics such as engagement rates, shares, and responses can provide insights into the successes or areas for improvement in outreach strategies. By analyzing feedback, custodians can adapt their messaging to be more effective in capturing interest and inspiring action.

In conclusion, leveraging media for wider reach is crucial in humanity's efforts to promote cosmic preservation and understand the significance of safeguarding life across the cosmos. Through strategic storytelling, creative collaborations, educational campaigns, and interactive platforms, custodians can foster public engagement, inspire collective responsibility, and amplify support for preserving genetic diversity. As we enter a new era of exploration, embracing the power of media will unlock pathways to illuminate the wonders of biodiversity and galvanize action, ensuring that life's essence continues to thrive amid the vast expanses of the universe. Through these collective efforts, we can cultivate a culture of stewardship that not only honors our connections to life on Earth but also resonates with the stars that beckon us forward.

16.3. Interactive Exhibits and Virtual Conferences

Interactive exhibits and virtual conferences play a critical role in broadening public engagement and enhancing education concerning the preservation of biodiversity in cosmic contexts. As humanity embarks on the ambitious project of establishing interstellar DNA vaults to safeguard the genetic blueprints of life on Earth, it becomes increasingly important to create avenues through which individuals can learn, participate, and contribute to these pioneering efforts. Interactive platforms offer compelling opportunities to bridge the gap between scientific knowledge and public understanding, fostering a culture of stewardship that aligns with our cosmic ambitions.

Interactive exhibits designed for museums, science centers, and public spaces can immerse visitors in the narrative of cosmic preservation. Utilizing state-of-the-art technologies, such as augmented reality and interactive displays, these exhibits can provide a multidimensional experience that captivates audiences. Imagine walking through an exhibit that allows visitors to visualize the intricate structures of DNA, explore virtual ecosystems, and engage with scenarios demonstrating the potential impacts of preserving genetic diversity. Through touchscreens and interactive simulations, users can manipulate variables such as temperature, humidity, and radiation to understand how these factors affect the viability of genetic material stored in DNA vaults. This engaging approach makes the learning experience both educational and memorable, prompting conversations about the importance of safeguarding life.

Moreover, the success of interactive exhibits hinges on collaboration between scientists, educators, artists, and designers. By inviting interdisciplinary teams to contribute to the development of educational content and engaging visuals, these exhibits can resonate with diverse audiences. Incorporating storytelling elements that reflect the interconnectedness of life not only fosters a sense of wonder but also inspires empathy toward the organisms we aim to protect. Artistic interpretations of scientific concepts can infuse creativity into the narrative, making complex topics more accessible and captivating.

Virtual conferences serve as powerful platforms for disseminating knowledge, fostering collaboration, and engaging communities globally. As we navigate the challenges posed by cosmic preservation, virtual conferences enable experts, researchers, policymakers, and advocates to connect, share insights, and discuss strategies for addressing the multifaceted issues in this field. The ongoing COVID-19 pandemic has highlighted the importance of digital communication, prompting institutions to explore virtual formats that facilitate wider participation and accessibility.

These conferences can encompass presentations from scientists exploring advancements in genetic research, discussions around ethical considerations in cosmic stewardship, or workshops focusing on the development of sustainable practices applicable to both terrestrial and extraterrestrial contexts. The ability to record sessions and provide materials for on-demand access allows individuals from diverse backgrounds to engage with content at their convenience, illuminating pathways for lifelong learning and participation.

Additionally, as the reach of virtual conferences expands, there is significant potential to incorporate public involvement through interactive Q&A sessions, social media engagement, and online forums. Encouraging individuals to ask questions and contribute their perspectives not only democratizes the conversation but also fosters a sense of community around shared goals. The dialogue between experts and the public creates a culture of collaboration, reinforcing our collective commitment to cosmic preservation and encouraging deeper connections to the issues at hand.

Integrating feedback mechanisms into both interactive exhibits and virtual conferences will ensure that the content remains relevant and resonates with audiences. Regular evaluations, surveys, and focus groups can provide valuable insights on public perceptions, understandings, and interests, allowing future initiatives to adapt based on feedback. By continuously refining the content and delivery methods, custodians of cosmic preservation can effectively bridge the gap between science and society.

In conclusion, interactive exhibits and virtual conferences are instrumental in cultivating a culture dedicated to cosmic preservation and the safeguarding of biodiversity. By engaging individuals through immersive experiences and fostering public discourse, we can empower communities to become active participants in conservation efforts. As we strive to establish DNA vaults among the stars, it is vital that we illuminate the importance of these initiatives, ensuring that knowledge of life's interconnectedness resonates across generations. Through collaboration and innovation, we can inspire a committed movement, driven by the collective aspiration of preserving the essence of life—for Earth and the cosmos alike.

16.4. Community-Supported Projects and Involvement

In the context of "Arks Among The Stars: DNA Vaults and the Preservation of Life," the notion of community-supported projects and involvement is fundamental to realizing our vision of cosmic preservation. As humanity sets forth to explore and secure the genetic legacies of life from Earth, the engagement of global communities becomes a vital keystone in the endeavor to promote ethical stewardship and collective responsibility for biodiversity conservation. This subchapter delves into the various forms of community engagement, the significance of local partnerships, and the strategies to foster active participation in preserving life's intricate tapestry.

Community-supported projects resonate deeply in the fabric of ecological and cosmic stewardship. These initiatives harness the enthusiasm and expertise of local populations, empowering individuals and groups to become stewards of the environments they inhabit. By fostering a sense of ownership and involvement, communities can strengthen their connections to biodiversity and recognize their role in the legacy we seek to protect. Such participatory approaches can be employed through local conservation projects, educational programs, and collaborative decision-making processes that integrate the voices of various stakeholders.

One prevalent model for facilitating community involvement entails collaboration with local organizations and educational institutions. Schools can serve as hubs for awareness, allowing students to engage in hands-on projects related to biodiversity, conservation, and cosmic stewardship. Students might participate in citizen science initiatives, conducting ecological assessments, or monitoring local ecosystems, fostering an understanding of global challenges while simultaneously cultivating a passion for stewardship. When students become active participants in these projects, they transform into informed advocates for the preservation of life, nurturing a culture of environmental awareness that can extend well beyond their immediate communities.

Community-supported agriculture (CSA) is another model worth exploring in the context of cosmic-related stewardship initiatives. By creating local networks that promote sustainable practices, we can inspire communities to celebrate and support biological diversity. These agricultural systems empower local producers to share their knowledge about sustainable land management, responsible resource use, and the significance of genetic diversity in crops. In this way, the principles of community-supported projects resonate with the overarching goals of cosmic preservation, emphasizing the interconnectedness of local and cosmic systems.

Funding community-supported projects is critical for their success and sustainability. Public-private partnerships present a powerful avenue for securing financial resources to empower local initiatives. Governments, non-profit organizations, and corporations can collaborate to provide grants, scholarships, and investment opportunities that bolster community-led actions related to biodiversity conservation. Such partnerships not only enhance the practicalities of launching and sustaining projects but also embed a sense of shared purpose in pursuing the preservation of genetic diversity, both on Earth and in the cosmos.

Furthermore, technology can serve as an enabler of community-supported projects by enhancing accessibility to information, resources, and opportunities for involvement. Online platforms and social media can facilitate knowledge sharing, allowing varied stakeholders to connect and collaborate across distances. Virtual forums enable communities from different regions to exchange best practices and lessons learned in biodiversity conservation, democratizing access to valuable information and fostering a sense of global solidarity.

Public initiatives aimed at raising awareness about cosmic preservation and encouraging community engagement are essential in shaping the discourse surrounding biodiversity. Educational campaigns that promote the importance of protecting genetic diversity locally, nationally, and globally allow citizens to reflect on their roles as custodians of life. Outreach efforts should emphasize the connections between personal actions and larger environmental outcomes, empowering individuals to contribute positively to cosmic conservation efforts.

In conclusion, community-supported projects and involvement represent a cornerstone for advancing humanity's endeavors in cosmic preservation. By nurturing local partnerships, fostering active participation, and promoting engagement through education and technology, we can elevate collective responsibility for safeguarding life. This collaborative spirit encourages individuals to embrace their connections to biodiversity, reinforcing that the preservation of genetic diversity transcends terrestrial boundaries and resonates within our cosmic aspirations. As we chart our course toward a sustainable future among the stars, the involvement of communities will inspire a shared commitment to protect the intricate web of life that defines our existence, ensuring that the genetic legacies of Earth thrive in the universes yet to be explored.

16.5. Funding the Future Through Public-Private Partnerships

In a world where the preservation of life takes on unprecedented dimensions, funding the future through public-private partnerships emerges as a pivotal mechanism for advancing cosmic biodiversity preservation initiatives. As humanity endeavors to safeguard Earth's genetic legacy while exploring the cosmos, collaboration between governmental entities and the private sector becomes essential for mobilizing the resources, technologies, and expertise needed for long-term sustainability. This section delves into the synergistic potential that arises from these partnerships, emphasizing the importance of strategic investment, innovative funding models, and shared goals.

Public-private partnerships facilitate the pooling of resources from both sectors, thereby creating a foundation upon which ambitious projects can be realized. The intricacies of space exploration and genetic preservation require substantial funding, often exceeding the financial resources available to public institutions alone. Governments, recognizing the intrinsic value of cosmic preservation, can leverage partnerships with private companies to access expertise in engineering, biotechnology, and cutting-edge technologies. These collaborations can lead to the development of innovative solutions while alleviating some of the financial burdens associated with research, development, and deployment.

Investments in technology and infrastructure play a significant role in enabling public-private partnerships to flourish. The design and construction of DNA vaults capable of withstanding the harsh realities of space—with robust monitoring systems, radiation shielding, and sustainable energy sources—present complex challenges that require specialized knowledge. By channeling private investments into the development and refinement of these technologies, partnerships release the potential for rapid advancements that might not be possible through public funding alone.

Innovation in funding models also presents exciting opportunities for cosmic preservation. Traditional grant mechanisms often come with limitations that may not align with the ambitious timelines and unique requirements of space exploration. Alternative approaches, such as venture philanthropy, impact investing, and crowdfunding, open new avenues for securing financial support. Through these models, both public and private stakeholders can harness collective enthusiasm and investment from individuals and organizations interested in supporting the preservation of life's genetic diversity across the cosmos.

Bilateral agreements between governments and private entities can also help to establish clear roles, responsibilities, and shared objectives. By developing comprehensive frameworks that articulate the commitments made by each party, partnerships can cultivate transparency, mutual accountability, and long-term dedication to cosmic preservation. These agreements serve as touchpoints for monitoring progress and aligning ongoing efforts with the evolving landscape of scientific research and technological advancements.

Furthermore, as public-private partnerships evolve, they can promote the importance of education and outreach efforts tied to cosmic preservation initiatives. Engaging the public is essential for raising awareness and garnering support for broader conservation efforts. By integrating education and outreach into funding strategies, stakeholders can forge connections with communities, highlighting the importance of preserving Earth's genetic legacy and fostering a culture of stewardship that extends to cosmic ambitions.

In addition, the collaborative spirit fostered by public-private partnerships can lead to innovative approaches to optimizing resource utilization and recycling practices. Sustainability becomes a core principle in the design and implementation of DNA vaults and related technologies, ensuring that operations align with the fundamental values of cosmic stewardship. This shared commitment to sustainability can culminate in synergistic solutions aimed at addressing pressing terrestrial challenges while reinforcing the vision of protecting life across the universe.

Ultimately, funding the future through public-private partnerships represents a dynamic approach that requires a commitment to cooperation, innovation, and shared responsibility. As we move forward with cosmic preservation initiatives, these collaborative efforts will not only enhance our capacity to safeguard especially vulnerable genetic materials but also illuminate pathways for sustainable practices that resonate across both terrestrial and cosmic contexts. By working together across sectors, we can cultivate a future where the preservation of life's genetic legacy is not only feasible but thriving, securing a rich diversity of existence for generations to come amid the infinite mysteries of the cosmos.

17. The Sustainability of Cosmic Endeavors

17.1. Analyzing Long-term Viability and Efficiency

Analyzing long-term viability and efficiency is a pivotal undertaking as humanity embarks on monumental endeavors to preserve genetic diversity through cosmic DNA vaults. The analysis allows for a comprehensive understanding of how these vaults can effectively safeguard Earth's biodiversity while also evaluating the ecological, technological, and operational frameworks necessary for maintaining life in extraterrestrial environments. Setting the stage for effective genetic preservation requires us to not only assess current practices but also chart a sustainable and coherent path forward, ensuring that our initiatives yield tangible benefits for generations to come.

A key factor to consider when analyzing long-term viability is the adaptability of organisms we choose to preserve. The effectiveness of genetic preservation hinges on our ability to select species with inherent resilience traits capable of adapting to changing environmental conditions. Factors such as climate change, habitat loss, and pollution necessitate a focus on organisms that exhibit genetic diversity, allowing for adaptability across various ecosystems—whether terrestrial or extraterrestrial. Assessing the long-term viability of stored genetic material means understanding how species might fare in conditions far removed from their traditional habitats, promoting a commitment to conservation efforts that respect ecological integrity.

Moreover, operational efficiency involves a detailed examination of the technologies and methods utilized to preserve genetic materials. This encompasses assessing cryogenic systems, vacuum storage techniques, and monitoring technologies employed within the vaults. We must evaluate how these systems sustain optimal conditions over extended periods, considering not only their effectiveness but also their energy requirements and environmental impact. The aim is to develop practices that maximize efficiency while minimizing resource consumption and ecological footprints, creating a sustainable paradigm that aligns with our cosmic ambitions.

Additionally, the durability of the genetic data being preserved is a crucial aspect of long-term viability. We'll need to embrace adaptive technologies in the field of data storage that can withstand not only environmental stressors but also emerging challenges related to cyber threats and data integrity. This means establishing protocols for routine checks and updates on both biological samples and their associated data. Continuous engagement with advancements in biotechnology and data management will be essential to ensure the longevity and usability of preserved genetic materials.

Resource utilization—both in terms of energy consumption and raw materials—is equally vital when considering long-term efficiency. Establishing self-sustaining systems, particularly in extraterrestrial environments, necessitates innovative designs that harness renewable energy sources. Incorporating solar power and advanced energy-efficient technologies can create a feedback loop, allowing systems to function sustainably while preserving life. Implementing closed-loop systems further enhances resource efficiency by recycling materials and minimizing waste—an approach that mirrors ecological processes already present in nature.

Developing robust relationships between technological advancement and ecological considerations is integral to achieving long-term viability in cosmic preservation. By establishing partnerships with technological innovators, environmental organizations, and local communities, we can foster a collaborative spirit that transcends traditional boundaries, uniting diverse perspectives in our shared quest. This collaboration should involve coordinating research projects, sharing knowledge and resources, and engaging in outreach efforts aimed at promoting awareness of the intrinsic value of preservation efforts.

Furthermore, as we analyze long-term viability and efficiency, we must incorporate frameworks for ethical reflection. The decisions we make regarding which organisms to preserve, how to manipulate genetic material, and the potential impacts on ecosystems should always be underscored by ethical considerations. Engaging in dialogues about the implications and responsibilities associated with genetic preservation serves as a guiding light in ensuring that our actions reflect a commitment to the intrinsic value of life.

In summary, analyzing long-term viability and efficiency is a crucial endeavor as we establish DNA vaults aimed at safeguarding Earth's genetic diversity. By prioritizing adaptability, evaluating operational efficiency, enhancing resource utilization, fostering technological collaboration, and upholding ethical principles, we can shape a sustainable path forward. The insights gained from this analysis will inform not only our current practices but also our aspirations for cosmic preservation, ensuring that the legacies of life endure across time and space. As custodians of biodiversity, this commitment to thorough analysis reflects our dedication to responsible stewardship and empowers us to navigate the complex realities of protecting life among the stars.

17.2. Optimizing Resource Utilization and Recycling

Optimizing resource utilization and recycling is essential in the context of establishing interstellar DNA vaults and ensuring the sustainability of cosmic preservation efforts. As humanity extends its reach into space, the understanding and application of efficient resource management become crucial not only for the protection of Earth's genetic legacy but also for fostering a new paradigm of ecological stewardship across the cosmos. This subchapter examines innovative strategies that can promote efficient resource use, minimize waste, and enhance the overall sustainability of our initiatives in cosmic exploration.

The first step in optimizing resource utilization lies in the design of DNA vaults and their associated technologies. Advanced engineering techniques must prioritize energy efficiency in both construction and operation. As these vaults will exist in environments far removed from Earth, it is vital to integrate renewable energy sources, such as solar panels, into the design. Utilizing solar energy not only minimizes reliance on finite resources but also establishes a self-sustaining ecosystem capable of maintaining vital systems over extended periods. The incorporation of energy-efficient appliances, insulation materials, and automated monitoring systems further enhances the capacity of these vaults to function with minimal energy expenditure.

Recycling resources is another key consideration that can significantly contribute to optimizing resource utilization. Closed-loop systems, which mimic natural ecological processes, can be employed to recycle waste products and repurpose them within the vaults. This might include the transformation of biological waste into nutrient-rich compost for potential future habitats or even the recycling of water through advanced purification processes. By integrating these principles into the vault's operations, we can create a sustainable cycle that reduces the need for external resources and promotes efficient use of what is available.

Additionally, the materials chosen for constructing the vaults must also align with sustainability objectives. Utilizing advanced materials capable of enduring the harsh conditions of space—such as radiation, temperature fluctuations, and vacuum environments—ensures long-term viability. Selecting materials designed for durability and recyclability reinforces the commitment to sustainability while minimizing the ecological impact. Implementing a materials selection framework can guide decision-making processes, encouraging the use of environmentally friendly materials that can be repurposed if the vaults require decommissioning or upgrading.

The incorporation of smart technologies and artificial intelligence into resource optimization strategies provides significant advantages for operational efficiency. AI-driven monitoring systems can continuously evaluate resource consumption, alerting custodians to anomalies or opportunities for improvement. By analyzing patterns of resource usage and performance data, these systems can suggest modifications to enhance efficiency and sustainability in real-time. Employing predictive analytics allows for informed decision-making that can lead to better management of materials and energy, ultimately reinforcing the vault's self-sustaining capabilities.

Moreover, recycling initiatives should extend beyond the vaults themselves. As humanity embarks on cosmic exploration, implementing policies regarding the recycling and repurposing of materials used in spacecraft and other systems becomes essential. By adopting a cradle-to-cradle philosophy where waste is minimized and materials are reclaimed and reused, we can establish practices that normalize resource efficiency as a fundamental aspect of space exploration.

To promote a culture of sustainability and resource optimization, education and outreach efforts must emphasize the importance of these practices. Through workshops, public campaigns, and educational curricula, we can raise awareness about the significance of efficient resource utilization and recycling, encouraging individuals and communities to adopt sustainable habits both on Earth and in their aspirations for cosmic engagement. The establishment of community-supported initiatives that focus on conservation and recycling can foster grassroots movements that align with planetary stewardship.

International collaboration can amplify these resource utilization efforts, as nations gather to share best practices, technologies, and methodologies for optimizing sustainability in space missions. Aligning global standards for resource consumption and recycling can help mitigate the risks associated with pollution and waste generation, emphasizing shared responsibility in protecting the cosmic environment.

In conclusion, optimizing resource utilization and recycling within the context of cosmic preservation is a multifaceted endeavor that demands forward-thinking strategies, innovative technologies, and global collaboration. By establishing practices that prioritize sustainability, we can ensure that the genetic legacies safeguarded in interstellar DNA vaults are protected not only against the uncertainties of the cosmos but also from the rampant resource depletion and ecological destruction threatening life on Earth. Through these concerted efforts, humanity can rise to its responsibilities as custodians of life, nurturing resilience amid the beauty and complexities of the universe. As we set forth into the cosmos, the commitment to resource optimization illuminates the pathway for preserving the intricate tapestry of life and celebrating the remarkable journey that lies ahead.

17.3. Promoting Green Technologies for Space Missions

In the realm of space exploration, the promotion of green technologies for missions emerges as a pivotal theme in ensuring that humanity's cosmic endeavors align with principles of sustainability and ecological respect. As we set our sights on establishing DNA vaults among the stars and safeguarding Earth's genetic biodiversity, it is critical that we focus on innovative, environmentally friendly approaches to all facets of space missions. This commitment to green technologies encompasses everything from spacecraft design and energy utilization to waste management systems and life support mechanisms.

The journey toward cosmic preservation begins with the design of space vehicles that prioritize energy efficiency and sustainable materials. Traditional rockets, while ingeniously engineered, often rely on fossil fuels and emit significant quantities of greenhouse gases during launch. In contrast, green technologies such as electric propulsion systems or renewable energy sources—like solar sails—offer transformative alternatives. These advanced propulsion methods harness energy from the sun or utilize ion thrusters, which provide efficient means of movement while minimizing the environmental impact associated with traditional launch methods.

Moreover, the potential for in-situ resource utilization (ISRU) presents an exciting avenue for developing self-sustaining ecosystems on other celestial bodies. By tapping into the resources available on the Moon, Mars, and beyond, we can significantly reduce the cost and environmental footprint of long-term space missions. For instance, extracting water from Martian ice caps or regolith can refuel return missions, create oxygen for crew members, and support the cultivation of food crops within biodomes. Integrating ISRU into mission planning can lead to the establishment of circular economies in space, where resources are continuously recycled and repurposed, further emphasizing our commitment to a green future.

Promoting green technologies also extends to the implementation of sustainable life support systems. The challenge of creating habitable environments within spacecraft or lunar bases can be met with innovations that mimic Earth's natural ecological processes. Closed-loop systems, which recycle air and water while producing food, maximize efficiency and minimize waste. These systems can be modeled after regenerative processes in nature, ensuring that the resources consumed during long missions are replenished and sustained, creating self-sufficient environments that reflect our commitment to preserving our planet's ecosystems.

Furthermore, the deployment of waste management systems that prioritize recycling and composting aligns with principles of sustainability. As we venture into the cosmos, the generation of waste presents significant challenges, particularly in confined environments. By innovating methods for treating organic waste and reusing materials from expired supplies or equipment, space missions can promote a culture of resourcefulness akin to Earth-based sustainability practices. Such strategies echo broader goals of harmonizing human activities with ecological principles, celebrating our responsibility as custodians of both Earth and the universe.

Educational outreach initiatives are vital for promoting green technologies and instilling a culture of sustainability in future generations. By engaging the public through awareness campaigns, interactive workshops, and educational curricula that emphasize the significance of green practices in space exploration, we can inspire curiosity and collective action. Raising awareness about the sustainability practices employed in cosmic missions makes tangible the connections we share with our environment, reinforcing the importance of stewardship beyond the confines of Earth.

International collaboration and knowledge sharing remain paramount during this endeavor, as countries seek to promote green technologies and sustainable practices in cosmic missions. By forming partnerships among space agencies, research institutions, and private enterprises, nations can work together to pool resources, share best practices, and develop innovative technologies aimed at minimizing environmental impacts. Such collaborative efforts can foster an international culture of stewardship that emphasizes responsibility and accountability as we venture into uncharted territories.

In conclusion, promoting green technologies for space missions underscores humanity's commitment to cosmic preservation and stewardship. By prioritizing sustainable practices in spacecraft design, employing in-situ resource utilization, innovating life support systems, and engaging in educational outreach efforts, we can align our cosmic ambitions with the ethical mandate of protecting the environment. As we look to the stars with hope and aspiration, let us remain steadfast in our commitment to ensuring that our foray into the cosmos reflects a dedication to preserving the intricate tapestry of life on Earth and beyond, securing our legacy as responsible custodians across time and space.

17.4. Developing Self-sustaining Ecosystems

Developing self-sustaining ecosystems is pivotal in the grand vision for cosmic preservation, particularly as humanity embarks on the ambitious journey of creating DNA vaults among the stars. These ecosystems not only represent a commitment to safeguarding genetic diversity but also serve as models for resilience and harmony in environments where life may face stark challenges. As we delve into the intricacies of designing these ecosystems, we find ourselves tasked with innovating strategies that promote sustainability, integration, and ethical stewardship, ensuring that life flourishes both on Earth and beyond.

At the core of self-sustaining ecosystems lies the principle of closed-loop systems. Just as nature has perfected its processes over eons of evolution, we must draw inspiration from these natural systems to create environments that recycle nutrients, water, and energy efficiently. In terrestrial ecosystems, nutrient cycling is facilitated through the interactions between producers, consumers, and decomposers—each playing a vital role in maintaining balance. Similarly, in the context of DNA vaults and potential extraterrestrial habitats, fostering these relationships will be essential for creating resilient systems capable of thriving amidst the uncertainties of the cosmos.

To create closed-loop systems for cosmic ecosystems, we can employ technologies derived from both biological and engineering disciplines. For example, bioreactors—where microorganisms break down organic matter—can be integrated with hydroponic systems to nourish plants while simultaneously recycling waste products. This symbiotic relationship establishes a self-sufficient habitat capable of producing food while effectively managing resources. By mimicking natural ecosystems in these environments, we can cultivate a balance of flora and fauna that is sustainable and ethically sound.

The cultivation of diverse plant and microbial species becomes essential in developing self-sustaining ecosystems. The selection of organisms should prioritize those with adaptive traits, ensuring they can survive in new or alien environments. These selections might include extremophiles capable of withstanding harsh radiation levels or temperature extremes, thereby enriching the genetic diversity and resilience of the ecosystem. Furthermore, understanding how these organisms interact will be key to creating integrated systems within the vaults, enabling seamless nutrient cycling and energy flow.

Energy management is another critical component in developing self-sustaining ecosystems. By harnessing renewable energy sources such as solar or wind power, we can ensure that the ecological systems thrive without depleting finite resources. Advanced energy storage solutions, such as bio-batteries, can store captured energy efficiently, ensuring that the ecosystems remain operational during periods of low energy availability. Implementing smart technologies equipped with AI can enable real-time monitoring and optimization of energy use, preventing wasteful practices while maximizing the efficiency of various ecological processes.

Water management stands as another fundamental pillar in creating these self-sustaining environments. Recycled water should be the default practice in maintaining ecosystems, utilizing technologies like atmospheric water generators or water purification systems designed for space applications. Establishing systems that recycle wastewater into potable forms will not only conserve resources but also promote the sustainable use of water in closed-loop environments. This practice draws upon the principles of natural water cycles and reinforces the idea that sustainability is integral to preserving life.

As we venture into the cosmos, the ethical considerations of developing self-sustaining ecosystems must remain at the forefront. The introduction of Earth-based species into extraterrestrial habitats raises significant ethical dilemmas surrounding potential ecological impacts and the responsibilities we hold in shaping life on other worlds. Engaging with philosophical inquiries about what constitutes acceptable ecological manipulation encourages deep reflection on our roles as custodians. Establishing guidelines for ethical stewardship of all organisms involved in cosmic ecosystems ensures that our efforts resonate with a commitment to ecological integrity and promote harmony between nature and technology.

The human aspect of developing these ecosystems cannot be overlooked. Education and outreach play vital roles in cultivating a sense of ownership and responsibility among individuals, encouraging communities to engage with the principles of cosmic preservation actively. Programs that highlight the significance of biodiversity and the interconnectedness between organisms foster awareness and inspire collective action, reinforcing the idea that everyone has a role to play in stewardship.

In summary, developing self-sustaining ecosystems in the context of cosmic preservation involves integrating scientific innovation, ethical considerations, resource efficiency, and community engagement. By drawing upon the principles of resilience seen in nature, we can create systems capable of thriving amidst the unpredictable realities of space. This commitment to sustainability extends beyond preserving Earth's genetic legacy; it embraces a broader vision of stewardship that nurtures life itself. As we chart our way into the cosmos, our dedication to developing these ecosystems will ensure that life—both on Earth and among the stars—can flourish and thrive across time.

17.5. Creating a Blueprint for Cosmic Biodiversity Sustainment

Creating a blueprint for cosmic biodiversity sustainment involves a comprehensive approach that synergizes scientific innovation, ethical considerations, and cross-disciplinary cooperation. As humanity stands at the threshold of ambitious endeavors such as establishing DNA vaults in space, the task of ensuring the protection and continuation of life amidst vast cosmic challenges calls for deliberate planning and strategic foresight. This blueprint serves not only as a guide for preserving Earth's genetic legacy but also as a foundation for cultivating life in various extraterrestrial environments.

The blueprint begins with a thorough understanding of genetic diversity and its critical role in ecological resilience. Preserving genetic material involves identifying a wide array of species—including plants, animals, and microorganisms—that embody a rich tapestry of evolutionary potential. The selection process must prioritize organisms with adaptive traits, ensuring that even in the face of environmental stresses, they can thrive. This proactive approach underscores the importance of a holistic view of biodiversity, where the preservation of genetic material transcends traditional conservation efforts to encompass future adaptability.

Central to the blueprint is a commitment to leveraging cutting-edge technologies for storage and preservation. Advanced cryogenic systems, innovative vacuum storage solutions, and sophisticated monitoring technologies must be integrated into the vault designs to safeguard genetic material for extended periods. Continuous environmental monitoring utilizing artificial intelligence will enhance the robustness of these systems, ensuring that deviations in temperature, humidity, or radiation are detected and addressed promptly. By establishing protocols that prioritize both reliability and efficiency, we can create secure environments that stand the test of time in the cosmic expanse.

Furthermore, as we contemplate the environment in which we intend to reintroduce preserved species, it is crucial to understand the context of extraterrestrial ecosystems. The blueprint must include detailed assessments of potential locations to establish these vaults, including considerations of astrobiological influences, planetary characteristics, and the accessibility of resources essential for sustaining life. Identifying habitats capable of supporting genetically preserved organisms is vital for envisioning the future ecological landscapes we hope to cultivate on other celestial bodies.

Collaboration and international cooperation form a cornerstone of this blueprint for cosmic biodiversity sustainment. Engaging stakeholders from diverse backgrounds—including governments, scientists, ethicists, and the public—ensures that varied perspectives are integrated into cosmic preservation strategies. Forming partnerships with organizations dedicated to conservation and biological research can lead to fruitful collaborations that enhance technologies, promote knowledge sharing, and establish a sense of shared accountability toward cosmic biodiversity.

Education and public engagement are paramount to the success of this blueprint. Informing the public about the importance of biodiversity and genetic preservation fosters a culture of stewardship. Initiatives such as community workshops, educational programs, and digital outreach can instill a sense of connection between individuals and the living organisms we aim to protect. The success of these efforts relies on narratives that convey the significance of preserving life across the cosmos—narratives that encompass not only scientific expeditions but also the deeply human stories that underpin our relationship with nature.

As we consider the long-term implications of our cosmic endeavors, ethical considerations must remain central to the blueprint for cosmic biodiversity sustainment. Reflecting on humanity's responsibilities as custodians of genetic legacies embraces questions around the preservation of life, the complexities of genetic manipulation, and the implications of engaging with extraterrestrial ecosystems. By fostering dialogues that encourage moral reflection, we cultivate a sense of accountability and respect for all living forms.

Finally, the blueprint must account for adaptability and resilience in the face of the unknown. As advancements in science and technology continue to evolve, the strategies for cosmic biodiversity preservation should remain flexible, allowing for new discoveries and insights to inform operational practices. Embracing change ensures that our conservation efforts remain relevant and effective, paving the way for a future where life flourishes amid the vast expanse of the universe.

In conclusion, creating a blueprint for cosmic biodiversity sustainment serves as a vital guide for humanity's commitment to preserving life on Earth and exploring possibilities beyond our planet. By recognizing the interconnectedness of all organisms, leveraging advanced technologies, fostering collaboration, engaging the public, addressing ethical considerations, and remaining adaptable, we set forth on a harmonious journey toward safeguarding life's genetic legacies. In this intricate dance of preservation and exploration, we affirm our roles as guardians of life—dedicated to ensuring that future generations can celebrate the richness of existence, both on Earth and among the stars.

18. Futuristic Perspectives on Life Preservation

18.1. Predicting the Next Century of Genetic Science

As we gaze toward the next century of genetic science, we are poised to navigate an extraordinary frontier that intertwines the knowledge and aspirations amassed in our current era with the boundless possibilities that lie ahead. The journey of predicting future advancements in this field unfolds in the context of our global initiatives for cosmic preservation—where the preservation of Earth's biodiversity through interstellar DNA vaults takes center stage. Envisioning this trajectory allows us to appreciate both the profound implications of genetic science and the responsibilities we bear as stewards of life across the cosmos.

The advancements in genetic technology that define the next century are likely to revolutionize our understanding of life itself. With the rapid evolution of tools such as CRISPR-Cas9 and other gene editing technologies, we can foresee a time when genetic manipulation will become increasingly precise and controlled. This precision opens the door not only to enhancing traits that enable resilience to environmental changes but also to potentially reviving extinct species —offering avenues for biodiversity restoration that were previously relegated to the realm of science fiction. The ethical implications of these capabilities must be carefully considered; as we delve into the intricacies of genetic editing, we must remain aware of our responsibilities toward the organisms we aim to preserve or recreate.

Furthermore, the understanding of epigenetics—the study of how environmental factors can influence gene expression—promises to deepen our insights into the adaptability of life in varying conditions. By appreciating how genes respond to external stimuli, especially in challenging environments like those on extraterrestrial bodies, we gain invaluable knowledge that can inform our selections for cosmic preservation. As we look to preserve genetic diversity within DNA vaults, insights gained from epigenetic research may guide our understanding of which organisms are most likely to thrive should they be reintroduced into other planetary ecosystems.

As we contemplate advances in synthetic biology, the prospects of designing entirely new life forms for cosmic habitats emerge. Through the combination of genetic information and technological innovations, humanity has the potential to engineer organisms that fit perfectly within the desired ecological roles in extraterrestrial environments. This capacity, however, raises fundamental ethical questions about our role as creators and the implications of introducing synthetic organisms to existing ecosystems. By prioritizing thoughtful discussions and transparent frameworks around these technological capabilities, we can responsibly navigate the uncharted waters of life preservation while ensuring that diversity remains at the forefront.

The influence of space exploration on genetic science is poised to be profound. As human exploration of Mars and other celestial bodies intensifies, the knowledge we gain will significantly impact our understanding of evolution and adaptability. Observing groundbreaking experiments aimed at studying life in extreme conditions will provide insights that can be applied to both terrestrial and extraterrestrial conservation efforts. The discoveries made in these alien environments carry the potential to enrich our understanding of life's resilience and adaptability, leading to transformative advancements in genetic research.

In this era of cosmic preservation, the necessity for interdisciplinary collaboration will propel advancements in genetic science. Those in genetics, astrobiology, ecology, and ethics must unite, sharing their unique perspectives and insights to navigate the complex challenges and ethical dilemmas that arise from our pursuit of cosmic conservation. The beauty of interconnectedness in our endeavors is that varied expertise can yield innovative solutions, enabling us to preserve ecosystems while considering their cosmic contexts.

Visualizing new models of biodiversity protection will also be essential for the next century of genetic science. We must move beyond traditional paradigms of conservation and embrace visionary approaches that align with the realities of our scientific advancements. This includes integrating ecological strategies that leverage technology and nature to foster resilience, where restoration and preservation efforts resonate across terrestrial environments and cosmic landscapes alike.

Empowering creative visions of universal survival through the arts will enhance our commitment to these initiatives. As we conceptualize the cosmos, artists can capture the emotional essence of what it means to be stewards of life. Their works can evoke aspirations that propel humanity toward an ethos of cosmic guardianship, stimulating dialogue and reflection on the stories we live out as custodians.

Ultimately, redefining cosmic stewardship for tomorrow involves considering the intricate layers of responsibility that accompany our scientific endeavors. As we navigate the path ahead, the interplay between advancing genetic science and our aspirational cosmic stewardship must be embedded in a commitment to ethical considerations, sustainability, and the interconnectedness of all life. By fostering dialogues that explore these dimensions, we can craft a future where genetic diversity thrives as we explore the universe—embracing the evolving possibilities that lie at the intersection of humanity, science, and the cosmos.

In this future, the next century of genetic science will stand as a testament to our commitment to preserving the essence of life, ensuring that generations to come inherit a vibrant legacy of biodiversity across the cosmos. As we embark on this extraordinary journey, we will continue to be guided by our aspirations, ethical responsibilities, and our vision of a sustainable future, as dreamers and custodians of the rich tapestry of existence woven across the galaxies.

18.2. The Influence of Space Exploration on Future Generations

The exploration of the influence of space exploration on future generations reveals an intricate tapestry of cultural, educational, and ethical implications. As humanity advances into the cosmos, the aspirations and experiences stemming from our endeavors will resonate deeply with subsequent generations, shaping their understanding of life, our place in the universe, and our responsibilities as custodians of biodiversity. This influence manifests in various aspects, including educational initiatives, artistic expressions, and the moral imperative that accompanies the pursuit of cosmic preservation.

First and foremost, the legacy of space exploration will inspire a new generation of scientists, engineers, and dreamers. The stories of astronauts who have ventured beyond Earth's atmosphere, the missions that have successfully landed on other planets, and the ambitious plans to create interstellar DNA vaults will serve as powerful motivators for young minds. These narratives will foster curiosity, igniting a passion for exploration and discovery. As children dream of walking on Mars or unlocking the secrets of the cosmos, they are likely to pursue careers aimed at advancing our understanding of life and its preservation.

Education will play a crucial role in this transformation. By integrating space exploration and environmental conservation into curricula, educational institutions can nurture a sense of cosmic responsibility and inspire students to become active participants in the preservation of Earth's biodiversity. Hands-on experiences in STEM (science, technology, engineering, and mathematics) programs, empowered with the backdrop of cosmic ambitions, will equip young individuals with the skills and insights necessary to tackle the multifaceted challenges we face. Envisioning themselves as both scientists and guardians, these students will carry forward the legacy of cosmic exploration into their futures.

The artistic world will also be significantly influenced by space exploration. As artists seek to convey the wonder and mystery of the cosmos, their works will captivate audiences, instilling a sense of awe and reverence for the universe. The interpretations of humanity's celestial aspirations captured in literature, visual arts, and music will inform the values and narratives passed down to future generations. These artistic endeavors will intertwine with scientific understanding, creating a culture that celebrates exploration while acknowledging the responsibilities that come with it.

As humanity ventures further into the cosmos, discussions surrounding ethical considerations will become increasingly vital. Future generations will inherit the complexities of managing genetic resources and making decisions about the introduction of Earth-based life forms into extraterrestrial environments. The narratives they are exposed to will influence the ethical frameworks they adopt, shaping their understanding of cosmic stewardship. By engaging in collaborative dialogues that promote awareness of the implications of our actions, we can instill a sense of ethical responsibility that transcends cultural boundaries.

Moreover, the cultural interpretations of cosmic preservation will reflect the values of future societies. The exploration of other worlds and the potential for discovering extraterrestrial life will contribute to a philosophy that embraces interconnectedness—a realization that extends beyond Earth. Flourishing within this framework will be the understanding that every organism, no matter where it exists, plays an invaluable role in the web of life. Future generations, shaped by these perspectives, will likely champion the cause of conservation and advocate for greater respect for all life forms.

The influence of space exploration on future generations will encompass a holistic journey—one that intertwines scientific innovation, artistic expression, and ethical considerations. It will prompt individuals to reflect on their roles as cosmic custodians, instilling a commitment to preserving life not only on our planet but also in the vast realms of the universe. As we illuminate pathways toward cosmic preservation, we must imbue future generations with the knowledge and values necessary to navigate the complexities of cosmic steward-ship.

In summary, the influence of space exploration on future generations will be profound and multifaceted. The aspirations derived from our endeavors will inspire curiosity and engagement with science while shaping artistic interpretations of the cosmos. Through a collaborative commitment to education, ethical responsibility, and cultural dialogue, we can cultivate a culture of stewardship that honors the intricate tapestry of life across the universe. As humanity embarks on its journey among the stars, this legacy of inspiration will spark exploration, reverberating through time, and nurturing a future rich in possibilities and preservation.

18.3. Visualizing New Models of Biodiversity Protection

Visualizing New Models of Biodiversity Protection represents a transformative shift in how humanity approaches the preservation of genetic diversity in an ever-expanding universe. As we venture beyond the confines of Earth and contemplate the establishment of DNA vaults within the cosmos, it becomes increasingly evident that traditional models of biodiversity protection may need to be reimagined. This visionary approach aims to integrate cutting-edge technology with a deeper understanding of ecological interdependencies, thus ensuring the longevity and resilience of life across celestial frontiers.

At the heart of this new model lies the recognition that preserving genetic diversity is not merely about cataloging and storing genetic materials but about creating dynamic systems that interact with and adapt to changing environmental conditions. This involves creating sustainable habitats that employ advanced techniques to mimic, or even enhance, natural ecosystems. The application of synthetic biology can facilitate the development of organisms specifically tailored to thrive in extraterrestrial environments, thus expanding the boundaries of life's adaptability.

Integrating technology into biodiversity protection opens up innovative possibilities for monitoring and managing genetic material. The incorporation of remote sensing technologies, artificial intelligence, and machine learning will allow custodians to analyze vast amounts of data, predicting shifts in ecosystems and genetic health while dynamically adjusting preservation strategies. This data-driven approach enhances the ability to respond to emerging threats, ensuring that conservation efforts remain flexible and proactive rather than reactive.

Moreover, artificial intelligence may revolutionize our capacity to simulate potential ecological scenarios. By creating detailed models that visualize how organisms respond to different environmental variables—such as radiation levels, temperature fluctuations, or the introduction of new species—we can gain insights that guide decision-making processes for genetic preservation. These simulations can serve as valuable training tools for custodians, helping them understand the complexities of biodiversity maintenance and human interactions within various ecosystems.

A noteworthy aspect of this model is its emphasis on inclusivity. Involving a diverse range of stakeholders in discussions about biodiversity protection is essential for capturing various cultural perspectives, knowledge systems, and ethical frameworks. By engaging local communities, indigenous groups, conservationists, and scientists in collaborative dialogues, we can ensure that our approach to biodiversity is respectful, equitable, and informed by a multitude of voices. This collective wisdom becomes a guiding force in developing strategies that resonate with cultural values and traditional ecological knowledge, affirming the importance of preserving life in all its forms.

Visualizing these new models of biodiversity protection also entails embracing the narrative potential found in artistic expressions. The intersection of science and art empowers us to communicate the significance of ecological preservation effectively. Artists can bridge the gap between complex scientific concepts and public understanding, creating powerful visualizations that evoke emotional responses and inspire action. Through artworks that depict the diversity of life, the potential of alien ecosystems, or the fragility of terrestrial habitats, we can cultivate a culture of stewardship that honors the intrinsic value of life and the interconnectedness of all living entities.

In this vision of biodiversity protection, education becomes a fundamental pillar, allowing future generations to engage with challenges and opportunities in cosmic preservation actively. By instilling a sense of curiosity and responsibility in young minds, we nurture the stewards of tomorrow—individuals who will wield the knowledge and ethical frameworks to navigate the intricacies of genetic diversity in the cosmos. Curricula that integrate the principles of diversity protection, space exploration, and ecological ethics empower students to become informed advocates for conservation, setting the stage for a brighter future.

In summary, visualizing new models of biodiversity protection invites a bold reimagining of humanity's role as custodians of life in the universe. By embracing advanced technologies, interdisciplinary collaboration, inclusivity, and artistic expression, we can redefine our strategies for preserving genetic diversity that extends beyond terrestrial boundaries. As we embark on this cosmic journey, let us commit ourselves to creating dynamic, sustainable systems that celebrate the diversity of life while safeguarding its essence across the stars. Through these visionary models, we can ensure that the legacy of life endures and flourishes in the ever-expanding realms beyond our Earthly home.

18.4. Empowering Creative Visions of Universal Survival

Empowering creative visions of universal survival invites a profound exploration of the intersection between art, science, and the human spirit as we confront the challenges of cosmic preservation. In an era defined by rapidly advancing technology and profound existential threats to life on Earth, imagination plays a crucial role in shaping our understanding of cosmic stewardship and the aspirations that guide us toward safeguarding our genetic legacy. This endeavor is not merely a technical challenge; it is a cultural and philosophical journey that can draw upon creative expression to stimulate public engagement and inspire collective action.

At the core of this vision lies the potential for art to serve as a conduit for societal engagement with the principles and implications of cosmic preservation. By harnessing the transformative power of artistic expression, we can evoke emotional connections with the themes of biodiversity, conservation, and our responsibilities as custodians of life. Through visual arts, literature, music, and performance, artists have the capacity to translate complex scientific concepts into narratives that resonate deeply with audiences, inviting reflection and dialogue on our stewardship of life.

For example, visual artists can create compelling representations of ecosystems, highlighting the intricate interdependencies that support biodiversity on Earth. These works can inspire viewers to contemplate the fragility of life and the importance of preserving genetic diversity, ultimately cultivating a deeper commitment to conservation efforts. By showcasing the splendor of life, art can function as a powerful reminder of what is at stake and galvanize individuals toward action.

Furthermore, literature serves as an essential vehicle for exploring the moral and ethical dimensions of cosmic preservation. Fictional narratives invite readers to delve into speculative scenarios in which humanity encounters life beyond Earth, fostering critical inquiries into our responsibilities when engaging with extraterrestrial ecosystems. Authors have imagined futures filled with challenges and triumphs, enhancing our understanding of survival and the evolution of life across time and space. These stories capture the imagination and provoke thoughtful discourse on the implications of genetic manipulation, the ethical treatment of living beings, and the potential consequences of our actions in habitats beyond our own.

In addition to traditional forms of artistic expression, the development of new technologies offers innovative avenues for creative engagement. Interactive exhibits, virtual reality experiences, and immersive storytelling can transport audiences into scenarios that illuminate the importance of cosmic preservation. By fostering experiential learning through art and technology, we invite individuals to participate actively in preserving life and its continuity.

Embracing cross-disciplinary collaborations between scientists and artists can further enrich the discourse surrounding cosmic preservation. The merging of analytical thinking and creative expression allows for fresh perspectives and innovative approaches to exploring biodiversity. Scientists can provide insights into ecological processes and threats, while artists can translate these complexities into accessible narratives, fostering a broader understanding of the interconnectedness of life across the cosmos.

Moreover, empowering creative visions calls for a commitment to inclusivity and representation. Engaging diverse voices—particularly those from indigenous and historically marginalized communities —ensures that the narratives surrounding cosmic preservation encompass a rich tapestry of cultural perspectives. These stories can offer alternative understandings of stewardship and inspire new approaches rooted in localized wisdom, reinforcing our responsibilities as global custodians.

As we envision a future driven by creativity and collaboration, we must remain aware of the ethical implications that accompany our aspirations. The narratives we share, the art we create, and the technologies we develop must all reflect a dedication to respect and honor life's intrinsic value, both on Earth and beyond. The task of cosmic preservation demands not only scientific knowledge but also a cultural commitment to uphold the principles of stewardship across a diverse and interconnected universe.

In conclusion, empowering creative visions of universal survival invites us to embrace the potential of art, narrative, and interdisciplinary collaboration in shaping our understanding of cosmic preservation. By harnessing the power of imagination, we cultivate a culture of stewardship that honors the complexity of life while inspiring a shared commitment to protect and celebrate its diversity. As we embark on this collective journey, let us envision a future where creativity and exploration intertwine, illuminating the path forward for generations to come as guardians of life across the cosmos. Through this collaborative endeavor, we reaffirm our role as custodians, ensuring that the genetic legacies of Earth thrive not only on our home planet but within the grand tapestry of the universe.

18.5. Redefining Cosmic Stewardship for Tomorrow

The increasing urgency of preserving genetic diversity amid the challenges posed by both earthly and cosmic dynamics calls for a profound reimagining of stewardship that is not only rooted in scientific inquiry but also deeply engaged with ethical considerations and cultural understanding. As humanity embarks on constructing interstellar DNA vaults, we stand at a critical juncture where we must redefine cosmic stewardship for tomorrow, integrating lessons from our historical narrative, scientific advancements, and communal aspirations into a coherent framework that guides our interactions with life—both terrestrial and extraterrestrial.

To redefine cosmic stewardship, we must first acknowledge that it is inherently an interdisciplinary endeavor. The complexities of preserving life demand cooperation across the fields of biology, ecology, technology, ethics, and art. Cultivating conversations that transcend disciplinary boundaries allows for a holistic understanding of life's intricacies, ensuring that conservation efforts resonate with a diverse range of voices and insights. By fostering a collaborative spirit among scientists, policymakers, educators, artists, and communities, we create a robust framework grounded in shared knowledge and collective accountability.

In this context, the ethical dimensions of stewardship become paramount. As we explore the boundaries of gene editing technologies and the potential for modifying organisms for extraterrestrial environments, ethical implications regarding ownership, consent, and ecological impacts must be rigorously examined. The decision to manipulate genetic material or introduce organisms into new ecosystems carries weighty responsibilities, and custodians must engage in open dialogues about how these actions align with our commitments to ecological integrity and respect for all life forms. Establishing transparent ethical guidelines and protocols that prioritize both scientific advancement and ethical stewardship will create a solid foundation for our cosmic efforts.

Moreover, the vision of cosmic stewardship must be deeply rooted in public engagement and education. Efforts to raise awareness about the significance of preserving biodiversity should prioritize outreach initiatives that promote understanding and advocacy for conservation efforts. As communities become aware of their roles and responsibilities as guardians of life, they will be empowered to engage in meaningful actions that resonate beyond their immediate surroundings. Cultivating a culture that values stewardship will require imaginative and creative campaigns that inspire individuals to connect with biodiversity preservation, recognizing it as a shared aspiration for humanity's collective legacy.

Furthermore, the redefining of stewardship encompasses thoughts on technological advancements that enhance our capacity for conservation. As we develop advanced monitoring systems, employing artificial intelligence and data analytics becomes indispensable. Insights gleaned from these innovations will guide decision-making, empower custodians to respond dynamically to changes, and ensure the sustainability of genetic materials within DNA vaults. As such technologies evolve, their integration into our stewardship efforts must be carefully managed and aligned with the ethical principles that govern our actions.

The integration of narrative and storytelling emerges as a powerful tool for communicating and reinforcing our aspirations for cosmic stewardship. The stories we tell—through literature, art, and public discourse—shape our understanding of the universe and our responsibilities within it. Establishing a cosmic narrative that resonates with audiences fosters a sense of shared purpose. Engaging with diverse communities to craft stories that encapsulate the interconnectedness of life and the ethical obligations of stewardship can galvanize support and action, transforming abstract concepts into tangible commitments.

As we envision the future of cosmic stewardship, resilience must also be a guiding principle. The potential for unforeseen challenges— whether they arise from new technological advancements or ecological interactions—calls for a flexible approach that adapts to evolving realities. By embracing a framework of resilience, we commit to continuous learning and improvement, ensuring that our stewardship efforts remain relevant and responsive to the dynamics of life across the cosmos.

In conclusion, redefining cosmic stewardship for tomorrow requires a comprehensive approach that incorporates scientific inquiry, ethical reflection, creative expression, and community engagement. By fostering interdisciplinary collaboration and engaging in open dialogues about the moral implications of our actions, we can establish a harmonious vision for preserving life's genetic legacy. It is a vision rooted in responsibility, respect, and resilience—a commitment to ensuring that the rich tapestry of life continues to thrive and flourish amidst the stars. As we embark on this journey, we embrace our roles as custodians with humility, creativity, and a deep sense of purpose, envisioning a future where the legacy of Earth's biodiversity resonates throughout the vastness of the universe.

19. Safeguarding Against Cosmic Threats

19.1. Monitoring Asteroid Impacts and Space Weather

Monitoring Asteroid Impacts and Space Weather is a crucial subchapter that delves into the critical need for vigilant observation and preparedness as humanity progresses into the depths of the cosmos. As we work toward establishing DNA vaults among the stars to preserve Earth's genetic legacy, we must first grapple with the cosmic threats that might jeopardize our aspirations. Asteroids, meteoroids, and the unpredictable patterns of space weather pose significant risks to both exploration missions and any sustainable ecosystems we endeavor to create in extraterrestrial environments.

The relentless nature of space exposes our planet to a host of potential threats, with asteroid impacts being among the most visible dangers. The history of Earth is dotted with evidence of asteroid collisions that have reshaped the landscape and influenced biological evolution profoundly. Notable events, such as the asteroid impact that contributed to the extinction of the dinosaurs, underscore the gravity of this concern. To preserve life and genetic diversity, we must engage in comprehensive monitoring initiatives aimed at detecting and assessing potential asteroid threats.

Central to effective asteroid monitoring is the establishment of observational networks that utilize advanced telescopes and detection systems to track near-Earth objects (NEOs). These networks, comprising both ground-based and space-based instruments, must be configured to monitor the trajectory, size, and composition of asteroids that come within proximity of Earth. The launch of dedicated missions, such as NASA's Planetary Defense Coordination Office, exemplifies global efforts in this arena. By pooling resources and expertise, countries can collaborate to maximize the effectiveness of asteroid tracking systems, sharing data to create a more comprehensive understanding of the risks posed by NEOs.

In addition to monitoring asteroid impacts, understanding space weather patterns is vital for ensuring the safety of both spacecraft and any biological materials stored in DNA vaults. Space weather, characterized by solar flares, coronal mass ejections, and cosmic radiation, can lead to harsh conditions for both astronauts and sensitive technologies. The high-energy particles released during solar events can disrupt electronics, damage infrastructure, and adversely affect human health. Building robust monitoring systems that can forecast space weather events allows for proactive measures to mitigate their impacts.

Harnessing advances in technology is essential for improving our capabilities to monitor and respond to these cosmic threats. The integration of artificial intelligence (AI) and machine learning algorithms can enhance data analysis, enabling the early detection of potential asteroid impacts and predicting space weather events. By analyzing vast datasets collected by telescopes and spacecraft, AI-driven systems can identify patterns that may go unnoticed in manual analyses, leading to timely warnings and preemptive actions.

Furthermore, the development of effective communication frameworks is critical when disseminating information about potential threats. Countries, space agencies, and institutions must establish protocols for sharing data on NEOs and space weather phenomena, ensuring that stakeholders can respond collaboratively and effectively. Public communication of risks and the collaborative efforts to address them are also crucial for maintaining public confidence as we explore new frontiers.

Education and training programs play an equally significant role in preparing for the challenges posed by space threats. By engaging with students and young professionals in disciplines such as astronomy, meteorology, and engineering, we can cultivate a new generation of experts capable of tackling these challenges head-on. STEM (science, technology, engineering, and mathematics) education initiatives that incorporate cosmic monitoring and preservation can inspire individuals to pursue careers focused on addressing the threats posed by asteroids and space weather.

International collaboration further emphasizes the need for a unified effort in monitoring cosmic threats. The various space agencies around the world can lend their expertise to bolster global asteroid tracking initiatives and the management of cosmic weather risks, combining their strengths to strengthen planetary defense systems. Establishing dedicated forums for the ongoing discussion and response to celestial threats will ensure proactive action and preparedness for various possible scenarios.

In conclusion, Monitoring Asteroid Impacts and Space Weather represents a fundamental pillar of humanity's commitment to cosmic preservation and international cooperation. By investing in monitoring technology, enhancing our capacities for early detection, and fostering global collaboration, we can prepare ourselves for the challenges posed by cosmic threats. This proactive stance not only safeguards our aspirations for creating DNA vaults among the stars but also reinforces our role as responsible custodians of life across the universe. Our ability to navigate these potential perils will ultimately define the sustainability of our cosmic endeavors and ensure that the legacy of Earth's biodiversity can thrive in the vastness of the cosmos.

19.2. Building Protocols Against Cosmic Radiation

The preservation of life through the establishment of DNA vaults among the stars is a visionary undertaking that requires multifaceted strategies and collaborative efforts across various fields. One of the paramount concerns of embarking on such ambitious cosmic preservation initiatives is safeguarding against cosmic radiation, which poses significant threats to both human explorers and the biological materials intended for preservation. As we explore the intricacies of building protocols against cosmic radiation, it is essential to incorporate scientific understanding, technological innovation, and transparent communication among stakeholders.

Cosmic radiation encompasses a wide range of high-energy particles originating from outer space, including proton and heavy ion radiation, as well as secondary particles generated by interactions with planetary atmospheres or magnetic fields. These energetic particles can damage biological tissues and genetic material, increasing the risks of cancer and other health issues for astronauts and potentially compromising the integrity of stored genetic materials. Therefore, developing practical and robust protection protocols is essential for the long-term sustainability of DNA vaults in extraterrestrial environments.

To build effective protocols against cosmic radiation, we must begin by investing in research aimed at understanding the specifics of radiation exposure in space. This involves examining how cosmic radiation interacts with the materials used in constructing vaults and securing specimens. Detailed studies of the effects of radiation on various types of DNA and genetic material will inform the design of radiation shielding systems employed within DNA vaults. Relevant materials may include specialized polymers, metal alloys, and hydrogen-rich compounds that are particularly effective at absorbing high-energy particles.

The design of these vaults must incorporate comprehensive shielding —an act of protective architecture that accounts for the potential variations in cosmic radiation intensity across different environments. For instance, vaults on the lunar surface may encounter different radiation patterns compared to those situated on Mars or in orbit around celestial bodies. The incorporation of layered shielding mechanisms that adapt based on the specific locale will further enhance protection against radiation exposure.

In addition to passive shielding, advancements in active radiation protection technologies must also be explored. These innovative systems could involve magnetic fields generated by superconducting materials that redirect charged particles, creating a protective barrier around the DNA vaults. The exploration of such technologies can stem from work done in understanding geomagnetic fields on Earth and their role in shielding life from cosmic radiation.

Effective communication of radiation risks, mitigation strategies, and ongoing monitoring efforts must also underpin the establishment of protocols. Engaging with astronauts, scientists, and relevant stakeholders early in the planning stages helps emphasize the importance of safety. Transparent communication allows for the sharing of best practices and collaborative decision-making regarding protective measures. Furthermore, training programs for astronauts must include a thorough understanding of radiation exposure, how to recognize potential risks, and how to respond effectively to alerts.

Emergency strategies for lunar and Martian outposts further extend the conversation surrounding protocols against cosmic radiation. In the event of increased solar activity or radiation storms, having well-defined contingency plans is essential. These strategies might include providing safe zones equipped with enhanced shielding, preferably constructed using locally sourced materials, where occupants can take refuge until radiation levels return to normal. The establishment of rapid-response protocols will ensure that all personnel understand their roles during emergencies, minimizing risk and fostering readiness.

As we contemplate the realities of cosmic preservation, we must address the myths associated with the dangers posed by cosmic radiation. The fear of radiation can generate alarmist perceptions, potentially deterring individuals from engaging in space exploration efforts. Clear, science-based communications that educate the public about the realities and risks of cosmic radiation empower informed discussions and foster public interest in cosmic conservation.

In conclusion, building protocols against cosmic radiation is a vital aspect of humanity's efforts to establish DNA vaults among the stars and safeguard Earth's genetic legacy. By utilizing advancements in materials science, enhancing shielding technologies, promoting transparent communication, and developing comprehensive emergency strategies, we can create a resilient framework for cosmic preservation. These protocols not only protect the integrity of genetic materials and the safety of those exploring strange new worlds but also reflect humanity's commitment to stewardship in the cosmos. As we embark on this journey, embracing the challenges posed by cosmic radiation fosters a collaborative spirit, illuminating the pathway toward securing life's survival amid the wonders of the universe.

19.3. Emergency Strategies for Lunar and Martian Outposts

Emergency strategies for lunar and Martian outposts must be meticulously planned and executed to ensure the safety and survival of both human crews and any biological specimens preserved for cosmic conservation. As humanity extends its reach into the cosmos, particularly with ambitions of establishing permanent habitats on the Moon and Mars, unforeseen emergencies such as equipment failures, radiation spikes, or life support system malfunctions will require immediate and effective responses. The development of robust emergency protocols is paramount for managing risk and ensuring sustainability in these hostile environments.

First and foremost, understanding the potential emergencies associated with lunar and Martian habitats is crucial. The environments on these celestial bodies are harsh and unpredictable; extreme temperatures, lack of atmosphere, and high levels of radiation pose significant threats to human health and operational integrity. Thus, establishing a comprehensive risk assessment framework will allow for proactive identification of potential hazards—whether they stem from natural occurrences or equipment failures—and ensure that strategies can be developed to mitigate these risks.

One of the foundational aspects of emergency preparedness will be the training of crews in simulated scenarios that replicate potential emergency situations. Such training will encompass the array of challenges they may encounter, from settling issues like equipment failure or radiation exposure to coping with psychological stressors associated with isolation and confinement. By employing high-fidelity simulators that replicate the conditions of lunar or Martian outposts, crews will learn to respond effectively to various emergency situations. These simulations would not only focus on technical skills but also include elements of effective communication, teamwork, and crisis management, ensuring that crew members work cohesively under pressure.

Moreover, establishing predefined communication protocols for emergencies is essential. Efficient communication between lunar or Martian outposts and Mission Control on Earth can facilitate rapid troubleshooting or guidance during crises. Regularly scheduled check-ins and real-time communication systems will ensure that any deviation from established operational parameters is swiftly reported and addressed. Protocols must outline procedures for escalating issues and provide crew members with access to remote assistance from experts on Earth, who can offer valuable perspectives using telemetry data.

Developing a comprehensive inventory of emergency supplies and redundancies is another critical pillar of emergency strategy implementation. Outposts must be equipped with backup systems for power, life support, and communications while having adequate medical supplies, food, and water on hand to sustain crews during potential crisis situations. In the event of a contamination or radiation-related incident, protective equipment and decontamination supplies should also be part of the core inventory to safeguard both personnel and preserved biological materials.

Human factors must also be integrated into emergency strategies. Psychological resilience will be essential as astronauts navigate the stress of isolation, confinement, and operational challenges. Establishing support systems—such as peer counseling programs, access to mental health resources, and recreational activities—can help promote emotional well-being. Integrating psychological support protocols into the emergency plan ensures that crews can manage stressors effectively during crises, contributing to the resilience of the mission as a whole.

Situational adaptability is important when implementing emergency strategies, as conditions outside of anticipated parameters can be encountered. Continuous monitoring of environmental conditions —such as radiation levels or solar activity—will facilitate early detection of potential threats, allowing crews to respond proactively. Automated systems equipped with artificial intelligence can assist in making real-time adjustments to life support systems or environmental controls in anticipation of changing celestial phenomena.

Plans for evacuation and safe return to Earth in case of a critical emergency must be established. Identifying safe landing zones and escape paths for lunar or Martian crews ensures that rapid exit strategies can be executed seamlessly. The crew should conduct drills to gain familiarity with these procedures, making it possible to navigate quickly and efficiently in high-pressure situations.

Collaborative partnerships with experts in emergency management, risk assessment, and crisis response are vital for developing comprehensive strategies. Engaging with professionals in these fields and incorporating their expertise enables a holistic understanding of potential emergencies that may occur in lunar and Martian scenarios. Workshops and training involving interdisciplinary teams can enhance preparedness at all stages of mission planning.

In summary, emergency strategies for lunar and Martian outposts must be grounded in thorough risk assessments and preparedness protocols that encompass training, communication, supply management, psychological support, adaptability, and collaborative expertise. Crafting a comprehensive framework allows crews to effectively respond to potential crises while promoting the safety and health of both personnel and any genetic materials aimed at preservation. As we set forth in pursuit of cosmic conservation, a commitment to emergency preparedness becomes integral to our shared responsibility for life—ensuring that the aspirations to safeguard Earth's biodiversity resonate throughout the cosmos. Through these robust strategies, humanity stands ready to confront the challenges posed by the solar system's far reaches, ensuring not just survival, but a future in which life flourishes, no matter where it may be found.

19.4. Cosmic Rescue Missions: Realities and Myths

Cosmic Rescue Missions: Realities and Myths

As humanity embarks on the journey of cosmic preservation, the concept of cosmic rescue missions evokes both intrigue and skepticism. These missions signify our aspirations to save not just the genetic blueprints of Earth's biodiversity—enshrined within interstellar DNA vaults—but also to engage with the broader narrative of safeguarding life across the cosmos. However, the realities of these missions often diverge sharply from speculative narratives found in science fiction, prompting critical examination of what is possible versus what remains firmly rooted in the realm of myth.

One of the most prominent myths surrounding cosmic rescue missions is the idea that technology can easily transport life forms across vast distances, enabling immediate intervention at the slightest sign of ecological distress. While advancements in technology have certainly transformed our capabilities—ranging from propulsion systems that could one day facilitate interstellar travel to cryogenic preservation techniques designed for storing genetic material—the practicalities of executing a cosmic rescue mission are fraught with challenges. The vast distances of space, coupled with the limitations of current propulsion technologies, present significant hurdles to conducting timely rescues or interventions on distant worlds. The reality is that maintaining stable ecosystems requires patience, dedication, and ongoing efforts to monitor conditions rather than merely relying on the potential of rescuing species at a moment's notice.

Moreover, the intricacies of alien ecosystems further complicate the prospect of cosmic intervention. The idea that life forms from Earth could be introduced into extraterrestrial environments rests on an assumption that these new ecosystems will readily accept such organisms. However, the success of such introductions is far from guaranteed; ecological balances within alien environments may be delicate, and the introduction of non-native species could result in unintended consequences. Historical precedents on Earth serve as cautionary tales, illustrating how the introduction of invasive species can lead to the decline or extinction of existing life forms. Thus, the myth of effortless adaptation masks the complex ecological realities that must be understood and respected.

Additionally, the assumption that preserving genetic material within DNA vaults guarantees survival poses another complexity in the narrative of cosmic rescue missions. While safeguarding genetic diversity is undeniably important, the prospect of reviving or reintroducing preserved species demands a nuanced understanding of adaptations and ecological interactions. It is essential to consider whether the preserved genetics exhibit the necessary resilience to thrive in environments that may be vastly different from their native habitats. The journey from vault to ecosystem translates into a litany of variables that cannot be easily predicted.

The realities of cosmic rescue missions extend beyond logistics and ecology; they also involve ethical considerations. Engaging with extraterrestrial ecosystems necessitates careful reflection on our responsibilities as stewards of life. Questions arise regarding consent: do we have the right to introduce Earth-based organisms into new environments? The potential consequences of altering the ecological fabric of alien worlds pose profound ethical dilemmas that must be navigated with care. The narratives that celebrate humanity's might and ingenuity must be tempered by a commitment to cosmic ethics, ensuring that our aspirations align with principles of integrity and respect for life.

Despite these challenges, the excitement inherent in the idea of cosmic rescue missions cannot be understated. The prospect of saving endangered species or securing the continuity of ecosystems in the face of cosmic challenges reflects a deeply rooted aspiration within humanity—a longing to protect life in all its forms. As we continue to explore the cosmos, it is essential to ground these aspirations in a thorough understanding of our limitations, ensuring that our endeavors remain thoughtful, responsible, and meaningful.

Moreover, collaborative efforts among countries, researchers, and organizations become crucial in redefining the narrative of cosmic rescue missions. By pooling resources, knowledge, and expertise, we can navigate the complexities of cosmic preservation more effectively than any single nation or entity could. This collaborative spirit fosters a culture of shared responsibility, reinforcing the belief that the challenges we face are best addressed collectively, rather than through isolated pursuits.

In summation, while the allure of cosmic rescue missions is undeniable, the realities of such endeavors require rigorous examination and careful planning. By separating the myths from the practical challenges, we can approach cosmic preservation with a clear understanding of our mission and responsibilities. The aspiration to preserve life amid the stars beckons us forward, encouraging collaboration and ethical reflection as we strive to navigate the intricate dynamics of existence across the universe. Cosmic stewardship embodies not just a mission of genetic preservation but a commitment to honor the interconnectedness of all life forms, where the pursuit of knowledge is matched by an unwavering dedication to responsible guardianship. Ultimately, our legacy will hinge upon how we approach these cosmic challenges, defining our role as stewards of life as we venture among the stars.

19.5. The Art of Predicting and Preparing for Interspecies Threats

The exploration of interspecies threats in the context of cosmic preservation beckons us to engage with the complex interactions between diverse biological entities as humanity reaches for the stars. The necessity of predicting and preparing for these threats takes center stage as we consider the implications of introducing Earth-based life forms into extraterrestrial environments. This journey not only underscores the need for preparedness but also emphasizes our responsibility as stewards of life, ensuring that cosmic conservation reflects a holistic understanding of biodiversity and interdependence.

To effectively predict interspecies threats, we must begin with a robust understanding of the ecological dynamics that govern inter-actions among various life forms. Earth serves as a vital laboratory for studying these interactions, where numerous species coexist, compete, and form intricate relationships—ranging from symbiosis to predation. The mysteries of co-evolution, wherein the presence of one species can significantly impact the evolutionary trajectory of another, provide valuable insights. Recognizing these dynamics in terrestrial ecosystems equips us with the knowledge needed to assess potential interactions in extraterrestrial habitats.

As we envision the introduction of Earth species into alien environ-ments, an important consideration arises regarding the adaptability of these organisms to their new contexts. Species that have thrived in terrestrial ecosystems may not necessarily fare well in extraterrestrial ecosystems where conditions differ significantly. We must account for factors such as gravity, radiation levels, temperature extremes, and resource availability—each playing a pivotal role in shaping the survival prospects of Earth-based organisms. Understanding the parameters that dictate life's potential adaptability will guide our decisions concerning which organisms to preserve and possibly rein-troduce.

Moreover, the potential for invasive scenarios emerges when intro-ducing organisms in extraterrestrial contexts. Invasive species can disrupt existing ecosystems, leading to declines or extinctions of native life forms. The historical precedents on Earth underscore the risks associated with introducing non-native species into balanced ecosystems without thorough assessments of their potential impacts. As custodians of cosmic biodiversity, it becomes our ethical respon-sibility to consider how the organisms we protect may interact within alien ecosystems, ensuring that our interventions promote ecological harmony rather than disrupt it.

As we prepare for interspecies interactions, the development of contingency plans becomes imperative. These plans should encompass predictive models that simulate the introduction of Earth-based life forms into extraterrestrial environments. Utilizing advanced computational tools, we can model potential outcomes based on different variables, enabling us to anticipate and mitigate risks associated with these interactions. Engaging interdisciplinary teams comprising ecologists, geneticists, and ethicists will yield a comprehensive approach to addressing the complexities surrounding interspecies threats.

Furthermore, continuous monitoring systems must be established to track the behavior and adaptation of any species introduced to extraterrestrial environments. Employing advanced sensor technologies and AI-driven analytics allows for real-time assessments of how Earth organisms interact with (and adapt to) novel adaptive pressures. This proactive approach will empower custodians to identify shifts in ecological dynamics and prepare adaptive interventions as needed.

Education emerges as a fundamental tool in preparing for interspecies threats, promoting awareness of the importance of ethical stewardship. Educational programs should engage students, scientists, and the public in discussions about biodiversity, conservation, and the implications of moving species beyond their native habitats. Issues that arise from interspecies interactions should inspire critical thinking, reinforcing the idea that conservation extends beyond mere preservation; it encompasses understanding the intricate networks that define life itself.

Public engagement campaigns can serve to raise awareness of interspecies threats and cosmic preservation, utilizing creative storytelling, art, and digital media to convey the significance of these issues. By painting vivid narratives that echo the complexities of interconnections among life forms, we can cultivate a shared understanding of our responsibilities as cosmic custodians.

In conclusion, the art of predicting and preparing for interspecies threats in the context of cosmic preservation requires a multifaceted approach that marries ecological understanding, technological innovation, ethical reflection, and public engagement. As humanity sets its sights on establishing DNA vaults and exploring other worlds, it must engage with the profound complexities that arise from interspecies interactions. By employing predictive models, contingency planning, and proactive monitoring systems, we can safeguard not only the genetic legacies of Earth's biodiversity but also the intricate interconnections that define life across the cosmos. As custodians of these legacies, we must rise to our ethical responsibilities, ensuring that our actions reflect a reverence for life that resonates far beyond the confines of our planet.

20. Parallel Universes and Hypothetical Life Forms

20.1. Theoretical Physics in Cosmic Exploration

The pursuit of cosmic preservation has led humanity to an exciting crossroads where science intersects with artistry in profound ways. The initiative aims not only to safeguard Earth's genetic heritage through interstellar DNA vaults but also invites a vast array of artistic interpretations that embrace the wonders of the universe. This interrelationship between the scientific and artistic realms creates a platform for understanding, engaging with, and ultimately advocating for the preservation of biodiversity—enhancing our cosmic ambitions.

Imagining cosmic wonders through art allows us to conceptualize dimensions of existence beyond our immediate perceptions. Artists engage with the symbolism and narrative power of the cosmos, translating scientific ideas and explorations into visual and experiential forms that resonate deeply with the human spirit. By harnessing a variety of media—from painting and sculpture to digital art and installations—artists challenge viewers to not only contemplate the intricacies of the universe but also forge emotional connections with the notion of life beyond Earth.

Cultural interpretations of cosmic preservation further enrich the discourse surrounding the future of biodiversity. Diverse cultural perspectives can influence how societies perceive and engage with the cosmos—shaping narratives that integrate spiritual, ethical, and ecological dimensions. Exploring indigenous stories that emphasize the connection to land, sky, and ancestry allows for a more comprehensive understanding of how various communities embrace the implications of cosmic exploration. This cultural tapestry provides invaluable insights as we strive to foster global cooperation in protecting life across the universe.

As the interplay of science and artistic vision unfolds, opportunities arise to bridge gaps between disciplines, fostering collaborations that inspire new conceptual frameworks. Scientists and artists can engage in collaborative projects that explore the themes of cosmic preservation, infusing scientific observations with creative interpretations. These collaborations can lead to impactful installations or exhibitions that compel audiences to confront the beauty and fragility of biodiversity while reflecting on humanity's responsibilities as cosmic custodians.

Inspirational works by both artists and scientists act as beacons of hope, illuminating the path toward cosmic preservation. Numerous artists have captured the surreal beauty and wonder of the cosmos through their craft, communicating messages that resonate with the human experience. The images and ideas encapsulated in these works ignite curiosity and reflection, prompting societal discourse on our place in the universe and the need to uphold ecological integrity.

Exploring the future of space art poses exciting possibilities as well. As advancements in technology propel us further into the cosmos, the potential for artists to document and respond to space exploration in real-time presents compelling avenues for creative expression. The rise of augmented reality, virtual reality, and interactive installations can foster immersive experiences that transport audiences to new realms while invoking awareness of the importance of preserving genetic diversity.

In conclusion, the artistic interpretations of cosmic preservation offer essential contributions to humanity's collective journey into the universe. By imagining cosmic wonders through art, engaging with cultural narratives, and fostering interdisciplinary collaborations, we can enrich the dialogue surrounding biodiversity and cosmic stewardship. These creative endeavors will inspire generations to come, illuminating the path towards a future where the richness of life —both on Earth and beyond—is honored, celebrated, and protected among the stars. As we continue to embrace the power of imagination, let us strive for a harmonious coexistence with the intricate tapestry of life, ensuring that the legacy of biodiversity flourishes across the cosmos.

20.2. Speculative Biology of Extraterrestrial Ecosystems

As humanity contemplates the cosmos and the intricate weave of life that inhabits it, the speculative biology of extraterrestrial ecosystems emerges as a profound subject of inquiry. This exploration not only challenges our understanding of life as we know it but also invites us to envision the potential forms and functions that life might take in environments distinctly different from our own. By examining these possibilities, we can better inform our efforts in cosmic preservation, from understanding genetic diversity to developing strategies that ensure the survival of life on newly explored worlds.

The underlying premise of speculative biology begins with the acknowledgment that life evolves in response to environmental pressures. As we extend our gaze beyond Earth, considering the diverse celestial bodies within our solar system and beyond, we must ask: what conditions might give rise to alternative life forms? Each planet or moon presents unique environmental factors—such as atmospheric composition, gravity, temperature ranges, and availability of water—that could shape the very essence of life.

For instance, Mars, with its thin atmosphere and harsh surface conditions, challenges our understanding of what it means for an environment to support life. While current conditions seem inhospitable, researchers are exploring how life once flourished in wetter periods or under elusive subsurface conditions. The potential for microbial life, evolving to withstand the planet's extreme pressure and radiation, adds complexity to our understanding of resilience. This inquiry enhances our strategies for cosmic preservation, as we must consider how organisms evolved under these conditions may react and adapt to similar stresses in extraterrestrial environments.

Simultaneously, other celestial bodies such as Europa, with its subsurface ocean, provoke exciting speculation about life hidden beneath layers of ice. The interplay between tidal heating, chemical interactions in the ocean, and the potential for hydrothermal vents creates an intriguing landscape for astrobiologists to explore. Speculating on the forms life might take in such environments—whether it be microbial, multicellular, or entirely foreign to our understanding—fuels discussions about the genetic diversity we should preserve in our DNA vaults. It urges us to recognize that preserving Earth's life is not merely about what we know but also about anticipating the unknown.

Furthermore, considering exoplanets located in the habitable zones of distant stars introduces a planetary system approach to speculative biology. The diversity of potential life forms on such planets could vastly exceed our current understanding, driven by factors such as high atmospheric pressure, varying gravity, or even differing stellar radiation. As we explore the possibilities presented by different planetary systems, we must also reflect on the preservation strategies we deploy in our cosmic vaults—developing a framework that ensures the viability of the genetic material from Earth's biosphere as it adapts to extraterrestrial contexts.

Philosophical musings on the continuity of life also resonate profoundly within this discourse. What does it mean for life to exist in parallel across the universe? Are we alone in our biological richness, or does the universe cradle myriad forms of existence? The inquiries surrounding these speculative possibilities compel us to engage in broader discussions about humanity's role as custodians of life—not just on Earth but throughout the universe.

Equally significant is the understanding that our own biodiversity is shaped by millennia of evolutionary pressures, and thus the preservation of genetic material should also prioritize the adaptability and resilience of species. This perspective allows custodians to turn their attentions to species that exhibit traits likely to thrive across various conditions—even those akin to those we might find in alien environments.

In conclusion, the speculative biology of extraterrestrial ecosystems offers a fertile ground for inquiry that enhances our understanding of life and informs our preservation efforts across the cosmos. Imagining life beyond Earth—its potential forms, adaptational traits, and ecological interactions—allows humanity to embrace its role as stewards of genetic diversity, firmly recognizing that what we preserve today shapes the future of biodiversity in the universe. The convergence of scientific exploration and philosophical reflection generates a deeper appreciation of life, prompting a commitment to nurture and preserve its legacy in the face of earthly and cosmic challenges alike. Ultimately, the dialogue around speculative biology can guide our cosmic stewardship, ensuring that life flourishes, not just on our home planet, but across the infinite expanse of the cosmos.

20.3. Understanding Life's Potential Diversity

Understanding Life's Potential Diversity is a transformative exploration into the intricacies of the multitude of life forms that exist and may exist across the cosmos. As humanity stands poised at the threshold of interstellar exploration, the task of comprehensively identifying, preserving, and appreciating the various manifestations of life remains ever more critical. This contemplation not only intertwines scientific inquiry but also invokes ethical, philosophical, and cultural dimensions that compel us to reflect on our roles as custodians of life's diverse tapestry.

At the heart of this exploration lies the celebration of biodiversity itself—spanning the intricate relations among organisms, the roles they play in their respective ecosystems, and the adaptability that defines the essence of life. The potential diversity we encounter may range from the well-documented species that inhabit Earth to the speculative life forms that could exist on other celestial bodies. Each offers insights into the capabilities and resilience of life in response to environmental pressures, revealing a complex web of interactions that continually shape the narrative of existence.

To systematically understand life's potential diversity, we must first recognize the fundamental principles of evolution and ecology. The diverse adaptations that have allowed organisms to thrive in myriad environments illuminate the evolutionary pathways that have unfolded over millions of years. From extremophiles, which flourish in extreme conditions such as deep-sea hydrothermal vents or acidic lakes, to the countless plant species that have evolved to exploit different niches, the breadth of life is a testament to nature's ingenuity. This variability ultimately informs our genetic preservation strategies; selecting organisms for preservation necessitates an understanding of their ecological importance and adaptive potential.

As we navigate the cosmos, the possibility of discovering life forms that deviate from our terrestrial experiences looms large. The investigation of extremophiles on Earth provides a glimpse into what life might look like in environments once assumed inhospitable. In parallel, astrobiological pursuits aimed at identifying signs of life on planets and moons within our solar system—such as Europa or Titan —push the boundaries of our knowledge, inviting us to speculate on the myriad forms life could take. The study of these environments emphasizes that life may be more resilient and diverse than previously imagined, prompting a reevaluation of what constitutes potential biodiversity.

In essence, understanding life's potential diversity invites us to embrace an open-minded approach. As we expand our cosmic horizons, we must remain receptive to the possibilities of life's manifestations, where forms and functions may diverge dramatically from those found on Earth. This perspective fosters humility and curiosity as we approach the endeavor of cosmic preservation, recognizing that the genetic blueprints we aim to protect may one day offer insights into the resilience and versatility of life itself.

Additionally, the ethical dimensions associated with engaging with extraterrestrial life cannot be overlooked. The notion of introducing Earth-based organisms into new environments poses significant ethical dilemmas concerning ecological integrity. Respecting the intricate relationships surrounding life forms and their natural ecosystems reverberates across not only our responsibilities on Earth but also our aspirations for cosmic preservation. Ethically, custodians must grapple with the implications of interfering with cosmic ecosystems, weighing the potential consequences against the benefits of conservation.

The cultural interpretations of life's potential diversity ultimately enrich this discourse, inviting diverse perspectives on the significance of preservation. As we contemplate cosmic preservation, it is essential to recognize that different cultures possess unique lenses through which they observe and engage with life. By embracing these perspectives, we fortify our understanding of biodiversity, recognizing that life is a universal phenomenon celebrated through various narratives, myths, and traditions.

In conclusion, understanding life's potential diversity propels humanity into a realm of intricate discovery that marries scientific exploration with ethical reflection and cultural appreciation. As we foster this understanding, we establish the foundation for recognizing our roles as custodians of life's genetic legacies. The quest for safeguarding the rich diversity of life extends far beyond Earth, empowering us to embrace our interconnectedness as we journey to the stars. Through this lens, the care for genetic diversity transitions from a simple notion of preservation to a profound commitment to honoring the myriad forms of existence that define our universe, ensuring that life—wherever it may flourish—continues to thrive.

20.4. Multiverse Theories and Biodiversity Implications

Theoretical explorations of multiverse theories broaden the horizons of cosmic understanding, raising intriguing questions about biodiversity and our responsibilities as custodians of life. This chapter delves into how these frameworks interact with the preservation of genetic diversity, shaping our perspective on the complexities of existence beyond Earth.

Multiverse theories posit that our universe is just one of many, with each universe potentially having its own distinct set of physical laws, constants, and even forms of life. This imaginative landscape invites profound implications for biodiversity preservation. If life can arise under a multitude of environmental conditions and physical laws, the characteristics that define 'life' may be more diverse than we can currently conceive. This realization urges us to reconsider what genetic materials we prioritize for preservation, as they may not represent the full spectrum of life's potential.

The implications of multiverse theories extend beyond mere speculation; they challenge our understanding of genetic continuity and evolution. If multiple universes exist, each with distinct evolutionary paths, the potential for varied forms of life becomes a tantalizing concept. This dynamic may inform our efforts in safeguarding species, as it suggests that adaptations to extreme environments could shape life's trajectory in ways we have yet to grasp completely. The existence of life in alternate forms invites contemplation about its resilience, adaptability, and the possible genetic traits that define existence across the multiverse.

Furthermore, the philosophical musings surrounding parallel life continuity resonate deeply within the context of cosmic preservation. If life exists in multiverses, the ethical implications surrounding genetic manipulation raise questions about our role as stewards of not only Earth's biodiversity but the potential biospheres spanning alternate realities. The concept of life existing in myriad variations beckons us to adopt a more inclusive philosophy regarding existence, fostering a sense of interconnectedness that transcends earthly boundaries.

Our exploration of multiverse theories invites a deeper understanding of responsibility. As we endeavor to preserve genetic legacies, we must grapple with the possibility that our actions could reverberate across multiple realities, affecting not just our own biodiversity but the fabric of life beyond our comprehension. This philosophical inquiry serves as a reminder that our stewardship of life must always reflect respect for the interconnectedness of all organisms and the complexities inherent in the multiverse.

Integrating multiverse theories into discussions of biodiversity preservation reinforces the understanding that our stewardship transcends Earth and, by extension, time and space. This broader perspective compels us to think of conservation as a universal endeavor, where efforts to safeguard genetic diversity resonate across dimensions and ecosystems. The recognition that the tapestry of life may exist in countless forms across the multiverse should embolden our commitment to conservation, inspiring us to protect and celebrate the incredible diversity within our own context.

In summary, the interplay between multiverse theories and biodiversity preservation calls for an expansion of our understanding of life. The insights gleaned from these theoretical frameworks inform our responsibilities as custodians and encourage a holistic approach to conservation that honors genetic diversity in all its potential forms. By embracing the complexities of existence and acknowledging our role within this intricate tapestry, we can illuminate pathways for cosmic stewardship that extend far beyond our terrestrial confines, securing the legacy of life among the stars.

20.5. Philosophical Musings on Parallel Life Continuity

In the realm of cosmic preservation, the philosophers and dreamers of humanity have long posed questions about existence, connection, and ethical responsibility. One of the deepest philosophical musings emerges from the intriguing concept of parallel life continuity—a contemplation of what life might look like across alternate realities and the implications this has on our responsibilities as guardians of genetic diversity.

The idea of parallel life continuity suggests the existence of multiple universes, each with its own unique set of physical laws, environmental conditions, and potentially distinct forms of life. This speculation prompts us to reflect on the nature of existence itself, challenging our understanding of life's adaptability and resilience. If life can take myriad forms, shaped by the peculiarities of its respective universe, the definitions we attach to life become intricate, broadening the discourse on what it means to preserve biodiversity not only on Earth but throughout the vast cosmos.

As custodians tasked with maintaining the genetic legacies for future generations, we face profound questions: which species should be prioritized for preservation? How can we assure that our efforts in safeguarding genetic diversity align with the ethical commitment to respect life in all its forms? When contemplating parallel life continuity, we are invited to think of our preservation efforts as an interconnected web—one that spans different realities, species, and environments. This contemplation cultivates a sense of awe and responsibility; the choices we make today resonate both within our universe and beyond, shaping the potential narratives of life through-out existence.

In parallel realms, the ethical considerations expand considerably. If life emerges in diverse environments across a multiverse, does this inform our understanding of which life forms warrant protection? The multitude of adaptations, resistances, and symbiotic relationships that characterize life in different dimensions challenges us to recog-nize that our own biodiversity is but one facet of a much larger cosmic legacy. It instills a necessity for humility—an acknowledgment that we cannot fully grasp the complexities of life that may exist elsewhere but are tasked with honoring and preserving what we know.

Narratives surrounding parallel life continuity equally amplify our sense of stewardship as we craft frameworks for cosmic preservation. This task invites societal discourse around the ethical implications of genetic manipulation and intervention in life cycles, should we encounter life in alternative realities or cosmic extensions. The notion that our actions might ripple across dimensions ignites an awareness of the cosmic consequences of our choices. Each decision made in the name of preservation comes with the responsibility to consider its impact not just on our terrestrial ecosystems but potentially on other forms and expressions of life that we have yet to comprehend.

In undertaking this journey toward cosmic preservation, cultivating a cultural ethos embracing interconnectedness and ecological respect becomes essential. By engaging in dialogues that integrate various perspectives—scientific, philosophical, and artistic—we can foster a shared understanding of our responsibilities. The interplay between the worlds of science, technology, and art becomes a conduit through which we can explore the vast possibilities of existence while instilling in our culture a reverence for life in all its manifestations.

As we reflect on the larger implications of preserving life, it is crucial to consider the diverse ways in which humans engage with these concepts. The narratives crafted through literature, visual arts, and music evoke emotional connections that capture the imagination, amplifying our intention to explore the cosmos with a sense of wonder and purpose. This interplay serves as an invitation for individuals to become active participants in cosmic stewardship, reinforcing the view that protecting life is a moral obligation we collectively share.

In conclusion, the philosophical musings on parallel life continuity prompt us to expand our understanding of stewardship regarding cosmic preservation. The potential for diverse forms of life in alternate realities reinforces our commitment to understanding and protecting Earth's genetic legacy. As we navigate the complexities of existence, the interplay between imagination, ethics, and responsibility becomes integral to safeguarding life across the cosmos. By embracing the mysteries of life and recognizing our interconnectedness with all beings, we honor the narratives of existence that span time and space, ensuring that the essence of life endures—for ourselves and the cosmos at large.

21. Painting the Final Frontier: Artistic Interpretations

21.1. Imagining Cosmic Wonders Through Art

Imagining cosmic wonders through art serves as both a celebration of life's possibilities and a profound exploration of the ethical dimensions tied to cosmic preservation endeavors. In the context of "Arks Among The Stars: DNA Vaults and the Preservation of Life," art offers a unique lens through which we can engage with the complexities of our mission to safeguard genetic diversity as we reach for the stars.

Art has long been a gateway for imagination—transforming abstract ideas into tangible representations that resonate deeply within the human experience. Cosmic themes have inspired countless artists to envision what life beyond Earth may resemble, drawing upon landscapes that stretch our understanding of existence. Through creative expression, artists explore the interplay between humanity and the cosmos, illuminating the beauty of nature while also raising critical questions regarding our role as custodians of life across the universe.

The aesthetic interpretations found in visual art play a significant role in shaping public perceptions of cosmic preservation. Astounding depictions of celestial bodies, interstellar landscapes, and imagined extraterrestrial ecosystems invite spectators to contemplate what it means to preserve life in cosmos. For instance, an artist may create a mural that combines elements of terrestrial biodiversity—vibrant flora and fauna—with fantastical portrayals of alien life patterns. Such artworks encourage viewers to expand their understanding of what life can be and to appreciate the intricate connections that tie different forms of existence together.

Moreover, by embedding cultural narratives within their work, artists can invoke discussions about the rich diversity of life on our planet and the pressing need to protect it against existential threats. Integrating indigenous perspectives into artistic representations of cosmic preservation highlights the significance of ecological interdependence—inviting audiences to reflect on their own ties to nature and the responsibility they share in safeguarding biodiversity. Art that explores these themes fosters a communal sense of responsibility, linking local knowledge systems to planetary stewardship.

The interplay of science and artistic vision enhances our ability to engage with the scientific principles underpinning cosmic preservation efforts. Artists collaborating with scientists can create multi-faceted works that not only visualize scientific concepts but also resonate emotionally with audiences. For instance, an immersive installation might integrate augmented reality to allow visitors to explore the data surrounding genetic uniqueness and resilience, presenting the information in engaging and interactive ways. This fusion meticulously constructs narratives that educate while encouraging deeper connections between individuals and the scientific principles driving cosmic endeavors.

Inspirational works by both artists and scientists can catalyze movements that promote biodiversity awareness and the necessity of cosmic stewardship. Artists like Olafur Eliasson utilize materials and light to immerse audiences in environments that evoke ecological consciousness and climate dialogues. Meanwhile, scientists collaborating with artists to produce compelling images of the cosmos—such as stunning visuals of nebulae or the intricate patterns of DNA—allow for the creation of narratives that emphasize the wonders of scientific exploration while simultaneously igniting curiosity about life itself.

Looking forward, exploring the future of space art reveals exciting possibilities for how artistic interpretations can morph and adapt as we venture further into the cosmos. As technology facilitates space exploration, artists may capture the experiences of astronauts in real-time through visual media, documenting not just the technical achievements but also the emotional resonances of existence in the cosmic void. The potential to create public art installations that celebrate milestones in cosmic preservation initiatives engages communities and fosters a connection between people and the universe.

In considering the implications of artistic interpretations, we must also recognize the responsibility that comes with visualizing life in the cosmos. As narratives surrounding cosmic preservation evolve, the accuracy and integrity of these artistic representations must be upheld. Artists hold a unique position that allows them to wield influence in shaping public perceptions, and thus must ensure that their work respects the complexities of life while promoting a commitment to ethical stewardship.

In summary, imagining cosmic wonders through art enriches humanity's journey as we seek to preserve life across the cosmos. By intertwining artistic expression with scientific inquiry, we cultivate an understanding of cosmic preservation that resonates deeply with individuals and communities alike. This reciprocal relationship between art and science not only inspires us to protect genetic diversity but also illuminates the shared values that define our role as custodians of life, ensuring that future generations inherit a vibrant legacy that flourishes amid the infinite expanse of the universe. Through the visionary lens of art, we can boldly embrace our aspirations and responsibilities, engaging with the cosmos while nurturing the intricate web of life that binds us all.

21.2. Cultural Interpretations of Cosmic Preservation

Cultural Interpretations of Cosmic Preservation

Cultural interpretations of cosmic preservation invite us to examine the tapestry of humanity's beliefs, values, and narratives as we embark on the ambitious journey of safeguarding the genetic diversity of life across the cosmos. As we establish DNA vaults designed to protect Earth's biological legacy amid the uncertainties of space, we are equally tasked with recognizing that our cultural heritage profoundly informs how we view, understand, and approach the preservation of life. This exploration involves uncovering the myriad ways in which cultures perceive the cosmos, the ethical implications of life beyond our planet, and the roles we embrace as guardians of biodiversity.

At the heart of these cultural interpretations lies the notion that humanity's relationship with the cosmos extends beyond mere exploration; it is woven into the very fabric of identity. The cosmos has inspired myths, legends, and philosophical reflections across civilizations throughout history. Ancient cultures revered the stars as messengers of divine knowledge, with celestial bodies often serving as navigation tools and symbols that guide societal values. These perspectives contain wisdom that can enrich modern discussions about cosmic preservation—underscoring humanity's shared responsibility for protecting the intricate connections among life forms on Earth and potentially within the cosmos.

As we contemplate the preservation of genetic diversity through cosmic vaults, a crucial aspect to address is how different cultures view the ethical implications associated with manipulating life. Perspectives on genetic preservation and cosmic intervention are largely shaped by cultural beliefs regarding the sanctity of life, relationships to nature, and notions of stewardship. For instance, many Indigenous cultures emphasize the interconnectedness of all living beings and the responsibilities embedded within those relationships. Their teachings remind us that the preservation of life is not solely a scientific endeavor but a moral obligation that transcends cultural and geographical boundaries. Incorporating these beliefs into our cosmic preservation strategies enriches our understanding of ethical stewardship, anchoring our initiatives in respect and reverence for life.

The narratives communicated through literature, art, and media further reinforce cultural interpretations of cosmic preservation. Science fiction, with its imaginative exploration of life in the universe, delves into themes of existential risk, genetic manipulation, and the potential consequences of human actions. Stories about encounters with extraterrestrial life prompt audiences to reflect deeply on humanity's role in the cosmos. For example, films like "Contact" illustrate the philosophical dilemmas surrounding human interactions with extraterrestrial intelligence, compelling viewers to confront what it means to be custodians of life in a universe teeming with possibilities. These narratives not only captivate the imagination but also inspire discussions about the responsibilities we bear for other forms of existence.

Contemporary artists also contribute to the cultural interpretations surrounding cosmic preservation through their visual interpretations and creative expressions. Artists employ various mediums to convey themes of interconnectivity, loss, and hope in the face of environmental challenges. By translating scientific concepts into poignant and relatable works, artists spark dialogue and heighten public awareness of the ethical responsibilities tied to cosmic preservation. For instance, art installations that explore genetic diversity or depict potential alien landscapes could resonate with people in ways that science alone may struggle to achieve. These creative endeavors encourage individuals to contemplate the significance of their roles in protecting biodiversity amid the vast expanses of the universe.

Furthermore, we must consider that cultural interpretations of preservation extend beyond Earth and into the cosmos. As we embark on the cosmic exploration of life's possibilities across the universe, these narratives can foster deeper connections with the unknown and prepare us for our encounters with potential extraterrestrial life. Engaging with the stories, myths, and beliefs of various cultures equips us with a rich repertoire of perspectives that can inform our approaches to conservation and stewardship beyond Earth.

In summary, cultural interpretations of cosmic preservation encompass the diverse beliefs, narratives, and ethical considerations that shape our understanding of life, identity, and responsibility in the universe. As we endeavor to establish DNA vaults to safeguard life's genetic legacy, we must embrace the narratives that emerge from different cultures, recognizing the invaluable insights they offer in guiding our stewardship endeavors. By weaving together science, art, philosophy, and cultural heritage, we can cultivate a comprehensive approach to cosmic preservation that honors the intricate connections among all forms of existence. In doing so, we affirm our role as guardians—not just of the past, but as advocates for a thriving and diverse future among the stars.

The Interplay of Science and Artistic Vision

The interplay between science and artistic vision enriches humanity's understanding of cosmic preservation and serves as a powerful catalyst for engaging broader audiences. As we embark on the journey of establishing DNA vaults in space to safeguard the genetic legacies of life, the collaboration between scientists and artists emerges as a multifaceted avenue for exploration that honors both the rigor of scientific inquiry and the imaginative prowess of creative expression. This symbiotic relationship enhances our narratives surrounding cosmic stewardship, inviting diverse perspectives and fostering a collective commitment to the preservation of life.

The visualization of scientific concepts through art allows us to bridge the chasm between technical understanding and public engagement. Artists possess the ability to convey complex ideas surrounding genetic preservation and cosmic exploration in accessible ways, evoking emotions, curiosity, and inspiration. For instance, an artist may take the intricate structures of DNA and render them into compelling visual art—transforming abstract scientific data into tangible representations that invite contemplation and discussion.

The collaborative projects between scientists and artists serve to elucidate the significance of cosmic preservation in vivid, ethereal forms. Artists can create immersive installations that simulate environments, showcasing the importance of biodiversity while immersing audiences in an engaging, experiential narrative. Since visual storytelling captures attention effectively, these installations can serve as educational platforms, initiating discussions about genetic diversity, ethical stewardship, and the intricate interdependencies that define ecosystems.

Furthermore, literature's capacity to explore the human experience in connection with cosmic exploration extends to its potential to shape public perceptions about biodiversity preservation. Works of fiction that explore the dilemmas of genetic manipulation or depict hypothetical scenarios of life in the cosmos invite readers to confront the ethical implications of such actions. An example lies in the writings of Octavia Butler, whose narratives often examine themes of identity, adaptation, and interspecies relationships. Such explorations challenge readers to consider the responsibilities associated with preserving life while encouraging empathy for all forms of existence.

The rising influence of digital media amplifies these synergies, enabling artists to create dynamic visuals and interactive platforms that engage audiences on multiple sensory levels. Virtual reality experiences can guide participants through simulated ecological environments, allowing them to explore biodiversity's richness and understand the significance of protecting genetic diversity. These immersive experiences blur the lines between science and art, instilling a sense of connection that deepens engagement with cosmic preservation initiatives.

The influence of science on art extends to the development of creative narratives that engage the public's imagination. Artworks that capture the vastness of the universe—be it through breathtaking landscapes, illustrations of alien life, or representations of cosmic phenomena—can evoke wonder and curiosity, drawing attention to the significance of preserving life on Earth and beyond. By emphasizing the intrinsic value of biodiversity through artistic interpretations, we celebrate the interconnectedness of life and encourage the collective effort necessary for cosmic stewardship.

As narratives unfold through the interplay of science and art, it becomes increasingly relevant to acknowledge and advocate for diverse cultural perspectives. Engaging with Indigenous artists and storytellers enriches the discourse surrounding cosmic preservation, as these communities often possess wisdom and traditional ecological knowledge that resonate with principles of stewardship. By incorporating these perspectives into narratives, we reinforce the importance of viewing biodiversity not as a commodity to be harvested but as a heritage to be cherished.

In conclusion, the interplay of science and artistic vision plays a crucial role in enhancing our understanding of cosmic preservation and engaging diverse audiences in this essential narrative. By collaborating with artists to visualize scientific concepts, sharing compelling narratives through literature and media, and embracing cultural perspectives, we can foster a deeper appreciation of the significance of safeguarding genetic diversity. This collaboration invites creativity, sparks dialogue, and cultivates a sense of shared responsibility—one that illuminates the path toward a sustainable future for all life across the cosmos. As we endeavor to bridge the art of imagination with the science of exploration, we affirm our role as guardians of life, preserving its intricate tapestry amid the infinite wonders of the universe.

Inspirational Works by Artists and Scientists Alike

The journey toward preserving life through interstellar DNA vaults is enriched by the contributions of artists and scientists alike, whose inspirational works and collaborations illuminate the path forward. Their creative expressions serve to bridge the gap between abstract concepts and tangible action, ultimately galvanizing public interest, empathy, and commitment to cosmic preservation. By examining and celebrating these transformative collaborations, we can appreciate the profound impact that artistry and scientific inquiry have on our mission to safeguard genetic diversity across the cosmos.

Art has an intrinsic ability to evoke emotions and provoke thought, making it a powerful medium for inspiring action and awareness. Many contemporary artists have turned their attention to themes of environmental conservation and cosmic exploration, utilizing various forms of artistic expression—painting, sculpture, multimedia installations, and performance art—to address critical issues surrounding biodiversity and the cosmos. These artists often draw upon scientific concepts and research to inform their creations, bridging the dividing lines between disciplines and demonstrating the interconnectedness of life.

For example, artists who create large-scale installations showcasing the beauty and fragility of life often employ data from ecological research to inform their designs. By visually interpreting the patterns and tendencies observed in ecosystems, such as migratory routes of species or the diversity of genetic traits, they create immersive experiences that prompt viewers to reflect on the essence of biodiversity. The power of these experiences lies not only in their aesthetic appeal but also in their capacity to convey vital messages about the importance of preserving life on Earth and beyond.

Works by scientists similarly reflect the call to protect life, drawing from both research methodologies and artistic principles. Books and documentaries that convey scientific discoveries in engaging ways illustrate the interwoven narratives of cosmic exploration and biodiversity preservation. For instance, documentaries exploring the field of astrobiology lay bare the intricate possibilities surrounding life—a narrative enriched by stunning visuals of distant planets and thought-provoking discussions regarding the potential existence of extraterrestrial life. These representations serve to educate and inspire audiences, fostering a sense of curiosity and urgency surrounding the need to safeguard life across celestial landscapes.

Moreover, individuals and collectives dedicated to cosmic preservation have emerged in response to the pressing ecological crises we face. Initiatives that combine art with activism, such as campaigns advocating for sustainable practices or the protection of endangered species, draw public attention and amplify awareness through creative means. By mobilizing the arts, these movements cultivate community engagement while promoting the ethical imperative to preserve the interconnected web of life that exists on our planet.

Importantly, these collaborations between artists and scientists inspire future generations to engage with cosmic preservation efforts on multiple levels. Educational programs that invite students to explore scientific concepts through artistic projects enhance their understanding of complex topics while fostering a passion for conservation. By encouraging interdisciplinary approaches in education, we empower young individuals to envision themselves as stewards of life, capable of contributing to cosmic preservation initiatives that extend beyond traditional boundaries.

As we look to the future, it becomes vital to continue nurturing relationships between artists and scientists. By fostering interdisciplinary connections, we can transcend conventional paradigms of knowledge, paving the way for innovative and impactful approaches to cosmic preservation. By harnessing creative inspiration alongside scientific rigor, we can encourage dialogue and reflection while building a robust culture of stewardship.

In summary, the inspirational works of artists and scientists alike provide a vital narrative in our undertaking of cosmic preservation. By intertwining scientific inquiry with artistic expression, we create pathways for promoting awareness, empathy, and collaboration, illuminating the importance of safeguarding the genetic legacy of life. As the boundaries of exploration expand and we strive toward a future marked by resilience and sustainability, the combined efforts of artistic and scientific voices will assist in guiding humanity on its journey among the stars, fostering a deep commitment to protecting the intricate web of life we aim to preserve.

Exploring the Future of Space Art

The exploration of the future of space art represents a transformative journey where creativity and scientific inquiry converge, inspiring public engagement with the principles of cosmic preservation. As humanity sets forth on the ambitious quest to establish DNA vaults among the stars, the evolving landscape of space art serves as both a reflection of our aspirations and a catalyst for dialogue around the importance of safeguarding genetic diversity across the cosmos. This exploration highlights the potential for art to illuminate and enhance our understanding of life as we reach for the stars.

As new technologies and mediums emerge, the future of space art will likely embrace innovative forms of expression that capture the beauty and wonder of the cosmos in novel ways. Virtual reality (VR) experiences allow audiences to immerse themselves into stellar environments, granting them insights into the universe as they explore distant planets, celestial phenomena, and the intricate complexities of life. By creating these immersive experiences, artists can engage broader audiences in ways that traditional mediums may struggle to achieve, evoking emotions that deepen our connections to cosmic preservation.

Furthermore, interactive installations equipped with augmented reality (AR) may enable individuals to visualize genetic diversity and ecological interdependence. Imagine a display where viewers can manipulate and observe genetic data, witnessing the relationships that define ecological systems in real-time. These interactives go beyond mere aesthetics; they harness the power of technology to create educational experiences that empower visitors to engage with scientific principles and ethical considerations surrounding cosmic preservation efforts.

As space exploration missions intensify, artists will have ample opportunities to document and respond to the experiences of astronauts and scientists working in extraterrestrial environments. Innovative storytelling methods—such as live streams, blogs, and digital art projects—could provide insight into the emotional and physical realities of life beyond Earth. Venturing into the unknown, artists serve as interpreters of the human experience, transferring the lessons and stories gathered through cosmic exploration back to society—inviting them to connect with the broader implications of our collective journey.

Additionally, the future of space art will champion interdisciplinary collaboration, fostering partnerships between scientists, engineers, and artists to explore creative avenues that emphasize the significance of cosmic preservation. By synthesizing expert knowledge with creative thought, artists can visualize concepts such as genetic preservation, ecological resilience, and the ethical considerations surrounding life in the cosmos. Utilizing collective insights, these collaborations can yield works that not only captivate audiences but also spark critical discussions around our role as stewards of biodiversity.

Moreover, as artists engage with the themes of cosmic preservation, honoring diverse cultural narratives becomes essential. Collaborative projects that embrace Indigenous perspectives or the experiences of historically marginalized communities offer alternative interpretations of our relationship with nature and the cosmos. Elevating these narratives fosters a richer dialogue regarding the complexities of life and the moral imperatives we encounter as custodians—a profound acknowledgment that the stewardship of life resonates across cultures and histories.

The narrative potential embedded in space art can also be utilized to advocate for broader public engagement in conservation initiatives. Through campaigns that emphasize the significance of preserving genetic diversity, artists can rally communities to participate in local conservation efforts, ultimately fostering a sense of responsibility that extends to cosmic stewardship. By creatively communicating the importance of genetic preservation to diverse populations, we can spark curiosity and mobilize collective action toward cosmic conservation.

In summary, the exploration of the future of space art promises to amplify the discourse surrounding cosmic preservation as we strive to establish DNA vaults among the stars. By embracing innovative technologies, fostering interdisciplinary collaboration, and honoring diverse cultural narratives, space art will engage communities and inspire individuals to appreciate the beauty and significance of biodiversity. As humanity ventures forth into the cosmos, the combined artistic and scientific voices will create a tapestry of engagement that reflects our commitment to protecting the legacy of life across the universe—a legacy that bridges the past, present, and future of existence itself.

21.3. The Interplay of Science and Artistic Vision

The interplay of science and artistic vision is a vital aspect of humanity's journey into the cosmos, particularly as we undertake the ambitious project of establishing DNA vaults to preserve Earth's genetic legacy. This relationship extends beyond mere aesthetic representation; it functions as a powerful conduit for engendering public understanding, empathy, and engagement in the critical narratives surrounding biodiversity and cosmic preservation. As we examine this dynamic interplay, we unveil the profound connections between creative expression and scientific inquiry, underscoring the collaborative spirit necessary for safeguarding life in all its forms.

Artists have long drawn inspiration from the wonders of the universe, capturing the awe and mystery inherent in cosmic exploration. Their works reflect humanity's innate curiosity about our place in the cosmos and serve as vivid reminders of the intricate tapestry of life —a tapestry that we are charged with protecting. Through the use of visual arts, literature, performance, and digital media, artists illuminate the profound questions surrounding biodiversity preservation, inviting audiences to engage with these themes on emotional and intellectual levels.

For instance, artists such as Olafur Eliasson create immersive installations that confront viewers with the stark realities of climate change and biodiversity loss. By translating complex scientific concepts into compelling visual narratives, these works evoke emotions that compel audiences to reflect on their personal connections to nature. Such artistic endeavors not only celebrate life but also serve as platforms for raising awareness about the urgent need to preserve our planet's rich biological diversity.

Likewise, fictional narratives in literature provide fertile ground for exploring the ethical dimensions of space exploration and genetic preservation. Science fiction authors like Ursula K. Le Guin and Octavia Butler challenge readers to reflect on the responsibilities accompanying technological advancements and the preservation of genetic systems. Their hypotheticals invite us to consider our roles as custodians of life while encouraging critical examinations of the implications of our pioneering aspirations.

The relationship between science and art undoubtedly extends to technological innovations as well. The advances in data visualization and simulation technologies facilitate collaborations that enable scientists to present complex data in interactive and engaging formats. By employing virtual reality and augmented reality technologies, scientists and artists can create immersive experiences that allow audiences to visualize genetic diversity and ecological interdependencies. This innovative overlap fosters curiosity and enhances public understanding of the scientific principles underpinning cosmic preservation efforts.

As humanity continues to journey into space, the role of artists will be increasingly essential in documenting and interpreting the experiences of those involved in cosmic exploration. Artists can capture the emotional essence of astronauts traversing alien worlds or the scientific discoveries being made within distant ecosystems. By weaving these narratives into compelling stories, they forge deeper connections between exploration and stewardship, compelling individuals to reflect on the significance of preserving life amidst the wonders of the cosmos.

Moreover, as we navigate the complexities of cosmic preservation, engaging diverse cultural perspectives becomes imperative. Artists from various cultural backgrounds can contribute unique insights and interpretations that honor the rich tapestry of life. Indigenous artists, for instance, often embody a deep connection to the land and biodiversity, offering profound narratives that reflect the interdependence of human existence and ecological balance. Integrating these perspectives into artistic expressions fosters a broader understanding of what stewardship entails and highlights the importance of respecting local ecological knowledge.

Ultimately, the interplay between science and artistic vision provides a compelling framework for advancing the mission of cosmic preservation. By fostering interdisciplinary collaborations that intertwine scientific inquiry with creative expression, we create avenues for dialogue that resonate deeply with individuals and communities. Engaging narratives that incorporate vivid imagery, compelling stories, and emotional connections inspire a greater commitment to safeguarding life's genetic legacy.

In conclusion, the interplay of science and artistic vision fosters a vibrant discourse surrounding cosmic preservation efforts. As we establish DNA vaults aimed at securing Earth's genetic diversity, the collaborative contributions of artists and scientists will serve to elevate our understanding while galvanizing public support. Through the power of creative expression and scientific innovation, we can inspire a profound commitment to protecting the intricate web of life that unites us all—both on our home planet and among the stars. In this way, we embrace our roles as custodians of life, charting a hopeful course for our future in the cosmos, one illuminated by imagination, inquiry, and a shared commitment to stewardship.

21.4. Inspirational Works by Artists and Scientists Alike

As we navigate the complex landscape of cosmic preservation and the preservation of genetic diversity, the intersection of art and science becomes a vital narrative thread. This section explores the expressions and contributions from both artists and scientists who engage with themes of cosmic exploration, life preservation, and the ethical responsibilities that accompany humanity's ambitions among the stars. Through their collaborative efforts and creative visions, these individuals inspire a collective commitment to safeguarding life and forging new paths toward cosmic stewardship.

The inspirational works of artists often draw heavily from scientific principles and explorations, capturing the depths of human experience in the vast tapestry of existence. Artists like Olafur Eliasson create immersive installations that bridge the gap between scientific inquiry and emotional resonance—inviting audiences to grapple with concepts of climate change, biodiversity, and the interconnectedness of life. By transforming abstract scientific ideas into visual narratives, artists engage the public on both intellectual and emotional levels, fostering curiosity about cosmic preservation.

In parallel, scientists engaged in the field of astrobiology promote conversations through their research and discoveries. Their documented findings about extremophiles—the organisms that thrive in harsh environments—serve as both factual bases for cosmic possibilities and as foundational knowledge for thinking about which genetic materials to preserve for potential extraterrestrial environments. As these scientists share their insights, they inspire new questions and creative interpretations—prompting artists to envision life in cosmic terms influenced by biophysical dynamics.

As we look toward the future of space art, we anticipate a plethora of innovative expressions that celebrate the wonders of the cosmos while also invoking the need for responsible stewardship. Artists may utilize advancements in technology to create augmented reality experiences that allow individuals to visualize ecosystems flourishing in extraterrestrial settings. These experiential artworks prompt deeper discussions about the ethical considerations surrounding the introduction of Earth's species into alien ecosystems while inviting participants to reflect on their roles as guardians of life.

Furthermore, literature reflecting cosmic themes elevates the discourse surrounding preservation efforts, encouraging critical engagement with the ethical implications of manipulating life. Authors such as Ursula K. Le Guin delve into the moral complexities of interstellar existence while emphasizing hope, resilience, and the interconnected nature of existence—all valuable themes for contemplating our responsibilities as custodians of life across the cosmos.

As these narratives unfold, the importance of interdisciplinary collaboration becomes increasingly evident. Science and art must merge to craft compelling stories that resonate with diverse audiences, broadening public understanding and appreciation of life's intricacies. By leveraging these partnerships, artists can help convey the urgency of protecting our planet's biodiversity, emphasizing the interrelatedness of terrestrial and extraterrestrial ecosystems.

When artists symbolize the mystery of the cosmos through creative expression, they encourage society to dream big and cultivate a narrative of exploration and preservation. Their work serves to inspire future generations to engage in cosmic conservation efforts, promoting a legacy that extends beyond individual aspirations. By sharing the intricate stories of life and the potential for cosmic exploration, artists foster an environment where stewardship becomes engrained in our collective consciousness.

In summary, the inspirational works of both artists and scientists provide a profound framework for understanding and advocating for cosmic preservation. By harnessing the creativity of the arts alongside the rigor of science, we generate narratives that captivate the imagination while promoting a deep commitment to safeguarding life in all its forms. As we travel along this uncharted path, we collectively embrace our roles as custodians, illuminating a future where the preservation of biodiversity persists amid the beauty and complexity of the universe.

21.5. Exploring the Future of Space Art

As we stand at the cusp of a new era in the quest for cosmic preservation, the future of space art emerges as a vibrant canvas where scientific inquiry and creative expression intertwine to illuminate the path forward. The establishment of DNA vaults among the stars —repositories designed to safeguard the genetic legacy of Earth's biodiversity—offers rich opportunities for artists to engage with profound themes surrounding life, survival, and interconnectedness in the cosmos. Imagining the future through art invites us to envision a tapestry of cosmic stewardship marked by innovation, inclusivity, and ethical reflection.

The potential of space art expands with advancements in technology that enhance how artists can interact with the cosmos. As new mediums such as virtual reality (VR), augmented reality (AR), and immersive installations become more prevalent, artists are better equipped to create experiences that transport audiences into the realms of cosmic exploration. Envisioning environments that allow individuals to navigate distant planets, encounter alien life forms, or interact with holographic representations of genetic material sparks curiosity and fosters a sense of responsibility toward preserving the intricate web of life. These engaging experiences can deepen our understanding of biodiversity and encourage meaningful reflections on our roles as custodians.

The narratives crafted in space art will also reflect humanity's evolving relationship with technology. As artists explore themes of genetic manipulation, environmental ethics, and the implications of life beyond Earth, they present both utopian visions and cautionary tales. Works inspired by science fiction can challenge us to contemplate the ramifications of our aspirations, warning of the potential pitfalls associated with tampering in ecological systems while simultaneously promoting hope for resilience and adaptation amidst the trials of existence.

In this context, the influence of scientific advancements on space art will continue to resonate. Collaborations between scientists and artists can lead to groundbreaking projects that visualize complex data, elucidating the scientific principles that underpin cosmic preservation efforts. By creating pieces that integrate the findings of astrobiological research with speculative creativity, artists can offer profound insights that enhance public understanding of the intricate bonds linking ecosystems and the cosmic environment.

Moreover, cultural interpretations of cosmic preservation will find expression in the creative narratives of diverse artistic voices. Indigenous artists and storytellers may weave traditional knowledge into their works, revealing the valuable ecological insights passed down through generations. Integrating local perspectives will strengthen the discourse surrounding cosmic preservation, fostering respect for the connections between Earth's biodiversity and the larger universe.

These narratives underscore the importance of creating a framework of stewardship that transcends cultural boundaries, allowing us to learn and grow from one another.

As we contextualize the future of space art, it is essential to consider the role of education in fostering the next generation of artists, scientists, and engaged citizens. Educational programs must incorporate themes of biodiversity, stewardship, and space exploration, while actively promoting interdisciplinary collaboration. By nurturing creative minds able to blend scientific inquiry with artistic expression, we cultivate a culture that values cosmic preservation and innovation.

Furthermore, public engagement initiatives centered on space art can elevate awareness of the importance of preserving life, stimulating collective action. Through outreach programs and community exhibitions, we can bridge the gap between scientific understanding and public perception, prompting individuals to reflect on their roles as custodians of life in the cosmos. By skillfully utilizing digital platforms, we can reach audiences far and wide, ensuring that the imperative of cosmic preservation resonates with diverse communities.

In conclusion, the future of space art promises to serve as a powerful vehicle for inspiring engagement with cosmic preservation efforts. Through the innovative use of technology, interdisciplinary collaboration, and the integration of diverse cultural perspectives, artists can animate the narratives surrounding biodiversity and survival in ways that captivate and resonate with audiences. This creative exploration will not only enhance our understanding of cosmic stewardship but also illuminate pathways toward fostering a culture of responsibility that embraces the rich diversity of life in the universe. As we venture forth into the cosmos, let us celebrate and honor these artistic expressions that remind us of our roles as guardians of life—both on Earth and among the stars.